ROMANTIC CONFUSIONS
OF THE GOOD

ROMANTIC CONFUSIONS OF THE GOOD

Beauty as Truth, Truth Beauty

Marion Montgomery

ROWMAN & LITTLEFIELD PUBLISHERS, INC.
Lanham • Boulder • New York • London

ROWMAN & LITTLEFIELD PUBLISHERS, INC.

Published in the United States of America
by Rowman & Littlefield Publishers, Inc.
4720 Boston Way, Lanham, Maryland 20706

3 Henrietta Street
London WC2E 8LU, England

British Cataloging in Publication Information Available

Library of Congress Cataloging-in-Publication Data
Montgomery, Marion.
    Romantic confusions of the good : beauty as truth, truth beauty /
Marion Montgomery.
        p.   cm.
    Includes bibliographical references and index.
    ISBN 0-8476-8393-1 (cloth : alk. paper).—ISBN 0-8476-8394-X
(pbk. alk. paper)
    1. English poetry—19th century—History and criticism—Theory,
etc. 2. American poetry—History and criticism—Theory, etc.
3. Thomas, Aquinas, Saint, 1225?–1274—Aesthetics. 4. Good and evil
in literature. 5. Aesthetics, Modern. 6. Romanticism. I. Title.
PR575.A34M66 1997
821'.809384—dc20   96-36051
                                                    CIP

ISBN 978-0-8476-8394-9

Printed in the United States of America

∞ ™ The paper used in this publication meets the minimum requirements of
American National Standard for Information Sciences—Permanence of Paper for
Printed Library Materials, ANSI Z39.48–1984.

*The purpose of the study of philosophy is
not to learn what others have thought, but to learn
how the truth of things stands.*

—St. Thomas Aquinas

Contents

Acknowledgments

I am grateful to the Earhart Foundation for its generous support in preparing this work for publication, and especially to David B. Kennedy, President, and Antony T. Sullivan, Secretary and Director of Program at that institution. Since T. S. Eliot figures in these pages as a "Romantic" poet in progress out of modernist entrapments, he is quoted rather often. The required copyright notice for permission: Excerpts from *Collected Poems 1909–1962*, copyright 1936 by Harcourt Brace & Company, copyright © 1964, 1963 by T. S. Eliot, reprinted by permission of the publisher. Excerpts from "Burnt Norton" and "Little Gidding" in *Four Quartets*, copyright 1943 by T. S. Eliot and renewed 1971 by Esme Valerie Eliot, reprinted by permission of Harcourt Brace & Company.

Dedication

This book is given with my gratitude to some of my young(er) teachers: Deal Hudson, whose confident encouragement of my several works has been sustaining. It was he who set this present task. And to Russell Hittinger and John Hittinger, long supportive. It was Russell who called attention to the importance of St. Thomas's principle of proper proportionality as the theme I was pursuing, I ignorant of that principle in its formalities. And John Hittinger has helped me better ground my own intuitive understanding of the companionable relation of reason and intuition, through his treatise on reason and intellect in St. Thomas. The recovery possible through such understandings, or so I believe, will mean new life in our poetry. I am endebted to these lively persons, then, though they are but partly responsible for what now follows.

Preface

The whole of this book was occasioned by my invitation to speak to a gathering of the American Maritain Association at Fordham University in October of 1990. The announced theme of that gathering was "The Future of Thomism," and I felt as always an uneasiness at the temptation to prophesy, for reasons the following pages will make clear I trust. Among the dangers attendant upon prophecy about the future of an idea or theory or principle are those lying in the necessity to use history in defining the subject. A prophet becomes most vulnerable whenever he depends upon, or seems to depend upon, that spectral creature History, which we have elevated in our Modernist Parthenon through Historicism. The danger might be localized as the difficulty of reading with our present eye the world as it appeared to the eye in the past. We have some confidence that, since the past *was*, it must somehow therefore be at least steadying to our present sight, forgetting how unsteady is the present eye upon reality.

I feel somewhat buttressed, and think my eye less wavering in its prospect upon the past, as these pages will make evident in the epigraphs chosen for the chapters, by the work of St. Thomas Aquinas and by that work concerned with what we might call "The Past of Thomism(s)" written by Étienne Gilson and Jacques Maritain, who wrote book after book on that past and its intersection with our present. Not that I pretend to have digested St. Thomas, or all the work of Gilson and Maritain. But having read much of them I have a confidence from their exemplary work that I need not fear either History or Historicism as much as we have been somewhat conditioned to fear them. I recognize the need of some certitude in my present perspective upon past positions. In looking at what was yesterday predicted by influential minds about our own today, we measure in some degree against what we see of that prophecy in relation to present realities. As to the validity in my own seeing of the present in relation to past prophecy, these philosophers encourage me in that what I believe I see they also seem to see. And so my own wavering in seeing a supposedly fixed past at least is in a rhythm with their own.

The wavering is no doubt an inevitable effect of intellectual movement, and one cannot avoid it. One must, however, attempt as best one can to make it in concert with what St. Thomas calls the truth of things, itself somewhat wavering when seen in its relation to the only Unwavering Truth, which is the truth of all things, including my own intellect. But just how does one steady oneself intellectually to the accompaniment of such singers of being as St. Thomas and Gilson and Maritain? I suppose in the end that is the most central theme of the pages that follow. For the question is "How must I tune my intellect to the truth of things?" Examples of a persuasive tuning prompt one, though the music one's own intellect makes at last may not be concluded a determined effect of one's teachers, however desirable and even necessary it is to have such teachers.

And so that brings me to another confidence, an acknowledgment of my own sense of what it means to be a "Thomistic realist." Though most endebted to St. Thomas, and in a secondary manner to many, including Gilson and Maritain, I am required to make distinctions so that they are not burdened by my own conclusions.

I remember from my fond experiences the old Sears, Roebuck catalogues that used to come once a year, usually in the fall, since that was the time when crops were in and money, if any was to be had from the year's labors, was at hand. In addition, there was already the hint of autumn's decay into winter, the ambience in the year's turning that occasioned one of Keats's greatest poems in which he encounters "the last oozings" of the seasons in that "Season of mists and mellow fruitfulness" in which the "clammy cells" of summer are "o'er-brimmed." There's the poet for you, and the fall catalogue proved instigator of imaginative forays that Keats might well recognize. I am distinguishing here the *old* Sears, Roebuck catalogue from its contemporary descendent, which comes almost every month, with occasional supplements, and in "living" color. Such pretense to reality, alas, does not speak mellow autumn nor burgeoning summer nor timid spring, but rather a world in which it is, as with the Lotus Eaters, always afternoon. In that old dispensation of the Sears catalogue, there was the recognition that turning seasons were at hand to our immediate experience as most actual, as opposed to being present only to a Lotus Land fancy.

Not that fancy wasn't a credited presence in our responses to experience, as the catalogue maker knew well enough. For after all, even in those days the "bottom line" as we now term it, was important to the survival of a rather seasonless Sears, Roebuck, and Company headquartered in the Windy City, Chicago. So there would be pages of shotguns, what with quail season at hand, and bicycles, since Christmas wasn't far away. There would even be evening frocks for mothers and daughters in anticipation of an imagined spring, above and beyond those foundational garments so practically present. And there was also a careful presentation of work-shoes and overalls and long underwear and harness and shovels and hoes and the like, the most central justification of the catalogue, anchored as it must be in the pending necessities to family life, a life in which one experienced for the most part only faint intimations of any world in which it might be said it was always afternoon. There were evening dresses and double-barrelled .16-gauge shotguns and bicycles with pneumatic tires.

I am not ready to leave the directness of the catalogue in its ancient history quite yet in pursuit of a metaphor, but let me hint in advance that perhaps there might be some analogy between the Thomism which Gilson is intent upon in that old catalogue called the *Summa Theologica* and the Neo-Thomism he is disturbed by in new colored versions of that old catalogue. As for the actual old Sears and Roebuck one, in the old days, those "wish books" were firmly anchored in the reality of the thing as one knew it or had known it at hand. The signs used in the pages were without the obscurations of color, but were careful line drawings, as precise as the medium of paper and black ink would allow. The accompanying verbal description was as precise as the economy of space dictated. One could know whether the wagon would fit in the barn out there in the yard, and one knew the wood and metal in it, and so on. The intent was to give as precise a conception to the reader as possible of the *thing* itself—*conception* in its scholastic sense.

That we commonly spoke of these as the "wish book," then, was not so much a description of the book itself as an acknowledgment, humorously cast by the term, of an inclination in us to handle things themselves through signs in an unrealistic way. The old catalogues summoned imaginative speculation, even to the borders of fancy's land. Now, with the constant succession of colored catalogues, the intent seems to be to pre-empt our imaginative action, as if color could include content. But the imagination must at last reach that content *through* sign, in relation to that "content" of existences we call *beings*. It cannot be reached for us by any remote manipulation of "life," as if life were desirably a state of consciousness in which it is always afternoon. That, it is evident, is the pretense of our advertising, whether in periodicals or catalogues or on television, today.

If such a judgment as mine has validity, it may obviate any sentimental tears for the demise of the Sears, Roebuck catalogue, announced even as I write (January 1991). It is an announcement, however, not justifying celebration, for the reason given for suspending is the competition from that new species of mail catalogues that are specialized, that seek a strata of taste, based on information derived from computer characterizations of a class of individuals in the *res publica*. One knows the catalogues I mean. If one has an income of a certain level, he receives a catalogue of a certain sort. If one reaches "senior citizen" status, he begins to receive a quite distinctive sort, which has endless gadgets, for instance, anticipating the inevitable decay lying ahead. There are the catalogues for chocolate "freaks" or fruit "freaks" or cheese "freaks." And one can hardly deny an appeal in them, so skillfully produced they are. But to take one step backward is to wonder whether we are not beginning, through print technology, to establish a class system such as has not been seen before, based on *taste* as the criterion, supported by whatever economic resources available to that taste. Look critically at the ads on television, particularly those for cosmetics, whether aiding an April beauty maintain bounce in her hair or an aging September erase grey from his. John Keats' concern for the mystery of art as perhaps an alchemy distorting reality, if art declare that "beauty is truth, truth beauty," seems rapidly to be elevated from a suspect alchemy to the science of taste, wherein our devotion is to be made more and more to the accidents of being, used against intrinsic truth—lest we be forced to confront old mortality, the grey in our hair, or corns on the toe, or even pale spectre-thin lips of youth itself.

Which is to say that the old catalogue did not prohibit the imagination's inclinations toward the land of the lotus eaters, only that it also carried clearer reminders of the realities of things in themselves. Image tended to be image of the thing, not mirror to a vague desire in us. Imagination is inescapably fallible, since affected by innate desire whose proper end easily becomes distorted under the growing recognitions of the self by the self through the stirrings of desire. Desire perverted is, of course, selfishness, than which nothing is more distorting of the proper ends of our desiring. Therein lies the problem, and in the end our failures of desire are not to be charged to catalogues, old or new.

Now this is by way of introducing my recognition of an abiding problem for the particular intellect, in this instance my own, as it addresses itself to material and immaterial things. But it is not merely a matter of my own wayward fancy to suggest that we may, through desire fallen from its ordinate role in our intellectual becoming, misuse not only the old Sears, Roebuck catalogue, but the *Summa Theologica* as well. With this new, improved plow of 1875, the whole Western plain may be turned to grain. With the new metaphysical vision of 1300, wish may be converted to vision. In that press of desire for ends to be accomplished here and now, *being* itself may become susceptible to manipulations by intellect, even when intellect would not desire to do so, if we could but arrest and charge intellect with the attempt. That is why I have sometimes suggested that even Thomism is susceptible of gnostic uses, a suggestion that has not always met with approval from some Thomists.

As for that marvelous plow, whether out of Sears or the *Summa*, the poet sometimes recalls us to a marvel beyond even it. I've quoted Hopkins on the point, in a passage that for me has something of the old virtues of the Sears, Roebuck catalogue. That is, his words at once remind us of a throbbing signal of being in things themselves and of the steadiness of encounter necessary to our finitudes, which disallow our transport at once to a country where it is always afternoon—that substitute beatitude so doggedly pursued by modernism.

> sheer plod makes plough down sillion
> Shine, and blue-bleak embers, ah my dear,
> Fall, gall themselves, and gash gold-vermillion.

The plod of ploughing, the turning of earth in sheered cuts of furrows: there is the steadiness anchoring desire for vision within the realities of being itself. So that not simply the reflection of sun on the moist, glassy surface of the new turned clod meets the eye, but a stirring sense that there is another sort of light, out of *being* itself, a shining out of, not merely upon. Not only a leap of recognition by imaginative vision happens in this complex of words, but also a leap as yet anchored in the actualities of existence. The embers burning deep in the soil, turned as clods in sunlight, are "blue-bleak," and one must have witnessed what the words speak to, as one must in the old days have had some sense of the hold of a plow in ordering one from the old Sears. Damp soil in its shimmering of sun is underlain by an actual bleak blueness in some soil. They gall themselves, fall over when gashed by the plow in small avalanches, though gold-vermillion to the eye even as they fall.

Ah my dear, says the poet in recognition of a vision of the complexity of existence encountered by his fallible intellect, recognizing the rescue of the world in that incommensurate sacrifice of Christ, who is the poem's "dear," "ah my dear," always speaking in a present moment in this particular place, which we are required to endure in good cheer and not abandon for any lotus land, though imagination slip its bonds in reality, may take wing through fancy in a doomed seeking of that fancied land.

That condition of fancy in pursuit of the lotus land—that is what Gilson is speaking of when he says that, when thought substitutes itself for knowledge, those transcendentals (the good, the true, the beautiful) float in the air without knowing where to perch themselves. To the contrary, for "the realist, whose thought is concerned with being, the Good, the True and the Beautiful are in the fullest sense real, since they are simply being itself as desired, known and admired." And that is what Hopkins's words remind us of. It may well be that Scotus is more a presence in his intellect than Thomas, as is cogently argued by some. Very well. But what is of first importance is the reminder in such poems as "The Windhover" of the anchor of those transcendents in our desire to know and to admire the Good, the True and the Beautiful in a simplicity we intuit as possible to us, a simplicity in our complex potential, spoken of prophetically by intuition as Beatitude. But what is fundamental to that intuition, such is our nature—which is also fallen nature—is its necessary pursuit again and again in the context of reality itself: through our experiences of being; through the fallible instrument of intellect. Eliot, in his version of these words by Hopkins, has spoken of encountering in a deserted garden "roses that have the look of roses that are looked at." He might have followed that visionary moment with "ah my dear," as in the truth of his own spiritual and intellectual estate at that moment I am confident he did.

What I have been cautioning myself against is the problem of that desire, worthy and vitally necessary in intellect—without which I could not move or be moved toward Beatitude. But desire is also capable of a reduction to the level of wish, in which instance all creation becomes but a wish book. However real such wishing seems, grown out of a conception of some new plow or other—a real "thing"—such wishing inclines toward denying the engulfing realities the poet speaks of in metaphors of the turning seasons, the seeming whims of the world's weathers, whether those of a summer's day storm or the greenhouse effect. To ignore those *inclusive* conditions to the actual and potential of the plow in my own hands, perceived imaginatively with the support of concept, is to be prepared to blame the plow when the crop fails. Such is the misuse, the abuse, of the plow, whether we mean by *plow* a metaphor for our uses of nature or a metaphor for our peculiar, particular intellectual response to being itself. The error may be in mistaking the limits of our intellectual nature.

Such, indeed, is the gnostic address to reality, an address which requires no formal training at Harvard or the Sorbonne, no recovery of the history of intellect through the genealogies of ideas. All required is the misuse of that distinctive gift of ours, common to the sixth-grade dropout as to the multidegreed intellectual. For the gnostic may be literate or illiterate. As for myself as intellectual, as philosopher née poet, I must always remind myself of the necessity of sheer plod down sillion, for I too much desire imaginative leaps. And so I add to my epigraph from St. Thomas one from only yesterday, spoken by Eliot as he gives up the writing of poetry as Thomas at his end gave up the writing of philosophy. St. Thomas says, "The purpose of the study of philosophy is not to learn what others have thought, but to learn how the truth of things stands." And Eliot, in *Little Gidding*:

> Every phrase and every sentence is an end and a beginning,
> Every poem an epitaph.   And any action
> Is a step to the block, to the fire, down the sea's   throat
> Or to an illegible stone: and that is where we start.
> We die with the dying: . . . .
> We are born with the dead . . . .

We die and are born, says Eliot, "With the drawing of this Love and the voice of this Calling." Heard, we add, through *being* itself. Ah, my dear!

Introduction

"Our whole being is an individual by reason of that in us which derives from matter, and a person by reason of that in us which derives from spirit . . . . Evil arises when, in our action, we give preponderance to the individual aspect of our being."

—Jacques Maritain, *The Person and the Common Good*

As we have come increasingly to recognize, there occurs in Western thought since St. Thomas an accelerating shift of intellectual attention away from an engagement of existence at large, with an accompanying neglect of or rejection of a metaphysics that might order that shifting attention. Put cryptically: the introduction of Nominalism exploded into empirical fascinations, which when explored in material existence led at last to a new fascination with awareness itself as the phenomenon which must yield to analytic empiricism. The shift leads, in other words, to a fascination of intellect with itself, accompanied by a growing euphoria that encourages intellect to suppose itself the prime agent of being, however it chooses to define *being* in the development of thought from Descartes to Freud and Sartre. But if we observe the effects of that movement upon intellect, especially in evidence in the poet from Baudelaire to our own moment, we might conclude that the euphoria breeds a growing intellectual anxiety fathered by that intruding sense of isolation that is increasingly troublesome to intellect's presumption of its authoritative autonomy over being. The issue is a depressing ennui to replace what intellect might once have experienced as serenity through reflection or contemplation or meditation. Under that threat, a "busyness" becomes necessary, as distraction from thought. If one is in that state of "funk," which once might have been characterized as a disquiet of the spirit, the solution offered is that one must be up and doing. Something "useful" to nature or humanity; something in the name of some future dream, pre-scribed by a concurrent consent to some present intellectual authority.

Intellect thus discovers itself, through its narcissistic inversion of its own being by closure, to suffer a narcissistic end: the isolation of intellect from any relation to existence beyond intellect itself, however busily it strives to deny that isolation. For ignoring the pool as a thing other than a surface whereon images of the self are fed to the self, intellect can but become separated from the deeper waters of the world, of creation that willy-nilly includes and does not exempt the self from among pools and rocks and the multitudinous creatureliness of creation. Intellect not only suffers that loss, but also at the last even becomes uncertain of the reality of its own reflection and then of its own existence. Intellect in that mo-ment of panic is prepared to conclude itself but chimera, having long since forgotten St. Augustine's reassurance: If I am deceived about my own existence, I nevertheless exist; for I must exist if I am deceived. But intel-lect, in its "modernist" inheritance, continues largely arrested in a state of helplessness, if it pauses from its busyness to consider its present estate. That consideration is available through its reflection in and on the world. It is not the same thing as *reflection* in the merely imagistic sense associ-ated with Narcissus, the condition of intellect in which the substantiality of existence fades and fades. In that pause from recessiveness against real-ity, it may well experience at first a helplessness, attempting to deal with reflections seemingly isolated even from reflecting surfaces, whether that of a pool in a desert or any object taken as capable only of giving back to the senses a sensual awareness of the self as isolated.

That was an intellectual moment of terror for T. S. Eliot up to the 1920s. He was confounded by the mind as constituted of "a thousand sordid images" projected against the world as ceiling. Those images seemed to have neither a dependable referent beyond awareness nor any medium suitable of signifying beyond isolated images. Words, intellectual signs, appeared no longer dependable. For the body itself appeared separated from its intellect by willed autonomy, in a secularizing of Platonism. Still, the material world of which the body continued the most disturbing im-mediate problem threatened intellect. It was as if Narcissus's pool of water should begin to speak or try to speak to him. In that confused circum-stance of intellect's address to image in its awareness by sign—by word—sign revealed only a most uncertain anchor in image itself, let alone any object that might be the remote cause of the image afloat in intellect. Sign seemed, most confusingly, to exist if it existed at all as *out* of intellect; but it also seemed only available to the isolated intellect. It was a consequence, as Eliot would later recognize, of that isolation of the self which had been accomplished in the name of power, in the name of intellectual autonomy. There is an ironic dimension to this condition of intellect, not always recognized by that intellect itself under the pressure of its isolation, an isolation it increasingly fears to be absolute. For however deep intellect's fear, the encroaching sense of isolation does not destroy its insistent use of the sign. Our world is surely louder with sign than ages before us in time. And the ironic implication in that very loudness is that somehow sign must signify.

I have spoken of intellect in the singular, as we generally shall. But here I have also been speaking of a sweep of our intellectual history, with the term *intellectual* as a collective signifying a plurality of intellects continuous in time. To speak of intellect historically necessarily implies intellect in a plural, Averroes to the contrary. We are speaking here, then, of a community of intellectual concern extending from the past into our present. And to use the term *community* as we have just done requires a clarification. For the community I am characterizing as unified by its emphasis upon intellect's power as autonomous is not inclusive of all intellects. Thomistic realism, for instance, sets itself athwart that presumption. To this distinction of communities of mind, then, one wants to add—lest the Thomistic realist overlook an import ally—that the common sense which is resident in each intellect, each person of whatever calling, sets the generality of mankind outside that community of patrons of intellectual autonomy.

That this is true is witnessed by the day-to-day acts of persons living in a community separate from the modernist intellectuals, those inheritors of the principle of autonomous intellect. And we recognize as well that even those who purport to live under that principle themselves inescapably display commonsense response to reality in their own day-to-day existence. Their actions speak a dependence upon reality separate from intellectual autonomy. If they did not, they would starve soon, or be run down in traffic, or become victim to some effect of complex reality independent of their discrete intellectual actions. At the same time, we must recognize that it is this separate "plurality" of persons, drawn to the reality through common sense, who constitute intellects susceptible to recruitment by the modernist intellect. They are a means required to the reductionist ends which a modernist, autonomous intellect may be ravenous to effect by intellectual actions subversive of reality.

The plurality of intellects represents the necessary source of power needed if modernist intellect is to control and restructure what it only allows to be a shadow world. This reading of circumstance as it appears to the modernist intellect I have sometimes spoken of as inverted Platonism. It is a position achieved through a strategy whereby reality is assumed the shadow of intellectual autonomy, despite the contradictory conduct of such intellects in relation to that "shadow." The self as an existent intellect is exorcised from reality in its bid for intellectual eminence over the existential world. Plato's transcendent realm is denied, but Plato's shadow world is accepted. This autonomous intellect emerges as the sole reality, the idol to be worshipped in a pseudo-transcendence of intellect over existence. That both common sense and reason, responsive to the realities of creation, refute such a strategy in no way denies its considerable effectiveness in distorting intellectual vision of reality.

Of course, *transcendence* here is ambiguous and in my use intended metaphorically, since it names for the modernist position a separation from both creation and any cause of creation except finite intellect itself. It is a term here descriptive of a presumption to godhead by intellect. That it has been a relatively successful strategy seems conspicuous. Through its loudness of sign, autonomous intellect by its presumption of authority has gained the unreflective consent of common sense among so many persons that it effects an intellectual deracination of common sense in those persons, who become useful collectively to gnostic ends. The malaise of homelessness, of alienation, permeates the structures of community, its symptoms emerging as variously as from the chaos of the academy down to the disintegration of the family. One need only examine the uses of sign in advertising to take the point, whether that in academic catalogues, political campaigns, or cosmetic and headache remedies on that besieging cyclops, the television set, the local manifestation at the hearth of the god through whom deracinations of person are exploited. Consider, meanwhile, with what residual religious inclination we embrace the authority of intellect as it is distorted in its limits and ends, that autonomous intellect which is manipulative of discrete intellect now so random in the disintegrating structures of community and longing for some rescue.[1]

It is to the recovery of our inclination through intellectual nature, from which may follow intellect's recovery to *being* in its manifestations of truth and beauty and goodness, that Thomistic realism is called in our day, an end beyond the first necessity of refuting the false intellectualism we describe in the epithet "modernism." Thus modernism's history becomes important to this recovery of common sense to elemental truths, long distorted by intellect's self-deceptions. And here we emphasize that the singular intellect is always the beginning ground. It is always *my own* intellect with which I must begin. With such a beginning, out of the actual experiences by my own intellect of things which are not intellect itself and out of reflections upon those experiences, I may come to believe such a proposition as this: *Intellect* in the singular designates a particular, discrete unity in relation to a specific, unique *soul*—a *person, myself* larger than my intellect. That is the point St. Thomas argued long ago, in his *On the Unity of the Intellect*, against the Averroists, a treatise which was at once abandoned when contending intellects turned toward establishing the principle that intellect is autonomous, the first step necessary in its dream of power through knowledge. That dislocation of intellect from reality pointedly characterizes what we speak of as *modernism*, or in Eric Voegelin's term, *modern gnosticism*.[2]

I say that Thomas's argument was abandoned. But it might be more correct to say that the truth of his argument was partially appropriated, while his larger vision of intellect's relation to reality was rejected. That is, his concern for the truth of things, in this instance the truth of the nature of the specific intellect, was as a principle perverted and the context of that principle—his metaphysical vision—discredited. For in each instance of the particular modern gnostic intellect, one discovers its actions proceeding out of an assumption of its *own* unity, however subtly sophisticated the disguises of that assumption. It was necessary to this new gambit of intellect, which in a larger perspective proves but the very old one spoken of in Genesis, to abandon the grounding of intellect in that realism which St. Thomas celebrates in vigorous treatises. It was necessary, if the particular gnostic intellect was to summon as old Averroist error to forge its present instrument of power. The power was to be gathered out of the general common sense response to reality in the plurality of humankind, the generality of discrete human persons. The very vigor of Thomas's attack upon the Averroist error, and especially the somewhat uncharacteristic challenge to *any* antagonist to refute his argument, shows how crucial Thomas understood this particular issue in the future of Western thought. Thus his conclusion:

> But if there be anyone boasting of his knowledge, falsely so-called, who wishes to say something against what we have written here, let him not speak in corners, nor in the presence of boys who do not know how to judge about such difficult matters; but let him write against this treatise if he dares; and he will find not only me who am the least of others, but many other lovers of truth, by whom his error will be opposed or his ignorance remedied.

The final clause shows Thomas's recovery from the threatening excessiveness of his challenge, confident of other defenders against the error, though not many subsequent to Thomas will prove greater than he in his love of the truth of how things stand.

The Averroist error which Thomas refutes has two aspects, both important to our understanding of how we have come since Thomas to such
conditions as Eliot experienced as would-be philosopher. In an early
poem Eliot reduces the soul to being "constituted" of a "thousand sordid
images," both soul and images chimeric beyond intellectual certitude. As
Beatrice H. Zedler puts the matter in her introduction to her translation
of Thomas's treatise on the intellect, the Averroist error lies in asserting

> (1) that the possible intellect is a substance that is separate in its being from
> the body and not united to it as its form; and (2) that this possible intellect
> is one for all men.

If the *possible intellect* is a substance separate in being and therefore not
integral to the discrete body as a form; and if, further, intellect is a substance separate from any intellectual creature, being one for all such creatures, then a most radical definition is introduced of the *person*, or the
discrete, explicit *soul*. Thomas saw this, and he saw it with some anger in
his opposition to that contemporary appropriator of Averroes, Siger of
Brabant. That Averroist position requires a dangerous dualism, reducing
person to a *part* serving a *whole*. Its parallel we find Maritain speaking to
in our present epigram, in which *person* is considered as an individual in
relation to the structure of the world; in relation, that is, to social and
political structures that are temporal finitudes insofar as *person* is of concern to us in its ultimate end. Thus Maritain will say,

> As an individual, each of us is a fragment of a species, a part of the universe,
> a unique point in the immense web of cosmic, ethical, historical forces and
> influences—and bound by their laws. . . . Nonetheless, each of us is also a
> person and, as such, is not controlled by the stars. Our whole being subsists
> in virtue of the subsistence of the spiritual soul. . . . It is as person that we
> love, since "Love is not concerned with qualities." . . . For love is not con-
> cerned with qualities or natures or essences but with *persons.*"

But that new thought a-burning after Thomas must necessarily reduce
person to the control of the stars, and to that end *person* becomes reduced
to *individual*, toward becoming a mechanistic part serving the larger intellect. In consenting to serve that larger intellect there lies, however, a
presumption of that larger intellect as exterior to the controlling stars
themselves, though not transcendent of them. Such is the operation of an
argument appropriating but also inverting not only Plato but also Thomas
himself. It is the initiating gambit required to that new Western thought
which leads to a quasi-mythical reduction of *person* to a *part* in the shad-

owy machine, the universe. In a concession to that residual common sense, which still knows itself person and knows a hunger for Person transcendent of finitudes, the strategy requires a substitution of some concept for that of God. Fancy then is used to "personify" the purported shadow machine itself to placate the restless particular soul. The substitute is "Nature." In the Averroist error we might put it that intellect, still considered in Thomas's day transcendent, is argued manifest in nature as if a hydra: it is a *one* intruding into a multiplicity of heads, into individual brains but not losing its unity thereby. Some centuries later this version of intellect will emerge in its residual presence to thought in fascinations with immanence in the machine of the universe.

What is either ignored or deliberately subverted in the Averroist argument is the intellectual distinction recognized in *person*. The sense in intellect of desiring a transcendence to its *particular* perfection must itself be deconstructed. (A late remnant signifying the success of that deconstruction, one is tempted to say, is the prestige of *committee* in our world, in which as often as not we have the Averroist error writ small.) The first step in the reduction of the unity of intellect in the discrete person is to transfer *intellect* as concept to a limit of the stars, to the limits of "Nature." Thus may be subverted the transcendent end of intellect—known by intellect in its nature but forgotten by its fascination with concepts. Such is the beginning of the secularization of creation. For the hunger for transcendence, the desire for immortality, can but disturb the efficiency in the gnostic intent. And so by granting a limit of the stars in that concept "Nature," stirring a pride by conquest, intellect is limited from its transcendence by a closed system. It was necessary to this incipient "modernist" inclination in intellect, then, to repudiate Thomas's argument for the essential unity of intellect in relation to the discrete person, while at the same time appropriating Thomistic truth to the personal limits of the manipulating intellect. One must search long indeed, we are saying, to find the gnostic activist who will consent to *himself* as an individual among individuals, a part among parts, instead of being the exception to that reductionist version of humanity. The system is closed, for he closed it. But he closed it as he exited it. In operating from a denial of personhood in the Thomistic sense, that gnostic nevertheless functions as a person and will not relinquish that nature, though transforming it to the convenience of his intended action against being. That is, the gnostic will be found again and again to be a *person* in whom person is perverted. The perversion of personhood, Thomas would say, is the perversion of love in its relation to Love. It is that perversion which we call *self-love*.

And so, such perverse intellect appropriates Thomistic truth, which is true, not because articulated by Thomas, but because it is that knowledge given intellect from reality itself. It is an appropriation to the personal limits of the manipulating intellect which is intent on power gained by its pursuit of its own absolute autonomy. The source of that power is seen as possible by appropriating "Nature's" power to its own authority, to be exercised in turn upon "Nature," including human nature. That is why the concept *plurality* becomes increasingly important to such a "director" of that power in his reconstitution of "Nature," which is in its fundaments the intent to restructure being. For a concept like *plurality* allows a residual sentiment in the separate self, echoing a known but forgotten sense of *personhood*. *Plurality*, as a principle justifying activism in some degree, rescues the loss of *person* indicated by the formal and austere *individual*, in which term there is the suggestion of *identity*, so that the particular person becomes indistinguishable in the realm of Nature when reduced to individual—not actually so, but technically so, and technique leading to technology will obfuscate the distinction. That is, by the letter of the law propounded by gnostic intellect, *equality* is eroded to *egalitarianism*, supported by the lingering moral sense proper only to the reality of personhood.

One might survey Western history since the nineteenth century and discover that such is the confusion distorting common sense, with the seeming anomalies of, say, the French Revolution and Stalinism, totalitarianism by committee or by single dictator—always, of course, justified by the confused assertion of *dignity* in the *individual*, made proportionate by the exercise of the gnostic power ascendent in the historical moment. What is necessary to the lord or lords of gnostic power, then, is the atomizing of community, if the "Prince" or a "Collective Prince" is to maintain authority through power seized from, or seduced from, the *persons* in *community*. Such was the necessity to the appropriation of power over being, but it is not an interest actually proper to intellect in its nature nor to the truth of things. It is, in fact, a perversion of nature, in respect both to the *person* and that larger diversity, the body of creation.

In the Averroist error, the unity of intellect is declared transcendent of created existence by the logic of the proposition of its *separate* unity, thereby removing it from its essential limit in *person*. In this strategy, it might be said, intellect is conjured down to creation by the Averroist concept of intellect, out of the realm of Platonic Idealism into a shadow world which does not thereby cease being Plato's shadow. Thomas must have seen a species of the same error in the contemporary uses of Aristotle, and indeed much of his labor was spent in resisting this sort of Platonizing of Aristotle whereby there as an increasingly unsuitable pretense that material existence is a shadow world. Aristotle, Thomas objected, was a stalking horse used to capture the Aristotelian realist to a secularized Platonism, to a Platonism entrapped by cosmology which Greek philosophy had struggled to escape. It is significant that Thomas opposes this Alexandrian manipulation, returning to the complete texts of Aristotle, insofar as he could find them, to rebuke the distortion being made through a selectivity practiced on Aristotle.

Now this appropriation of Plato and Aristotle by the Neo-Averroists with whom Thomas battled bears an ambience of spiritual respectability, residual from Plato, though the spiritual particularity of the created soul is put at once at risk. That is to say, by the appropriation, Platonic Idealism is transferred toward the shadow world away from the transcendent world, but done progressively so that there is no sudden panic from the loss of orientation to the transcendent. Indeed, rather the opposite occurs, an exhilaration of spirit we speak of as the "Renaissance Spirit," given to exploration of the world in all its dimensions. That is the first ambience of spirit in the new dispensation. Its last will be that of ennui as we suggested, as celebrated by Baudelaire, though after much struggle rejected by T. S. Eliot. Meanwhile a ground is sufficiently prepared for evil's flourishing in our actions, as Maritain observes, through our giving a preponderance of consent to man as individual, at the expense of man as person. Given its effect in Western thought and action as we may observe it from our vantage of retrospection, one suspects this transfer of Platonic Idealism to a proximate habitation in the shadow world and in select intellects to be less a principle out of intellectual conviction of the truth of how things stand than a pragmatic advantage to the standing of the particular intellect who is interested in manipulative uses of power.

It is a secularizing of Platonism: the universal is set aside from the transcendent, as *individual* is set aside from *person*, and a new "spirit" is posited in God's stead, with the emerging advantages of Nominalism as the instrument for the dislocation. Or should we rather say "new spirits," since the name of this new unknown god shifts under the pressures of event: there is the spirit of nature, the spirit of history, the spirit of humanity, the spirit of science, the spirit of the state—any number of names used as signs to woo a common sense reduced by the popularity of the new name. The name becomes an object, captor of persons into a collectivity of opinion: the "Spirit" of the moment. The common principle to this shifting from an *end* to the *means as the end* is the gradual denial of any transcendent cause to either spirit or shadow, so that the shadow may be thus given the illusion of being made substantial by the action of the consent of collective individuals. There is in this strategy, I suggest, a recognition that unsophisticated intellects at least require some sense of religious end to any intellectual principle. Only in accommodating that incipient hunger in the individual, which is a hunger for a recovery as *person*, may the principle be used to control a siphoned power to the interests of the particular gnostic intellect.

We are aware today as never before of the implications of that Marxist shibboleth: religion is the opiate of the people. To the sophisticated intellectual, that was a "truth" justifying the condescending manipulation of those "religious" individuals. We are even more aware of that truth at our century's close, given the bankruptcy of Marxism, because we now may recognize the cleverness of the strategy. For Marxism wasn't simply intent on removing the superstitution of "Christianity," the shibboleth of "religion as opiate" used as a stalking horse requiring a steady, quiet approach to the beast to be slain, Christianity. The very stalking was itself a most deliberate opiate to intellect. In that clever deception, one religion— *materialistic determinism*—was raised on an altar to the new god, the ideal state, which became the new chimera worshipped by intellect, as imminent. The separation of the intelligentsia from the people, whether as manifest in Solzhenitsyn Russia or in our own country, is clearly an effect of this clever ruse of intellect. In the end, what has proved most bitter to the intellectual is his own self-betrayal, for it has become impossible by now to deny that the god has failed the intellect that created it. Making that failure even more bitter is his growing recognition that he, too, required that opiate, religion, whether focused (if but vaguely) in the "state" or "humanity" or in these latter days the "environment."

In studying Western intellectual history, we observe that particular persons, particular intellects, are caught up by this turning of the self upon the self in its self-love. And that entrapment underlines again and again the truth which St. Thomas defended against Neo-Averroist appropriations of the ancient heresy: intellect, Thomas insists, is a discrete unity peculiar to *this* person, certified by its experience of its own reality. What becomes fatal to intellect is the conclusion from that experience of unity that it is autonomous. For in that conclusion its capacity for an open response to things other than itself is damaged. So handicapped, intellect is well along the way toward the further conclusion that all not awareness itself is antagonist. However much Occam or Bacon or Descartes or Hume or Hegel asserts his argument as intending the general good as its end, by the inclination to, or presumption of, intellect as autonomous he sets himself outside the general good by that principle underlying the argument. The presumption that my intellect is autonomous must in the end issue in the belief that I am the single king, the single god, of being.

To that end, implicitly or explicitly, such argument advances a severely limited vision of the truth of things. In a sort of concession to humility, whereby one demurs from himself as king or god, there follows an elevation of demigods such as Progress to intellect's Parthenon. Progress as an emerging god is inclusive of a multiplicity of names—History, Humanity, and so on. But what it signifies primarily is a progress of intellect both in and against the world, a fulfillment of autonomy over being.

Let us insist on this point, justified by Thomas's argument, that intellect necessarily acts with clear evidence of the truth of its discrete unity, whatever the distance between its potency and act. And it is well enough to say as well that, in dealing with such intellects, we are not so much contending with infidel intellect as with heretical intellect. That is at least a concession we may make to afford some respect to good intention, even when it paves the road to the hell of intellect's separation from being. As for heretical intellect, T. S. Eliot suggests that the difficulty with it is that it is partly right.[3] That is why it is difficult to deal with. As to a possible presence of intellect as infidel, we may remark that an intellect may pretend otherwise—may pretend to a consent to the Neo-Averroist principle while secretly convinced of its own possession of intellect as undivided, as possessed fully through gnosis. Its pretense is through a species of intellectual deism, speaking in signs *as if* intellect were separate from particularities such as *person*, suggested as pervasive of the shadow world and requiring only its revelation by the elected intellect manifest in himself, the anointed priest—self-anointed by gnosis. Thus the dualism again in asserting a universal cause to what may then be taken as diverse extension. But one is in a very curious intellectual milieu when thus required to reconcile pervasive spirit to pervasive shadow. Little wonder the confusion in our own day, when the particular intellect operates from a position that must implicitly assume its own substantial unity, which by its operation it must as intellect also deny. Little wonder that image, that inescapable point of departure in intellectual action, is the most disturbing presence of all. It is disturbing since, by its very presence it raises the fundamental question: how may image anneal dualism? How may intellect come to that satisfaction of its secret hunger for unity against a discomforting dualism between the shadow world and its own sense of substantial being, which on its principle of revolt from being it must assert as disjoined? The cry of Husserl last century, *"back to the thing itself,"* is distraught intellect's cry against that dualism, out of its sense of alienation consequent in the modernist principles of the autonomous nature of intellect.

That is why we increasingly become aware of intellectual confusions.

For we must, on every hand, deal with particular intellects who operate by these means of contradictory principles from a position which implicitly assumes the substantial unity of their own intellect. Such are the operators so destructive in our world, the would-be "directors" of being against whom Eric Voegelin has warned us, the "modern gnostics." For these, through intellectual power operated in material manifestations of power, assume the physical world by reducing it from its sacramental relation to the transcendent, though requiring personifications echoing existence as sacramentally taken. It must act with this contradiction if public consent to restructuring the shadowy material world is to be granted. Thus "Nature," we suggested, is born, like Aphrodite rising from an amorphous shadowy sea, through a presumption of image as incorporating symbol in the command of gnosis. The communal *body* of humanity reduced to civil *crowd* requires that transformation, lest the power latent in *crowd*, as opposed to spirit in a *body*, not be collectable. The arresting assertion of that disjunction is put as a question, against the position of Thomistic realism, in words almost universally known but not communally understood. "How many divisions has the Pope?" Stalin is infamous for having asked that question, but some species of that same question is always at hand to any gnostic intellect bent on power.

Being in the Thomistic sense must of course be denied, though the gnostic manager must be very much aware of its residual presence as a knowledge held by the intellect precedent to intellect's concept and so always susceptible to a recovery through common sense. It is nevertheless a reality which must be appropriated through essential particularity, in order to transform the essential to gnostic power. That collection is possible if particularity can be disguised as a random effect in "Nature," and thereby made available as a sort of prime matter to the derived power exercised upon it in restructuring particularity to fit concept. The reality of "Nature" is thus to be used to *subvert* reality itself. Thus the uneasy sense of committing a transgression of reality, the twinge of *sense* in common sense stirred by gnostic appropriation, may be somewhat stilled. At this moment, its most threatening manifestation seems to be out of a Darwinian genetics, with a multitude of disturbing questions increasingly forced upon us in this latest dream of a god who will not fail intellect. But reflection here gives one discomfort. The modern state itself sprang from the brow of Hegel and Marx in response to the necessity in the dualistic principle of intellect as divorced from the rest of creation. Mystical though it may appear, genetic determinism has the same roots, a concept in which gnostic manipulation of *particular* beings (through gene adjustment) is a parallel to the manipulation of the "gene" as person in the body social. Always, it is common sense which is the threat to gnostic manipulations of being, a common sense stirred by conscience, which stirs awareness into at least a gloom of indefinite guilt. But the fitfully stirring conscience may yet be explained away. There is a general concern within the popular mind for the deleterious effects of television upon intellect, especially upon our young. But never fear, I have before me, from the "Science/Medicine" section of the Atlanta *Journal-Constitution*, reassurance, under the headline, "Can't turn TV off? Genes may be culprit." Not the devil, but the gene made me do i̇.

The initial Averroist error about intellect which St. Thomas so vigorously opposed may be described metaphorically as hydra-headed, though a single being in its body. The transformation of that error to modern gnostic ends requires an inverse appropriation. Now there is one intellect, the gnostic manager's, existing by extension to the several parts of being that are to be transformed, the parts named *individuals* in the collective intent prescribed by that gnostic intellect presuming its own oneness. To say *one* here does not necessarily mean to say any particular discrete intellect. *Stalin* or *Hitler* are convenient signs, but their recent manifestations might as easily be designated *Committee*. The submissiveness of discrete persons, though possessed of common sense, to such experts of being is too conspicuous to require demonstration.

There is no longer even the tenuous Averroist recognition of the transcendent. The transcendent reduced to a universalism—that is, reduced to creation as closed cosmology—followed by universalism separated from actual existence by Nominalism, leaves the expert or the experts in intellectual command through the sign as now enslaved to instrumentality. Thus is justified an isolation of intellect or intellects in a transcendence of the shadow world, within which drifts those shadows called individuals. To borrow from a poem by Wallace Stevens, "The Idea of Order at Key West," the gnostic intellect, sometimes in plural concert as a body of experts in a limited vision, concludes itself the *only* world, and furthermore a world that exists only by its authority over sign, an authority denied to those shadowy separate intellectual worlds, any one else. The rationalization of that presumption one finds in such arguments as Jean-Paul Sartre's. Argument most contradictorily advanced, of course, since if the argument is true there is no need to argue, no need to attempt persuading other intellects whose existence must be, by the extension of the Sartrean principle despite denials, dependent upon the grace of his own intellect as act.

If one spoke as Old Testament prophet on this matter, he might observe that this progression into modernism since Thomas is but the continuation of an old revolt, signaled by the ancient shibboleth prophetic of intellectual isolation: *non servium*. Thus the fundamentalism at the heart of modernism proves ancient indeed. Milton stated it in the older terms in *Paradise Lost*. We see it in Percy Bysshe Shelly, who appropriated the Satanic but disguised it as mythically heroic, as Promethean. Indeed, there has been a general masking of the diabolical itself through Romantic appropriations of Prometheus, made in the name of Humanity, the name which is used to justify a range of aberrations of the human. The spectacles of those aberrations are everywhere about us. That modern religion Humanism as founded formally in our century when examined in its consequent manifestations reminds us, or should remind us, of the perversions being made possible by old Nominalist assumptions. One need only think of the typical humanist's position on abortion, "pro-choice." Or one need only explore the humanist dimension of political thought in the West following World War I, which raised in its wake a political consent and support to Stalin's cause. Little wonder that we have difficulty, intellectually, dealing now on the one hand with Stalin's slaughter of the Kulacs or Hitler's exterminations, and on the other with the slaughter of innocents under the justification of a freedom of the self called abortion.

Little wonder that intellect, when it is called back to reality, finds itself desolate. By the waters of being, it sits down first to weep, before turning to that question it must at last engage: "How shall I sing the Lord's song in a strange land?" In that new estate of intellect, beginning a spiritual recovery, it is not likely that intellect shall ever be content to look into those waters and see only its own wavering self.

1

Mind as Its Own Place

Evidently, it is because I am that I think, but it is not in the least
evident that it is because things exist that I think of them.
—Étienne Gilson, *Methodical Realism*

Let us here recall, to suggest how pervasive the disjunction of intellect
from reality, a writer for whom this is a principal theme, James Joyce.
Joyce's artist, Stephen Dedlaus, advances himself as the creating Christ of
a shadow world, who through art makes an imagined world substantial.
Stephen affirms as his own Satan's cry: "I will not serve." It is the artist's
principle, lest credit in his making must be shared beyond himself. So
Stephen rejects family, country, church. Milton has put a telling word in
his Satan's mouth describing the position necessary to this total rejection:

> The mind is its own place and of itself
> Can make a heaven of hell, a hell of heaven.

That such a mind is doomed to be inhabited by a thousand sordid images
as a residue of the rejected world, images seemingly unsubmissive to ordering in an intellectual recovery to reality, is a sufficiently Dantesean
punishment. It is a moment of intellectual estate, let us confess, that we
each most probably experience in some degree, and more acutely at some
moments than at others. For if we do not accept it as inevitable to that
condition of our finite existence, wherein we are touched by original sin,
it is a moment nevertheless forced upon intellect in a myriad of ways by
our daily breathing in "the spirit of the age." We are acutely aware of the
threats to bodily health of "passive smoking," such are the warnings is-
sued by the Surgeon General for our bodily health; we are seldom aware
of the threats to intellectual health from breathing in a polluted intellectual climate. For who defends the intellect in this regard? The Church?

As for this "Spirit of the Age" adrift in reality, Thomistic realism intends to stand against it. This realism affirms an anchor in *being*, from which deracinated intellect has deliberately cast its moorings. That casting away from reality is intellect's act of assuming, as the only acceptable principle of its existence, an insubstantial shadow world of chaos which is dependent for any ordered substantiality it may have upon this particularizing action of this particular intellect at the particular time of that action. It is a decree by intellect of being, so that any existence is thereby supposed an effect of intellect. I have attempted here an abbreviated characterization of the recent history of intellect in its revolt against being, from St. Thomas's *Being and Essence* to Sartre's *Being and Nothingness*, I trust without too much caricature, having explored this history at length in other works. It is a span of our history dominated increasingly by what we might term, following Gilson, *Cartesian Idealism*, though the origins of this aberration are antecedent to Descartes himself on the stage of history. It is, I hold, an inclination in intellect to ideological authority more accurately oriented in respect to an abiding reality in our nature as "man's first disobedience," to borrow once more from Milton.[4] Such survey, though brief, has been necessary preamble to our attention to intellect's recent growing discovery of itself as separated from, rather than tenuously a part of, the world as created reality. It is a condition, we are contending, which is opposed to the one explicated by St. Thomas, for whom intellect is seen as a part of, not the cause of, reality.

Intellect in its recent manifestations of authority is seen to have reached a point of lamentation over its separation. That lament is a major burden in our art, and most especially in our literature over the past two hundred years. Such a strain in his song is likely to gain for the poet the epithet "Romantic," whether uttered pejoratively of him or in praise. This term *romantic* we must deal with progressively and not by abbreviated definition, for we have not advanced our understanding of the "Romantic" condition of intellect when we enumerate symptoms, as when it is said that "Romanticism" is an effect upon intellect from the dominance in it of *imagination* over *reason*, or when we find in that condition only an impulse to escape unpleasant circumstances. Or say that in the "Romantic" state of mind one may well discover merely a nostalgia occasioned by a separation of the *individual* from the *crowd*, or his submergence in *nature*, and so on. Symptoms require exploration deeper than catalogue, but also deeper than the merely psychological rationalizations of that state of intellect that has been dominant since the time Eliot, himself in revolt against "Romanticism," declared himself a Classicist. Very soon he was to recognize the inadequacy of such terms to the questions about reality which intellect must ask to recover itself to reality.

If the "Romantic" mind sometimes laments its sense of separation, of alienation, it may as easily celebrate that separation as a justification of its intention to power over being. In the affairs of civil and political action, that celebration may be spoken of as the power intellect would exercise over Nature. That celebrant of intellectual authority, rejecting so he believes the "Romantic" disposition of intellect, will very probably understand himself to be a "Realist." Indeed, it is this "Realist" intellect that is likely to apply the epithet "Romantic" pejoratively to whatever intellectual opposition it meets in Nature's arena. For that intellect which exhibits misgivings about its separation from reality is a clear and present danger, requiring a term upon which to accrete pejorative connotations, though the term itself may not speak directly to the thing it would name when used by the "Realist." For a gnostic in "Realist's" clothing knows vulnerability and is quick to defend against the hint of opposition by the "Romantic" mind. Of course, the rising spirit in what we have come to call the "Romantic Age" in our literature and philosophy provided a variety of evidences to such accretion, particularly in the wake of nineteenth-century science. Victor Hugo's "liberalism in literature" in opposition to the restraints of a supposed "classicism," Heine's observation of medievalism as feeding the "Romantic" ideal, Pater's attention to the strangeness of beauty as opposed to order as beauty's ground: these and many symptoms, elevated to Romantic principles by the would-be Romantic, provided ground to pejorative imputations that Romanticism is merely the weak intellect's attempt to escape from the "real" world.

In consequence, there comes about a false antithesis between *Romantic* as epithet and *Realist* as epithet, an antithesis whose proximate ground of origin is the eighteenth century. The "Romantic" in his revolt is acclaimed or stigmatized by the "Realist" as possessed by nostalgia, his sense of a "something" lost being fed by dreams of the "long ago and far away," the strange and outlandish, the unique, and so on. The "Romantic" position is seen as looking away from the present to the past. But the "Realist's" position has emerged more and more as turning from the present to an ideal future. Both "Romantic" and "Realist" may thus be seen as avoiding a problematic present, the one dreaming the future as a past idealized, the other dreaming a future as a future substantiated through abandonment of the past. What we shall be concerned to show is the likelihood that both these minds are victim to similar intellectual dislocations from reality, when seen from a Thomistic perspective. It is the partial, limited, position each holds that occasions our setting the names in quotation marks above.

So conspicuous have these antipathetic minds appeared over the past two hundred years that a considerable critical industry supports itself in analyzing them in the academy—in philosophy departments no less than in literature or history departments. Scholars explore the degree to which intellects in a century or in a decade, or the discrete intellect of a particular person, is given to the one or to the other position—to being "Realist" or "Romantic." One may be struck however by similarities if he considers the emphasis by each upon the symptoms of the two conditions as detailed in a people or a group or movement or an individual, and especially as nostalgia must face its dream when it proves illusion, as in that disjunction of intellect drawn to the good old days on the one hand through lamentation or on the other to its seeming obverse, the "Realist" program for a glorious future to be accomplished by the gnostic passion for its own dream, which has had cataclysmic displays as illusion at the end of our century.

What we suspect as a deeper symptom, binding Romantic and Realist, the symptom we are to explore, is that both are disquieted by an insistent *present*. The Romantic may be cast as lamenting the present because of an antagonism from his fellows who call themselves Realists. The Realist may be disquieted by the presence of the Romantic, who has a disturbing habit of calling the Realist's own present in question by calling in question the reality of his projected ideal. Such a tensional antipathy leads to the prominence of those two genres of literature so popular in our day, history and prophecy, which share a common emphasis on politics, economics, and social structure but differ in as they are propounded by historian or prophet, the one emphasizing the past in an ambiguous present and the other the future as potential in the ambiguous present. But each contends with the other for the support of the popular spirit *in this present*.

What becomes lost in this contention is an unchanging and inescapable condition to intellectual action: the only point at which any action, significant or insignificant, is possible is this present moment. The complexities of our present moment are not escaped by turning away into the past nor toward a projected future, insofar as such turning effects a disjunction of the present from the past and future. Intellectual, social, or spiritual action is always a present condition to thought, whether the action be Adam's or Plato's or Marx's or Sartre's. Which is to say that the terms *Romantic* and *Realist*, as they have grown out of recent history and become codified by academic disciplines of literature, philosophy, and history—those terms at best designate two species of the dissociation of intellect from reality. I would characterize them together as "Romantic," insofar as that term carries pejorative connotations. For in this war of terms, it is evident that the "Realist" has controlled that war since the mid–nineteenth century. In either address, that of Romantic or Realist as we have so far used the terms, and whether in respect to social or political or literary interests, the position is founded on confusions of thought occasioned by intellect's disruption from the always insistent circumstances of intellection: reality as perceived by intellect in this present moment. Only a willfulness of intellect can make that relation obscure, with whatever intent.

It is precisely against this willfulness of the Realist or the Romantic that Thomistic realism stands opposed, and on the grounds stated as the necessary point to intellectual reflection—the initiating ground of circumstances to intellectual being perceived in this present moment of its existence. The Thomist would thus reject both the pathos of the defeated spirit reflected in nostalgia, which has so generally affected our recent literature, despite the disguise of experimentation in respect to form, and the unrealistic pretense to a progressive command of being directed by the intellect as Realist, which until recently threatened to dominate all of our sciences. Thomistic realism insists that, while the Romantic poet may become adept at forgetting the present misery of intellect by a nostalgic journey either into his own past or the world's past—into his childhood or into some version of the childhood of the race—such an escape is but illusional, foretelling the inevitable return to this present moment. Similarly, Thomistic realism would also reject the "Romantic" realist's error in ignoring himself as a part of the present context of creation, a principle inescapable to Thomistic realism. Indeed the Thomist might even suggest that the Realist's too is a species of nostalgia, a lingering expectation of the vindication of eighteenth-century Enlightenment thought that so firmly elevated Progress to godhead.

One sees easily enough the temptation to the "Romantic" realist (we shall presently abandon such awkward terms) to discount himself as a part of the larger whole of existence in this present moment, for he must believe himself separate from, not a part of, reality lest his determination to power over being require some adjustment by his recognition of that truth about the way things stand. The separation implies an abandonment of the past and at best a tenuous acceptance of the present, in the interest of a future to be born of imaginings in the name of Progress. If he accepts the truth of things experienced here and now, the imagined future is called in question. That such dreams are indeed illusions does not mean that they are not consequential in their effects upon the body of creation here and now. The history of our own century demonstrates such consequences again and again, though the lessons so often made seem not often learned. C. S. Lewis, in his *Abolition of Man* (1947), shows the final end to which such willfulness must lead. Since Lewis's little book, we have seen that abolition progressively accomplished, whether we look to technology's alchemy through artificial intelligence or technology's alchemy in engineering biological genetics.

The realist mind as dominating the sciences is in rapid decline, though still very much a force intending to dominate. *Time* magazine, with some of its proclivity as supermarket tabloid, ran a piece on "In Search of Artificial Life" in its August 6, 1990, issue, with the subtitle enticement reading: "Some scientists believe that things inside their computers are actually alive. What's really scary is that it may be true." It can advance that "truth" of things artificial, since "surprisingly, there is no clear definition of 'life.' " Similarly, I am tempted to say, we may hold it "true" that a cat has five legs if we avoid any clear definition of *leg* and count its *tail*. It is in respect to this manner of confusion that Roger Penrose writes his *The Emperor's New Mind: Concerning Computers, Minds, and the Laws of Physics* (1990). His is a welcomed, skeptical examination of the claims presently advanced by the disciples of artificial intelligence (AI), examining their advocacy of AI as actual intellect justified by physics. Suspending for the moment the question of whether Penrose is of the country of the heretic or the country of infidel, in relation to our earlier note on this concern, consider his incisive questioning of the advocates of the latest homunculus, AI.

The basic ground of the AI advocate, says Penrose, is that "mental activity is simply the carrying out of some well-defined sequence of operations, frequently referred to as an *algorithm*." (17) The "algorithm" is "a calculational procedure," instances in the history of AI analyzed by Penrose. Now there are among the advocates of AI both moderates and fundamentalists, not always comfortable with each other, as proves true of such division elsewhere—as among Baptists or among Conservatives and the like. The fundamentalists in any division have the virtue in debate of underlining the crucial point in contention. Within the advocates of AI, the fundamentalist is called a "Strong Artificial Intelligence" advocate (SAI, for our economy). He holds that, in Penrose's characterization, "the difference between the essential functions of the human brain (including all its conscious manifestations) and that of the thermostat lies only in this much greater *complication*, or perhaps 'higher-order structure' or 'self-referential properties,' (or some other attribute that one might assign to an algorithm) in the case of the brain." What is crucial to a proper alarm about these extremist fundamentalists of AI is that the immediate effect of the simple analogy may so easily woo consent. After all, thermostats work for us in many applications, like a good servant, not even wanting holiday or a Saturday night off. The Japanese very early recognized this advantage, and it has brought them to a technological power in this economic moment that leaves us confused.

The confusion in our response to this new world power lies in part, perhaps, in our not identifying clearly its cause. We know more or less how to respond to military power, even to economic power as justified by the authority of force in that more primitive dimension of economic and military warfares. But there is a new presence: we are at once awed and disturbed by the power of the microscopic chip capable of commanding actions of nature, in some respects defying nature. Frankenstein's new monster is so refined as to disappear from sensual representations, becoming a minute fragment of silicon as an altar at which this new holy ghost, intellect independent of human intellect and of nature and nature's God, is to be worshipped—if its fundamentalist advocates are to be credited. The meaning of "life" becomes ambiguous indeed. There is a flaw in the fundamentalist position which Penrose recognizes, though I do not think he makes as much of it as is warranted, largely because his perspective is limited by his devotion to physics as the ultimate perspective upon the truth of things. We note his remarking the necessity of "attributes" by the SAI advocate as a point of departure. We note as well *algorithm* as "a calculational procedure." And what we discover is that, in redefining "life," the AI advocate must submit to metaphor. It is a submission, however deliberately ignored, to an anchor of its alchemy in the truth of things, in existence precedent to this manufacture of its own new holy ghost, AI. That is, such an advocate must move from a recognition of the truth of that existent, *his own intellect*, as the calculator, as the attributor, in the restructuring of the meaning of "life." This restructuring is dependent ultimately, I suggest, on an acceptance by that amorphous creature, the Popular Spirit of the Moment, so that the object and end is a conversion of that spirit to this new religion of AI.

What we might explore is the question of whether the advocates of artificial intelligence are dependent upon an analogy of attribution, though necessarily pretending it to be an analogy anchored in the realities of the given and unexplained—namely, the actual living intellect on the one hand and the body of the world on the other. What is downplayed in AI, or ignored or unnoticed, is its dependence upon the "I"—which does not represent intelligence in the manner of the thermostat, a position always dependent upon a continuing superstition resting in Darwinian evolution, but the "I" of discrete consciousness. This dependence upon the "I" of consciousness is troublesome to itself precisely because the "I" is an existing "life" and not artificial. And so, troubled by its finitudes as an awareness under the pressures of its desire, it is (as common sense tells us) discombobulated. One hardly anticipates computers as counselors to computers that are troubled by such a disturbed awareness, though one might write a satiric science fiction account of that necessity. Which is to suggest that AI is intellect sterilized of life and so a shadow—a mechanistic shadow—of intellect, dependent upon a hidden god: namely, the intellect of its creator. What is most studiously required, if this experiment in man's making of "life" is to be credited by an always hungry popular spirit, is the distinction between *knowing* and *understanding*, the distinction so carefully made by St. Thomas in respect to the given nature of intellect. For, as Penrose remarks, "The mind-stuff of strong AI is the logical structure of an algorithm." That is a "mind-stuff" reduced from its fullness of being as a nature among natures to an abstraction.

Penrose makes a telling point about the logical position assumed by the fundamentalist AI advocate: "There is a remarkable irony in this fact that ... the standpoint of strong AI seems to drive one into an extreme form of dualism, the very viewpoint with which the supporters of strong AI would least wish to be associated!" It is not desired, because the presence of any dualism reflected by intellect raises metaphysical questions. The dualism, says Penrose, results from the algorithm's having a sort of "disembodied 'existence' which is quite apart from any realization of that algorithm in physical terms." It is to Penrose's credit that he underlines the difficulty, though he himself would prefer not to engage metaphysical questions, rather limiting the problem to physic's domain. So long as "algorithms" are restricted to the realm of physics, keeping the whole realm of physics itself free of metaphysical speculation, the always intrusive hunger for understanding may be kept somewhat at bay. When the "algorithm" is seen as a thing separate from its embodiment in actions of a process, it calls attention to a dualism, whereby the relation of spirit to body in the created thing has been obscured. The algorithm's dependence in its "body" chip, no less than the dependence of both upon the intellect which creates their conjunction—the "I"—raises significant questions. Those questions are metaphysical ones, rising in the "I" when the electrical impulses through the chip bear undeniable effects in nature. A process, we might say, which requires a critical perspective by the "I." What is thus underlined is the parameters of such thinking, prescribed by the "thinking" creator. The process turns back upon its cause, with disturbing questions about the finitude of that agent, the "creator" of this homunculus now abroad among us. What is desired by the SAI religionist, above all, is free will in the creature he has made, the last frontier in the battle between finite and infinite intellect. What stands in the way of its victory is itself as the determinate cause of the free spirit such an "I" would create in the AI. What is ironic, almost to the level of comedy, is that it is a *finite* determinate cause, attempting an infinite being as an effect of its finite creator.

Penrose's position, as I have underlined it, is that of physicist, so that his good service to us in establishing the central questions about AI serves only to delay those ultimate questions beyond the purview of physics. One discovers that he accepts his premises out of an evolutionist faith, though he holds that faith "metaphorically" and not fundamentally, putting him in the position of skeptic, not only toward the claims of AI but toward the claims of the Thomistic metaphysician. He recognizes in his own argument a degree of confusion occasioned by "anthropomorphic terms," which are acceptable so long as understood to be merely metaphorical. What he does not say is that such metaphor is attributive analogy, left suspect therefore in reference to the actuality of the being of both the machine (AI) and the being of mind itself alive, the "I" as creator of the machine.

He says: "it might be argued that there is an artificiality about imposing such 'goals' [as pleasure, pain, and the like in relation to the actions, the process of AI] on our device according to our whim. But this is not so very different from the way that natural selection has imposed upon us, as individuals, certain 'goals' which are to a large extent governed by the need to propagate our genes." Aside from the weasel words—*to a large extent*—there is a presumption of natural selection as intentional, so that Penrose wavers from his recognition of "anthropomorphic" supposition as merely metaphorical. *Intentionality* is an aspect of intellect, for which there is no attributed agent save "natural selection," which term answers no question of agency. And so Penrose himself implies the problem of a dualism that is circular in its Darwinian sophistications about the gene as determinate of particular beings. Does the moose have long legs because it feeds in shallows, or does it feed in shallows because it has long legs? The latest mystical fascination with genes introduces such fascinating complications out of empirical discoveries that the old cliché, to which science or meta-science must return willy nilly, is for a moment delayed: which came first, egg or chicken? That is its ancient metaphorical formulation. The inescapable *question* is that of agency, which we are returned to again and again by the one inescapable *presence* of agent in creation, man himself as intellectual creature.

We are concerned here with questions speculative, and so it may seem of little consequence in our work-a-day world upon which we rest such confidence. That is the world of "reality," we are like to say, in which the excesses of ideas are put straight. But in truth, that world of reality in which we vest faith is the world in which the process of accidents is supposed as managed by the "realist." To ask questions about the moose's legs or the chicken's egg may appear a parlor game, when it is more crucially a game likely to be played out in the laboratory, and without crucial speculative questions having been asked. For if we look closely at the implications in the actions of the practical intellect, which enjoys a general consent, we must discover that those actions rest at last on speculative actions of intellect, and as often as not actions not well founded in reality. Speculative questions require a solid foundation, but receive rather (in crucial instance) only a circular isolation from reality. The practical intent of the rationalist mind justifies the speculative, rather than the other way round. And it inevitably does so since truth itself is justified by the intellect rather than intellect by truth.

We are in a region of concern, here, most central to those concerns of the "Romantic" poet who is made disquiet by this circular approach to reality. We are not, of course, speaking simply of the nineteenth-century poet, nor merely of the poet as writer of verses, but of that intellect responding to its intuitive inclination, whether the issue of the intellectual engagement with such questions results in our calling the particular intellect a poet, or philosopher, or scientist. That is why, though our general concern in these pages is principally with the poet, this initial engagement is crucial and not the luxury of an aside from our principal concern. For it is one thing to engage esoteric questions—or seemingly esoteric questions—about the limits of artificial intelligence. It is quite another to recognize how effective so-called artificial intelligence has been in solving practical problems in the real world. And in that impressive accomplishment, there accrues to the idea of "artificial intelligence" an authority demanding a general consent, given the general favor the public mind directs to practical solutions to its work-a-day problems. Gradually, then, there easily occurs a shift in our thinking whereby, through initial consent to the principles upon which practical problems are resolved to the general good, we come to rest a faith in principles which have not been rigorously examined.

From that will follow an ideology pervasive of our thought, indeed so pervasive that we are not likely even to recognize our individual consent to it as being used to justify a relocation of desired ends to the acclaimed means as end. One might well say that we are experiencing, at the end of this century, just such a shift, more subtle and dislocative of intellect than the more limited applications of that same principle which we have witnessed in the rise and fall of Marxist economics out of Hegel. What is most dangerous here is, in effect, the emergence of a new religion, vague in its fundamentalism but basically requiring that intellect submit to the principle that the universe is a closed machine which in some wise has cast up intellect, which in turn guides that machine. Such threatens to be the triumph of circularity. To what purpose, and toward what end, continues unclear in this dislocation, which continues to require some species of Utopian projection not unlike the several already attempted and defeated, based in that same principle, since the early Renaissance.

This point we have made emphatically because it is crucial. As for our consent to the principal as if a religious response to a vision of ultimate truth revealed to the Realist's mind, one must look closely at the pseudo-religious evangelism that permeates the ecological movement—without, need I say, suggesting that one does not have a moral responsibility to existence, to the good health of creation. For what increasingly emerges is a secular deism, well illustrated by James Lovelock's *The Ages of Gaia: A Biography of Our Living Earth* (1988). The old myths of Mother Earth, as ancient as Homer, are given an illusion of substantiality out of the latest sciences. If writers such as Lovelock are the theologians to this emerging religion, neither is it without its philosophical doctors, one school of which we have touched upon in remarking the elevation of artificial intelligence. At a midpoint between the abstract scholastic who deals in artificial intelligence and the evangelical preacher such as Lovelock, there is a school set upon a justification of both to the popular mind. Its principal spokesman of the moment, complete with the prestige of a position as distinguished scientist in a distinguished university, is E. O. Wilson, the founder and proponent of *Sociobiology: The New Synthesis* (1975). Here is a scholastic doctor requiring attention.

The name which Wilson gives his thesis, *sociobiology*, is indeed a metaphor for the "synthesis" proposed, a sort of *Summa Theologica* for the new age. Now it is my contention that we known an intellect most surely through the metaphors it uses, metaphor being that species of sign whereby a particular intellect attempts to synthesize its vision in a concentrated articulation, lest the complexity of what it cannot say overwhelm the truth it has perceived in its vision of reality. For that reason, let us look closely at the signs given us by this father of sociobiology. By good fortune, given our present attempt, the January-February 1991 issue of *International Wildlife* gives us a point of departure. In it Don Lessem, a close observer of E. O. Wilson, devoted (one gathers) to the principles underlying sociobiology, contributes a portrait called "Dr. Ant." Wilson's passion as scientist is the complex social life of the ant in its multitudenous species, the Central American *Atta* his favorite. What we are interested in is the nature of the language used by Wilson in speaking of his fascination. First Lessem: "by one of Wilson's favorite calculations, these ants' [the *Atta's*] routine task is equivalent to a human running a mile in 3 minutes 45 seconds while wearing a 500–pound backpack." Wilson himself remarks that "An ant colony is a huge family, made up of fertile queens and their many offspring." What Wilson is led to, from such observations (and we are using his particular concern for the ant, though his observations are much more general) is that "Among animals . . . the urge to protect one's shared genes in children and siblings influences all manner of actions, from establishing a territory to dividing labor."

One needs only a cursory reflection on the use here of *family, children,* and like terms to determine that a new species of anthropomorphism is underway, whereby, by first humanizing the ant, Wilson may then anticize humanity. Such a reductive simplification of existence finds its central symbol in the gene, of course, the ploy very common now whereby intentionality as imminent in the universe is focused upon the gene—supported by the sophisticated analysis, chemical and other—upon that image of the universe writ small by the DNA theory that has swept all biological questions before it. In that avalanche has been swept aside those questions which one would raise against this strictly mechanistic reading of existence in its pseudo-disguise of imminent intentionality which gives an aura of "life" to the machine. It is thus that all "animals" have "the urge to protect [their] own genes in children and siblings." It is from such visions of reality that Wilson advances the new scientific discipline of sociobiology. "It may be called evolutionary psychology or bisocial anthropology," he says of it, "but it's taught everywhere, including China and the U.S.S.R." One is shocked, I hope, by the naivete of the statement, since where more than anywhere would the anticizing of the Earth Mother be more likely to be embraced than in China or the U.S.S.R.? ("I never worry about pest control," Wilson says when asked what one must do when over-run by ants.) Little wonder that a Harvard colleague, Stephen Jay Gould, is quoted by Lessem as finding sociobiology "dangerous nonsense." And yet it is a discipline widespread, and growing.

And as a discipline, given the present understanding of the uses of such disciplines, once established as respectable academic thought it must project practical uses in the body social. In 1983, along with Charles J. Lumsden, Wilson published *Promethean Fire: Reflections on the Origin of Mind.* In a critical review of that work, Howard Kaye, a student of social and theoretical implications of modern biology, remarks that in boldly announcing "the discovery of the positivist grail: a true scientific account of the human essence," Wilson aims at extending "Darwinian analysis beyond the physical traits of organisms to their behavioral and social characteristics." (*Commentary*, Oct. 1983) In Wilson's (and Lumsden's) words, that essence is "a machine created by genetic evolution." Out of that conclusion, it follows that the "selection of social and economic roles" and the "goals and principles that organize our daily lives" are rules susceptible to adjustment. As Kaye remarks of this gnostic intentionality in Wilson, "since many of the epigenetic rules . . . are now obsolete, inefficient, and downright harmful, they must be retooled by scientist/social engineers." What we might say in summary of Wilson's philosophical theology about the essence of humanity and its future is that its perfection lies just ahead, accomplished by the new ant queen, the scientist as social engineer. There is an antiquated, eighteenth-century Enlightenment pall over Wilson's mind, made popular by nineteenth-century Darwinian theory and the miracles of twentieth-century technology. It is indeed a frighteningly "dangerous nonsense," dangerous because it is so largely embraced as a new sense of human destiny to that Lotus Land in which it is an eternal afternoon.

Against this nonsense, this secularized dualism whereby the body of the earth and the spirit of the earth constitute a closed system demanding human intellect's consent on the authority of the latest Darwinian genetics, there are many spokesmen, not only from among Thomistic realists but more surprisingly also from an alarmed Darwinian fundamentalist set of mind. The vague issue of a pagan gnosticism that clouds Wilsonian thought clearly has its roots in that intellectual dislocation which Gilson succinctly analyzes as Cartesian Idealism in his *Methodical Realism* (1990). The amalgamation of Descartes's "mathematicism" and Kant's "Newtonian physics" contributes to the necessary theology, despite the disturbing implications emerging out of particle physics, about which more must be said on an appropriate occasion. [5]

Of this amalgamate of Descartes and Kant, Gilson remarks that "He who begins with Descartes cannot avoid ending up with Berkeley or with Kant." The intellectual deism of the emerging position and the nonintellectual paganism necessary to assure popular support prove companionable, in that science out of the *one* (the mystery of the gene) provides many of a paganized populace with particularly the many things that are supposed to satisfy appetite. The result is a "communal" reduction of being, against which Chesterton spoke long ago in distinguishing our acts of *giving* from our acts of *sharing*, a distinction we certify by experience of the everyday world of reality as we must live in that world. Fr. James Schall brings Chesterton to bear in his own discussion of *Religion, Wealth and Poverty* (1990), a work suitably applicable to our common concern for this new paganism. In Chesterton's essay "Why I Am Not A Socialist," he remarks that "Almost all Socialist Utopias make happiness . . . chiefly consist in the pleasures of sharing. . . . Now there is a real pleasure in sharing. . . . But it is not the only pleasure, nor (I think) the highest or most human of altruistic pleasures. I greatly prefer the pleasure of giving and receiving."

Chesterton is, in his final sentence, being ironic, as if the preference were a private one, when it is rather a pleasure founded more largely in his Christian position as articulated by Thomistic realism. What he might well have pointed out as underlying the socialist concern for sharing is that it is—when charity is not its motive, whereby sharing is transformed to giving and receiving—a principle out of Hobbesian conclusion about the nature of our existence in a "state of nature." What that means, as Gerhart Neimeyer has pointed out, is, in Hobbes's phrase, "war of all against all." With that premise, Hegel gives it an altruistic direction, not established in the charity required of the individual soul but vested in the inevitability of history, which direction in turn gains momentum out of Darwinian theory, reaching such frightful consequences in the work-a-day world of this century as to require some alleviation. One may at least pray an alleviation to be found in sharing, the argument runs. But happiness proves always an accident, never found in its direct pursuit, as if happiness were not an accident to giving, sympathizing, controlling. Happiness as primary object always proves evasive of the soul. With the Marxist rationale for sharing in respect to economic things, socialism advances to its support a "humanitarianism," as if to relieve us and turn us to dreams of a continuous state of happiness in nature, a temptation to which we are susceptible simply because we are created creatures. The old belief in our willfulness, our sinfulness as creatures created in the image of God, no longer serves to counter the incessant war in us in our pursuit of happiness. *Sharing*, then, as an ideal to replace *giving*, attempts to soften the gnostic principle already accepted, as if sharing might soften determinism's necessity through our good intentions. Thus Hobbes's "war" of all against all can be made safe for the new religion of Mother Earth, raising to contemplative serenity our prospects upon the "Ages of Gaia" as defined by history.

The position we ourselves are taking in this matter is by now quite evident, the position of Thomistic realism. But there is a position from within the heart of modernist attitudes which have grown out of Hobbes and Hegel and Marx that we should note. There is such an intellect as the Darwinian fundamentalist, who can only see in Wilson's sociobiology a sentimentality obscuring the Darwinian purity out of the Hobbesian proposition that all is at war with all. To this Darwinian fundamentalist, Hobbes must appear something like an Old Testament prophet to Darwinism. The latest liberation theology such as that of sociobiology puts the true faith at jeopardy. There comes to hand an articulate fundamentalist objection to Wilson's "dangerous nonsense," as his colleague called it. It is an objection to scientific sentimentality from one who is clearly not of Chesterton's party. Charles W. Morgan, in a letter to *Science News* (November 3, 1990), takes strong exception to the trend he sees in the pages of *Science News.* "Whenever one of your articles implies, suggests or states that a trait was developed to do such and such (aid in survival, attract a mate, protect from predation, etc.), it assumes an anti-Darwinian, anti-natural selection posture, promoting myth as scientific fact." Our own instance, out of a popular "nature" program used for educational purposes, was the relation of the moose's legs to its feeding habits. Mr. Morgan insists that such traits "may well serve the function in question," but "it was neither designed to do so nor did it evolve to do so. In hindsight, the existence of a function served may suggest the successful implementation of a design solution, but this is an illusion created by the viewpoint." The evidence of purpose, he goes on, is merely accumulated observations of general distribution in this moment, or in some moment, of "history." But since "evolution (natural selection) is neither farsighted nor purposeful, any attempt to establish the purposeful, any attempt to establish the purpose for which a trait originated, is a search for the nonexistent."

The point is well taken, though in that taking we remark that it purifies logically the false principles upon which a sentimentalizing of scientific evidence since Hobbes is founded. It does not follow that those principles are in themselves acceptable, only that the strict logic in relation to the mechanistic principle, implicit in Hobbes and advanced by Darwinian theory, may not be gainsaid by those who are intent on building a view of existence on those principles. Our own position is, of course, quite the contrary. For Mr. Morgan's position against "design" focuses upon the Darwinian vision of a closed creation, and his objection is to a myth of design as imminent in that closed world. One quite agrees, without thereby abandoning the position that there is in creation a design, whereby there is implied a designer.

We may seem to have come a long way from our earlier concern for the "Romantic" realist and the "Romantic" poet, but not so. For one does not encounter in the course of Western thought in these matters many pure determinists such as Mr. Morgan seems to represent. The most severe realist cannot escape nagging suggestions of design, any more than he can escape, while in the body, his daily encounter of the realities of creation which speak design. He may rationalize, in an impure reductionism such as Mr. Morgan charges him with, a "spirit" of some sort, whether symbolized by "Nature" or "Gaia," or whatever term. But what he is left with is a reduction that is itself impure in relation to his announced principles. It continues impure, since his own intuitive recognition of being complicates the severe fundamentalist reductionism that would "purify" intellect's relation to reality—that is, would sever intellect from dependence in reality as Mr. Morgan would require.

And so the Romantic realist is no less susceptible to practicing illusion than his Romantic poet antagonist, though it is often more difficult to discover in his deliberate deceptiveness that realist who is ravenous to sacrifice intellect upon the altar of Progress. That is why Mr. Morgan's account of the Darwinian realist's sentimentality as scientist proves so devastating. It is far easier to discover naivete in the Romantic poet who is seduced by nostalgia than in the Romantic realist who would, like Wilson, readjust genes to his limited vision of an Eden of things first atomized or anticized and then reconstituted. In that vision, the problem lies in the Eden imagined as a seeming object, but whose actuality is the present body of existence, the world. The dangerous nonsense lies in a failure to know what is being manipulated, so that there is in such approaches the quality of somnambulant dream, wherein the dreamer destroys the world within which he dreams without noticing it—unless waked to horror, as with the explosion of the first atom bomb. The explosion out of inordinate dreams of restructuring human nature through manipulation of genes waits its own cloud of horrible awakening from the reductionist manipulations of being itself.

As for the Romantic poet, what the Thomistic realist (if I may for a moment attempt that position) might say of our present intellectual impasse, is that this naive poet in his mood of lamentation at least keeps alive, if but faintly, a recognition of his separation from reality. He would wake from his dream of wandering. And so his important contribution is that thereby he keeps alive a sense that it is an undesirable separation which he suffers. This poet bears at least implicitly in his lamentation a recognition of the desire for a community of intellect, to be joined through creation as creation may be engaged by his own intellect. The dominant modernist spirit, as we have observed, seems to make it increasingly improbable of achievement, especially given the very subtle shifting of desire in the popular mind to focus upon untenable visions of reality as if the proper end. What the Thomist says to the threat of despair out of such recognition of improbability is that a community intuitively desired is a community beyond the reach of those reductionisms of community to a mere worldliness such as dreamed possible by Hegel or Marx or Darwin or Freud or E. O. Wilson. In this respect that community is a "body" always present in this moment, in which moment are united discrete persons beyond history past, present, or future. It is this community, a mystically singular presence, that is always threatened by despair, though the crucial being at risk is not that community itself but the particular soul desirous of membership in it. The community in truth is beyond destruction, we are saying, and only the person desiring membership in that community is susceptible to being lost from it.

To recover this dimension in a present reality, to sustain the person's membership in that larger community, requires of intellect an engagement of this present reality which neither nostalgic euphoria nor utopian dream may prevent. Wherever two or three are gathered together, persons as persons, a body is made manifestly real, though not necessarily palpable to the gnostic mind, who nevertheless encounters that body through that body's circumstantial accidents. The growing, if chaotic, attempt to recover the religion of our fathers as witnessed to us in recent social and political events of the past two decades speaks that point. But that body is manifest beyond its accidents, we are saying, even though but two aspects of reality are recognized by the discrete, lonely, seemingly alienated intellect: *essence* in relation to *being*; my own particular *intellect* in relation to the *truth* of how particular things stand underneath all those things' accidents. It is the nature of intellect to perceive this even though it may not be acutely aware of that perception. It is this perception of *being* which stirs the intuitive intellect so characteristic of the "Romantic" poet.

2

Our Dark Woods Since Dante

In analogicals it is not *diverse realities* which fall under consideration but diverse modes of existence of the self-same reality.

—St. Thomas Aquinas

I have admitted the temptation to believe it increasingly improbable that we recover a community of intellect in its only proper ground, reality, because of the present dominance of the modernist mind. It is a circumstance that might well make one nostalgic for the court of King Louis, with the hulking presence of Thomas confounding the Manicheans in the midst of chaotic court revelry. The improbability which tempts such Romantic longing for a true age of realism seems increasingly apparent and undeniable by a more severe retrospection, divorced of nostalgia—a survey of Western thought since St. Louis's and St. Thomas's time, a sweep which I think reveals that span of our history to be all a "Romantic Age." That is, by that character of intellect seen in that span of time, we see in motion an emerging species of intellect accelerating toward its own isolation unto itself. The anecdote of St. Thomas, thundering out against the Manicheans, delights us. But it does so, not simply by the seeming incongruence of Thomas's presence at King Louis IX's festivities.

One need only recall a similar scene so different in its epiphany: the beggar at the feast of Penelope's wooers. At that moment, when the chief wooers would ridicule the beggar's presumption in asking a turn at attempting to string the great Odysseus's bow, they at last consent, as one might consent to a ten-year-old's attempt to lift his father's car. The beggar

> in one motion strung the bow.
> Then slid his right hand down the cord and plucked it,
> so the taut gut vibrating hummed and sang
> a swallow's note.

19

If one thinks sophistications of "objective correlatives" a modern discovery, he need only look closely here, to this drawing to hushed silence
a chaotic gathering of unruly wooers, each of whom hears that swallow's
note. What follows is general carnage, consummately handled by this
great artist of the terrible, Homer. But attractive as the aesthetic marvel
of this handling of scene might be, that is not our first concern. Rather
we look to Louis's court, to the mountain of a friar in the midst of a feast
as lively as that at Odysseus's court. But it is an appropriate liveliness.
Thomas (as Chesterton tells us of it), "brought down his huge fist like a
club of stone, with a crash that startled everyone like an explosion," crying out, "And *that* will settle the Manichees." The unlikeness in these
like scenes: the feast in Louis's court goes on, but King Louis directs his
secretaries to go to that friar and write down the argument he has just
concluded in his head, because, again Chesterton's words, "it must be a
very good one."

One understands in the anecdote the true nature of patronage, as opposed to our own self-congratulatory version. For we lose an acceptable
patronage when we are removed from the virtues of existence as anchored
in being, spoken to by St. Thomas's principle of proper proportionality.
Our new system deals in proportions of a sort, of course, but proportion
as governed by attribution as abstracted from the accidents of reality,
and adapted in the attempt to balance social and economic and political
demands. The focus is removed from intellect's proper pursuit of the
truth of things. Thus if "x" is granted something of the state's largess on
the basis of personal and historical accidents of his particular existence,
then so must "y" be granted, though on quite different aspects of accidental existence. Thus, for instance, the term "affirmative action" becomes
the shibboleth for attributive actions toward an egalitarian balance of the
accidents of existence. It is not a principle grounded in the truth of things
themselves but in a denial, explicit or implicit, of things (including persons) in their discrete, particular natures. Thus such a term appropriates
to itself, through a disregard for the truth of how things stand in their
actual particular natures, a sentimental version of what might otherwise
be virtuous sentiment toward those particular things. Without regard for
race, color, sex, religion and the like, desirable principle when anchored
in the essence of the particular persons from whom such regard is set
aside, accomplishes nothing if not founded in a proper regard for what
each thing, each person, is. These enumerated negatives are, in the Thomistic view, accidents well enough, but accidents accruing to the essence
of a person, and not random in their own natures and so inappropriately
set aside in such an absolutist simplification. For the result then is, that

having set aside accidents as contingent upon essence, essence itself is ignored. One is then left of necessity to deal, not with persons, but with abstractions. The pursuit of justice in the affairs of mankind is thus made dependent upon rationing our collective regard for persons by the abstraction of statistics, advanced from the analysis of the social body, which body is conceptualized and not grounded in a body of humanity itself. Concept has as elements another abstraction, the State.

This questionable principle of this social order is that accidents and not essences are fundamental to order. And having long since rejected the accidents of birth, as for instance those of "royal" birth, as justifying the authority suited to the governance of a people, we seem only to have substituted the rejected principle in another guise, differing only in the class of accidents acceptable in determining the necessary authority. That is, the accidents of the person in relation to the social body are seen as expressing the truth of that person, since the social body is itself seen as an accident consequent to natural forces—such accidents as those used by Hobbes, Hegel, Rousseau, Marx, and the like to justify the state. But accidents attributed to the person as if essential are not virtual. That is, those accidents are not deeply significant of the proper, particular nature of this particular person. The accidents thus made adherent to the structure of the social body by collective abstractionism are concluded to be the essence of that body. Still, the actual reality of the person in his actual relation to the body of humanity in the realm of reality cannot be long ignored, and will not be ignored. We recognize an eventuality of such error in the present collapse of political institutions in Eastern Europe and in the Soviet Union. And there is a growing attention to similar confusions in the West, requiring only a thoughtful reading of the headlines of our evening paper and no extended explication here to confirm.

If we would discover the cause of the increasingly violent spirit fragmenting the body social in our day, a spirit at war with itself (as made apparent in a myriad of symptoms which the considerable maw of the daily media cannot take in but must register selectively), we find it at the level of our common pretense that accident is determinate of being rather than being as the limiting ground of accident itself. What is required is the intellectual courage to address this fundamental disorientation of intellect in relation to reality. Most conspicuous are the litigations that flood social discourse and threaten an arrest at the very center of the institutions of social order, forced inward upon them by the chaos on the periphery. The growing social disorder can only increasingly remind us of the necessity to regain intellectual courage. Were we to listen to Thomas, we might consider that accident is most immediately perceived—such is our nature as finite beings—as if it were the reality. Such is our nature as given that accident proves at last a helpful means toward conception, through which we approach an understanding of the complexity of reality. The necessary principle, which alone may at last serve social order: truth measures perception, not perception truth. But where our intellectual courage fails, our recovery of a community in that complex reality which truth teaches us will become increasingly improbable. Indeed, there is probable an accelerated degree of improbability of any recovery, an accelerated erosion of social consent. It was to this condition of the modernist world that one "Romantic" poet spoke, having recovered himself beyond the confusions of accidents. That poet, very nearly bordering on personal despair, remarks the "Difficulties of a Statesman" in words that speak directly to this moment of crisis as we must face it at whatever level—local, regional, national, international:

> A commission is appointed
> To confer with a Volscian commission
> About perceptual peace: the fletchers and
> javelin-makers and smiths
> Have appointed a joint committee to protest against
> the reduction of orders.

Out of which comes the public cry of the disoriented:

> We demand a committee, a representative committee,
> a committee of investigation
> RESIGN RESIGN RESIGN

Presently, more certain from a position understood as resting upon the rock of reality itself, that poet, no longer the "Romantic" poet, will say to us:

> What life have you if you have not life together?
> There is no life that is not in community.

That community, so we are arguing, is first of all the community of intellect with being, lest we remain at best described by epitaph as a "descent godless people," whose "only monument [is] the asphalt road/ And a thousand lost golf balls."

Meanwhile, we must do as we can, governed as we should be by the principle that truth is the measure of perception and not perception of truth. And if our concern is not that of Eliot's statesman but that of the artist, we may be led to reconsider what is suggested beneath such a term as *Romanticism*, when thought descends beneath its symptomatic manifestations. It is to this concern, as I have suggested elsewhere, that Dante becomes our first great "Romantic" poet, in whom we find the person of the poet elevated to a dignity as the protagonist of an epic, the *Divine Comedy*, representing the pilgrim soul. Here we move the term *romantic* to a consideration of the poet in whom there is the growing discovery of himself as lost in a dark wood and feeling called to a struggle to recover the path through the encroaching darkness. First, his concern must be for his own rescue, but more largely that becomes the possible rescue of community. We consider this recognition as thematically present in our literature, this awareness in the poet himself growing in its anxiety over its separation from reality: from Dante's dark wood to Eliot's wasteland desert, the place in which there "is no water but only rock. Rock and no water and the sandy road . . . winding above among the mountains."

The other species of the Romantic, intellect as self-imputed "realist," whether in the guise of poet, philosopher, or scientist, began to emerge most evidently with the Enlightenment: he is a more fleeting blossom in that desert, in the light of eternity, though contributing significantly to our own dislocation by his enticement to a various lotus land. We have emphasized his blossoming as out of the eighteenth century, or out of Descartes. But those indicators of time are to be understood as illustrative, not as locating the origin. Before Voltaire there was Descartes; before Descartes, Siger of Brabant and William of Occam. There was Francis Bacon, father of Utopianism—based in empirical arguments that made the future lotus land attractive, cross-fertilized ideologically by Hegel and Hulme and Locke and so on and so on. Before and before: even unto Adam in my own view of our present desert in which we dream gardens out of our intimations of a future bred in intellect by a dislocation of the virtues of intuitive knowledge to a focus in gnostic ends.

With the remainder of the largeness of nature's and history's canvas as a guard against simplifications, let us consider as exemplary two recent "Romantic" poets who confront intellect's dislocation from inclusive reality. They respond in quite different ways, each out of a sense of his dislocation. And each comes to a very personal discovery of his being lost in a dark wood, each at first taking it to be his own unique dark wood. What we value in each, first and last, is his ineradicable intuitive sense of reality which he feels compelled to recover. Each poet represents a species of Romanticism we have spoken of earlier: the nostalgic poet and the progressive, realist as poet. The second, the Romantic poet as realist (in the modernist sense) glories in being separated, at least he does so as much and for as long as he can. I mean here Wallace Stevens, who welcomes his dislocation as a warrant to an audacity with metaphor.

Stephens takes metaphor as dependent only *upon* and only as *out of* his own imagination. The other poet is that homesick Romantic, T. S. Eliot, who in his early poetry believes himself isolated beyond any possible rescue, since he accepts the authority of the dominant spirit of modernism which is pervasive of the intellectual community of which he finds himself member at Harvard University at the turn of our century. The seeming "reality" of his isolation will subsequently reveal itself to him as but a Cartesian Idealism which has become aggressive in the affairs of community. He will not come to that *recognition*, however, before agonies of spirit force him to it. As a student of philosophy, Eliot pursues this false reality in his doctoral dissertation, one chapter of which is called "Leibniz' Monads and Bradley's Finite Centers." That is the concluding chapter of his *Knowledge and Experience in the Philosophy of F. H. Bradley*, written on the eve of and in the first years of World War I, but only allowed publication in 1964.

The circumstances of the war are significant, a war his friend Pound will characterize at its end, viewing the carnage and the continuing confusions among nations, as fought on behalf of "an old bitch gone in the teeth,/ For a botched civilization." Eliot, turning aside from that grand sweep, looks to the nature of civilization's decay as lying in the nature of intellect itself. By some accident perhaps, his dissertation ends in a sentence fragment: "For if all objectivity and all knowledge is relative. . . ." The fragment is buried in a footnote in the edited publication, but it needs restoring to its proper and significant place, in that it so clearly signifies the dead end to which Eliot had come in his philosophical explorations. Whether a fragment by accident or as an acknowledgment of that dead end, the fragment shows the arrest out of which Eliot could not deliver himself by the exercise of his intellect unaided. The aid he received from his Harvard advisors was insufficient.

If all objectivity and all knowledge proves *relative*, then relative to what? For relativity is a concept still crying for some principle of measure. Eliot later will understand this aspect of our age's favorite concept, *relativity*, in its acceptable sense, in relation to Thomas's principle of proper proportionality. But that lies well in the future of his intellectual journey. At the time, such a concept seems related, if to anything, only to a subjective knowledge, which is itself relative unless intellect practices the arrogance of its own autonomy as the significant final measure of perception. One could hardly devise a phrase better than the dissertation's concluding fragment to point to the theme of his most widely known poem, whose emotional effect is that of nostalgic pathos, "The Love Song of J. Alfred Prufrock." In that poem the futility of self-love, the only love possible to intellect isolated from reality, echoes in empty chambers of that intellect we call Prufrock.

Of Eliot and his intellectual dilemma we shall have much more to say, even as we shall of Wallace Stevens, and with more detailed attention to their poems. But first, regarding the "Romantic" response of the intellect in its separation from complex reality as represented in them, the separation we see in a progress of our poetry from Dante down through Eliot and Stevens and on to Robert Lowell and Allen Ginsberg, it would be well to consider in preparation two of their intermediary fathers, not in respect to a calendar location of them but in relation to the history of intellect's separation from reality. In this respect we find William Wordsworth and John Keats at a midway station between Dante and Eliot and Stevens. Given our remoteness from Wordsworth and Keats, it might seem that we turn to a still point of the "Romantic" as its poet turns to gardens and prospects upon nature. But that is too easy a conclusion. Wordsworth and Keats are in personal turmoil such as is hardly to be measured by history's details from our distance. They deal, each in his separate way, with a present moment of encounter of intellect with reality, an encounter that is at once as disturbing as it is timeless in its actuality, such an encounter as one discovers in Dante before them or Eliot after them. Their moment in history could hardly seem to them so calm a weather of intellect as it may seem to us in retrospect.

From Wordsworth's and Keats's circumstances in coming to themselves in an increasingly dark woods in that first quarter of last century, their report of the oppressiveness of those woods seems a reading hardly supportable to us. We have experienced the violent flow of Western thought and history since their time as they could have hardly imagined. Still, those poets found themselves also isolated from a community with being no less than does Eliot. Each struggles, with varying intensity of spirit, to regain that community, to regain the way lost to his own intellectual journey. There is, for instance, a pleading note beyond surface affirmation in Wordsworth's insistence in his preface to *Lyrical Ballads* that the poet is a "man speaking to men." In our day the charge has become rather that the poet is man rarified. A common complaint is that the poet speaks only to other poets, against which charge Wallace Stevens agrees mischievously, insisting that the poet speaks only to himself. (But then Stevens violates that assertion, by publishing both poems and essays.) If poetry appears in many instances as increasingly inaccessible, we need not conclude it the poet's deliberate choice, out of his intention to speak only to other poets. And even when he himself on occasion asserts this a true charge (Stevens is not the only poet to give such consent), it may well be rather an act of desperation out of a sense of futility in the despair born of his conclusion of hopeless isolation.

Let us suggest here that the Romantic poet is moved, in his struggle to recover himself to reality, by an intuitive hunger in intellect itself, which demands satisfaction whether in Eliot's day or our own. In relation to any desperation, the poet's seeming disregard of audience may be a consequence of his primary regard for his own rescue caused by this demand. And should that rescue be accomplished, not only his personal recovery may be effected. He may thereby recover to us an opening upon our own possible recovery. The recent history of our response to the poetry of Eliot seems rather to make that point, for we cannot now read the body of that work without recognizing in it this development whereby as he recovers himself he turns toward a wider and wider audience. That will not mean, insofar as the poet continues to be committed to the truth of things, that he will be made easily accessible to us by that turning. For the very complexity of intellectual and spiritual journey, as intellect must address it, requires a firmness in him measured by reality and not by a secondary concern for audience. In the signs of that attempt, in the poems, there may be extreme difficulty to any individual intellect in our attempt to read reality through a poem which may seem at best a dark glass.

We observe as one of the consequences, in relation to Eliot's poetry, the divided judgment over the *Four Quartets* as poetry, some finding them a great falling off as poetry. But the argument turns, we may also observe, precisely upon the question of whether Eliot, in his enlarged concern beyond the personal witnessed by the *Four Quartets*, sacrifices poetry's virtues to that concern. It is a consequence of the escape from entrapment by Cartesian Idealism, an increasing awareness of the possibility of intellectual community, that affects Eliot no doubt. The result is his turning from irony to paradox, as he turns from the safety of masks to the more open and vulnerable deportment of speaking more and more in his own voice as the presence in his poem. What may possibly be involved in a critical faulting of Eliot as poet in his last works is not so much the quality of these poems as poetry, but an objection to a new direction of intellect: toward spiritual concern. If William Carlos Williams objected to *The Waste Land* because it returned poetry to the academy as he said, the objection to the *Four Quartets* may well be in reaction to those poems turning poetry back to spiritual concerns. That is a turning which when made by a superior poet is not easily forgiven by the modernist mind, long dieted on irony as disguise of intellectual sentimentality.

In his own day, Wordsworth too found Cartesian Idealism an insufficient food to satisfy that innate intuitive desire, however appealing it may have been made to seem by eighteenth-century "Romantic" rationalism. The species of Romanticism against which Wordsworth reacted, as we have said, appropriated intellect's disjunction from reality to its own elevation as autonomous authority, thus making itself independent of, not only nature and man, but of history as well, history becoming its more attractive target. For with the emergence of the illusion of Progress, the brake upon ideology out of history became less and less tolerated. (It will be Santayana, a hundred years after Wordsworth, who reminds us in a sentence often repeated in our day though little heeded that those who ignore history are doomed to repeat it.) Of course "Romantic" realism does, because it must, condescend to man and nature in the interest of a power over man and nature, lest it stir too much our sleeping common sense. But the nineteenth-century Romantic poet for the most part found the eighteenth century's "realist" position sharply antagonistic to his own understanding of the virtues of his own intellect. It is a circumstance of intellectual division too facilely prescribing the eighteenth from the nineteenth century. Eliot later speaks of it as a "dissociation of sensibility," a separation of "thought and feeling," which occurred earlier in his estimate. Eliot himself, initially opposed to "feeling" in its sway upon the nineteenth-century Romantic, did not recognize his own Romanticism, which would eventually lead him to a comfortable acceptance of Wordsworth. His was a stance initially more set against the Romantic nineteenth century than set on strict subscription of reason against feeling. There will follow, then, radical modification of his early position, dramaticized in "Ash-Wednesday" as we shall come to see.

Those Romantic poets Wordsworth and Keats, as unlike as they are in many respects and as they appeared to each other, nevertheless shared in the recognition that each has a tendency to surrender too easily a possible understanding of the knowledge each knows himself to possess by intuition. It is the knowledge out of immediate and personal experience of the immediate world. Put another way, each recognizes his own "thought" as a complication of that knowledge, seemingly making that knowledge suspect to some degree through thought itself. Again, the fear rising, in consequence of thought, is that intellect has surrendered on occasion to the dominance of rational intellect, even inclined to the province of science and the new philosophy, which were increasingly calling intuitive knowledge into question. Under the burden of rational intellect as exercised by eighteenth-century standards of intellection, each poet finds himself more and more in exile from that country perceived through intuitive intellect. Intuition suggests this perceived country is here and now, in the immediacy of experience through the senses.

What is lost in surrendering passport to this country, to which desire would lead one by intuitive intimations of that country, is any comfort to thought that it is anchored in reality. In that uncertainty, thought inclines to a conditional substitution for its indicative, that grammar of thought's assent to reality necessary to either mode of thought, the rational or the intuitive. Instead intellect feels forced by uncertainty to a detachment through the subjunctive. It supposes it may speak, even to itself, only with the conditional *as if*. *As if* knowledge of specific particularities were opening upon the essence that supports specific particularities. The conditional is proper, in the light of intellectual finitudes. But if it is taken as exclusive of any indicative address to existence, intellect will begin to wonder whether specificity is accident unrelated to essence. Accident then seems the only reality. Soon in that thought the subjunctive becomes its only indicative, but what is thereby *indicated* as the only sure *thing* is intellect's own exile from all save itself. Even its own existence comes in question, for awareness is perceived "as if a magic lantern threw the nerves in patterns on a screen," as Prufrock puts it. In short, what begins to be called in question—and the Romantic realist is adept in raising such doubts against speculative or intuitive intellect—is whether the shifting from a conditional *as if* to an *is* is only an exercise in wishful thinking whereby illusion is pretended to be vision. The intuitive knowledge of being, in the Thomistic sense of the terms, is concluded by the disoriented Romantic to be merely "unrealistic" thought. Was it vision, indeed, or but a waking dream?

So much for the poet in his concession to his own subjunctive, conditional response as translated by his own desire to an indicative—and thence usually to an imperative. Now let us reverse the charge and direct it to the Romantic realist. For the realist's knowledge, considered strictly indicative in his view of the truth of things, also results in the imperative of an intellectual action toward a future to be established by his "scientific" indicative: existence justified by the measure of his intellect on its march under the banner of Progress. That position also is prohibitive of any true vision when strictly adhered to in suppressing the intuitive, and nowhere more certainly than in his vision of "History's" future. The Romantic poet in his response may unfortunately seize by desperation upon *feeling* to oppose the rationalist's *thought*, as if that were to establish a viable antithesis. Thus feeling is made the acceptable avenue to vision through the dark wood, a vision eschewing reason. One has in this development only an antagonism between the two proponents of a vision of "realism," the one established by thought's reasoning, the other by feeling's thought. But there is a dissociation dooming either to a dead end, out of which no significant vision—that is, a vision signifying reality by conceptual action true to reality—orients intellect to the complexity of reality. As rationalist or intuitionist becomes entrapped, the trap itself makes reality the more remote. It is as if, to put our own conditional position in summary, it is as if the rational and the intuitive were not necessarily complementary modes of the specific intellect as in actuality they are, whether those of the "Romantic" poet or the "Romantic" realist—whether those of the poet or scientist or philosopher.

I need not demonstrate the poet's abandonment of the *ratio* to the Romantic realist as he seizes upon his own *intellectus* as the poet's limited or peculiar domain, to borrow Thomas's distinction of these modes of action in the intellect. Or at least I need not demonstrate beyond recalling the repeated accusations by poets themselves against science and philosophy, instead of against particular scientists and particular philosophers in their abuse of the modes. One instance, ironic in that the words are spoken by a would-be philosopher as he is pursuing his doctoral degree in that discipline: "all philosophizing is a perversion of reality; for . . . no philosophical theory makes any difference to practice." Thus Eliot speaks at the time he is a serious student intent upon what others have said about the truth of things, in a letter dated January 6, 1915, to the future father of cybernetics, Norbert Wiener. His attention to detail, the dating, would no doubt strike Eliot in its irony by the late 1920s when he would have recognized it as epiphany.

What our Romantic poet is apt to ignore, out of his feeling of a betrayal by both science and philosophy, is the implication of detail in relation to the truth which underlies detail. Thomas speaks of this truth as "the substantial nature of things" which "lies hidden under accident," or in respect to intellectual act "the meanings of words" which "lie hidden under words." What indeed lies under the numbered stipules of the lily, in the mode of the scientific rationalist's approach to that lily, or what lies hidden under such a notation as "January 6, 1915"? To explore such questions requires the use of the rational intellect, lest intuitive intellect leave the poet content with a subjective symbolism such as came to occupy the French poets in the late nineteenth century. It is pertinent that the French Symbolists influence later poets a various as Stevens and Eliot. So long as the poet does not suppose he has accomplished a comprehension of the lily (in the literal sense of the word *comprehension*) by the rational action of intellect in counting the lily's stipules down to its very genes (the charge the poet often raises against the scientist, justly), just that long must he welcome and employ the rational intellect to justify his intuitive knowledge. What he must guard against is an alternative and equally unacceptable attempt at comprehension, for which violation he is sometimes justly charged by the scientist or philosopher: a subjective response through feeling alone, taken as a revelation in full. When he makes such subjective response as if it were objective vision, his art is likely enough to employ images in an impressionistic manner, insufficiently grounded in the truth of the thing itself, the lily, though he think himself bearing witness to a vision.

We have been alluding to the advice one might find in Alexander Pope, who emphasizes in good eighteenth-century manner the importance of a precision in observation by the poet—his counting the lily's stipules—if he is to make image objective. By the time we come to Wordsworth, we find him wrestling with that concern, but not in relation to the nature of the lily as might be the botanist's concern. In his "I Wandered Lonely as a Cloud," that poem popular to secondary and undergraduate readings of Wordsworth, it is not the botanical particularity of daffodils that is at issue, though the poem may be too often read as if it were. Wordsworth's is an epistemological concern. The mystery of the mind itself is the fascination. One may record detailed historical circumstances of his encounter of daffodils, the place and the day and the time of day: a version of counting the lily's stipules. But the real mystery is the nature of that action and its consequent effect in subsequent intellectual actions; the mystery of memory itself in relation to image put in action within thought. If Wordsworth cannot solve that epistemological mystery, he can at least take some comfort that the gift of memory is a blessing to his whole being, even to his body no less than to his intellect and soul. Perhaps we are so long familiar with Wordsworth's conclusion that it seems more simple than it is. Perhaps, St. Thomas might suggest, more lies hidden under those words than we at first suppose:

> For oft, when on my couch I lie
> In vacant or in pensive mood,
> They flash upon the inward eye
> Which is the bliss of solitude;
> And then my heart with pleasure fills,
> And dances with the daffodils.

We need not linger here, except to point out that the movement of spirit being celebrated is that from *loneliness* to *solitude*. What is remarkable effect in his second intellectual event, remembered in saying the poem—

the new memory of subsequent actions of intellect while lying in-
doors—is a presence of a series of past experiences in an *actual* way unit-
ing that being, the poem's "I." What is arresting is the discovery to itself
of this intellect's discrete unity as it remarks the actual present event
called *thought*. It is not sufficient to see Wordsworth's fascination in the
poem as merely with his remembering a past encounter with daffodils,
the initiating event in time past. For what fascinates him is the actuality
of a present understanding of his present memory of a sequence of past
events. Experience of intellect, and so its existence, is actual now, whether
certified by deliberate thought or by sudden intrusions upon thought—
whether through his *pensive* or into his *vacant* mood. Intellect is actual,
and the engaging consequences of that recognition is the activity of the
body in its response to a memory of past actuality which effects a present
actuality. The moment is sensual as well as intellectual. For when Wordsworth speaks of his *heart* filling with pleasure and *dancing* with the daffodils, he is not being simply metaphorical. There is an actual sensual effect
occasioned by the images retained in intellect, which return out of memory. And his new recognition opens upon the significance of actual experiences of reality. Wordsworth on *his* couch foreshadows the Freudian
dislocations of this mystery of memory, the turning of mystery to the
mechanics of psychology. And that turning will for a time put Eliot off
the mark, to which he returns no doubt through St. Augustine and his
speculative concern for the mystery of memory in relation to image in
his *Confessions*. In that return, Eliot begins to see that there is more to
Wordsworth than his youthful disdain had allowed him to see.

3

Attribution: The Poet's Exercise in Confusing Proportionality

As Damascene observes, man is said to be made to the image of God, "image" in this context signifying an intellectual being who is free to judge what he shall do and has the power to act or not to act. . . . We should go on to consider His image, that is, man, inasmuch as he too is a principle of his actions, having as he does the freedom to judge what he shall do and control over his actions.

—St. Thomas Aquinas, Prologue, *Treatise on Happiness*

What is of concern to us is that the Romantic poet may succumb to the temptation of abandoning the *ratio* as necessary support of the *intellectus*. To do so will most likely lead him to a subjective isolation as the end of his partial, wounded, intellectual act. The concern for such a dissociation of sensibility, however, is more consequential than to the surface concerns of the poet's use of his signs, images in relation to feelings in poetry's entrapment of that subjectivity—represented so well by the Symbolist Movement. For that dissociation helps prepare the intellectual community as a whole for the intrusion and dominance of concerns for memory in relation to the actual by Freudian psychology. In Freudianism's emphasis upon intellect as mechanism, as an extension of neural physiology, there comes its attempt at a gnostic power over psychological being. We need only remember here that Freud himself refused to be "psychoanalyzed," for that is a procedure not unlike the questioning of God himself. And that reflection reminds us of C. S. Lewis's point that Freudianism can explain everything except Sigmund Freud. Which in turn reminds us of our own point already made: the gnostic intellect must exempt itself from the remaking of being. Persons are reduced toward integers in pursuit of gnostic power, but the director of that power would retain his own personhood. It is by that very retention that he becomes elevated to the godhead. For in a universe of integers, the lone gnostic person is the God of being.

What the Romantic poet, then, is required to discover, or else come to some degree of sad despair, is that to abandon the *ratio* in its complementary role to *intuitive* knowledge leads that intellect to confuse itself as the source of truth. The rationalist who abandons the intuitive elevates the rational, a counter error. Either failure effects an intellectual isolation from reality. That isolation brings Keats—and Wordsworth on occasion—to despair. The opposite course, that of the strict rationalist, is also one toward despair, though it appears less so. The rational as exclusive to intellect likely discloses itself as arrogant presumption of autonomous power, and that spectacle of deportment may disguise the despair of emptiness in personhood.

As poet, one deals with likeness in unlike things, whether in so simple a measure as "My love is like a red, red rose" or Wordsworth's juxtaposition of actualities and their effects in respect to the mystery of memory itself. But so, too, does the rational scientist traffic in likeness in unlike things. It is the philosopher St. Thomas who warns us, concerning this necessity to intellectual action in response to reality—to the truth of things in themselves—of the necessity of rational governance of our intuitive encounter of things in themselves. For that encounter may lead to confusions out of seeming likenesses in unlikenesses.

"In analogicals," Thomas says, "it is not *diverse realities* which fall under consideration but *diverse modes* of existence of the self-same reality." Such is St. Thomas's cautionary insight into analogy, reminding us that reality—existences founded in being—is always a present arena from which and within which diverse modes of existence blossom. It is not, therefore, through an accumulation of images juxtaposed that sound poetry proceeds, anymore than it is from an accumulation of facts that a comprehensive assertion of the fullness of any *thing* in itself may be made by the scientist. The Romantic poet again and again is led to the first of these errors. The Romantic realist (the scientist) again and again becomes entrapped by the second error. Because the error is so destructive to intellectual deportment in relation to existence—for poet or scientist or philosopher—it is worth our brief concern for St. Thomas's principle of proper proportionality as it relates to our concern for analogy.

St. Thomas explicates his principle in his treatise on *Being and Essence*, and we depend initially upon Fr. Gerald B. Phelan's extrapolation of Thomistic analogy from that principle in *St. Thomas and Analogy* (1941), though the topic is treated by many Thomistic scholars. Fr. Phelan remarks, "It is only when analogy of attribution is mingled with an analogy of proper proportionality that it appears to give a firm foundation for metaphysical demonstration." Perhaps *mingled* here presents a slight problem. For the intellectual inclination to attribution, in which the accidents of things are juxtaposed on the authority of the intellect rather than on the authority of the things themselves, is (we might say) an impulsiveness of intellect to satisfy its desire for an understanding of the wholeness of existence. Not the desire but the impulsiveness is the complication. Attributive analogy, inevitable to intellectual action, must be *governed by*, rather than *mingled with* the understanding of proper proportionality. That is, attribution is measured by, and so corrected by, proportionality, as concept is measured by and corrected by experience of reality. Such governance is not solely the province of rational intellect in its analogical actions, for the intuitive intellect responds directly to the truth of proportionality. It is the rational intellect which puts intuitive knowledge to the test. Robert Burns in his simile of his love compared to the rose is led to his analogy out of some moment's recognition of likeness between unlike things, those things already known in themselves in some degree before the juxtaposition. Or at least, surely such is the warrant of authority exercised by the poet.

And so Burns is not, in this respect, being merely fanciful, despite the disparateness of the things juxtaposed, in declaring his love to be like the red rose. The poet depends on the hearer's common sense to make a proper limitation in the correspondences between the rose and his Beloved. It is this dependence, incidentally, based in the poet's confidence in the immediacy of his hearer's experience of the existential world, that makes him so immediately available to his reader. Extended analysis by critical rationalism pretty soon calls in question such a simile, which is intended to touch only fleetingly upon correspondences common in experience. Burns, unlike Donne, moves on quickly to other similes, content with an effect through common intuitive knowledge of roses and beautiful women in his hearer.

Such "measure" by commonsense recognitions of proper proportionality is a reciprocal action of *knowing* by the intellect, whereby the instrumental intellect, in service to its discrete soul, is *justified* by its objects rather than by its will. In recognizing this necessity, the great poet through analogy characterizes, and his persona emerges as distinct, as a likeness to actualities. I think at once of Shakespeare's use of this truth about out intellect: by a person's use of analogy, he is revealed most clearly to be what he is. Consider, in *Henry IV*, Part I, the marvelous variety of persons projected by each's sense of analogy. One sets Hotspur beside Westmoreland for this regard; Hotspur beside Falstaff; Falstaff beside Prince Hal; Prince Hal beside Hotspur. And what that great poet himself depends upon, first and last, is his hearer's commonsense recognition of the principle of proper proportionality as learned from that hearer's experience of reality. It is in the character's failure of common sense that we know his weakness. It is the lesser poet in whom analogy of attribution overcomes his making, for attribution is intellect's probable first approach to reality in its own growing conceptual approach to that reality.

That is why we find the child's observations so "colorful," even arresting, as the child's intellect encounters correspondences among things in an innocence toward intrinsic order in things. The collocation of attribution and proportionality in the child's moment of awe, the moment of encounter with things in themselves, prove arresting to the adult mind by the very encounter as unresolved by the child's intellect. The instance that comes to my own memory is of a child waking to such wonder at the end of a summer. My child had been fascinated earlier by a gathering of yellow butterflies on damp ground. Then in September, a wind brought down a flood of small "butterflies," the leaves of autumn. What might come to mind next is a poem by a poet finely attuned to the relation of attribution to proportionality, Hopkins's "Spring and Fall," dedicated "To a Young Child." Such a poet as Hopkins, whom I include among the"Romantics" as that term has been used here, does not confuse his own intellect as the source of proportionality, while recognizing the inclination to attribution. He knows firmly that the measure of proportionality is in the thing itself and is not measured in its truth by our intellectual action, whether that action be excessively attributive or properly governed by proportionality. He knows, in brief, that truth justifies concept and conceptual devices such as our signs, rather than concept and device justifying truth.

Of course intellect, necessarily operating from and through its concepts of truth in its rational deportment, very easily may mistake concept itself as the justifier. That is the hazard to the necessity of thought that comes to establish the Cartesian Idealist in his error at a remove from the truth. For he so easily, given the fascination of his own awareness of himself, supposes his awareness to be the determinant of truth by the very fact of his having seized upon a truth. He will not recognize as prior to his act of seizing upon truth, truth's presence as knowledge in his intellect. It is in this dangerous ground of action within the discrete intellect, the ground of conceptual response to preconceptual knowledge, that one must distinguish, as St. Thomas does, between proper proportionality as intrinsic to the reality of the particular thing itself and our symbolic analogy, peculiar to human intellect, and a mode opening the soul to the truth but in no sense the cause of that truth in itself. Symbolic analogy, the articulation through sign of concept, is based in the effects upon the discrete intellect anterior to concept. Proper proportionality is based in causes independent of intellect, and ultimately dependent from that Cause of causes in things. In human intellect there is a coincidence which is occasioned by the particularity of intellect itself, its essential unity, whereby man as creature is said to be not only *the thing man is* but as well to have been created *in the image of God*.

This dangerous ground we are exploring, that of human intellect, is the one in which, and in which alone, the self may properly "come to itself," come to know itself to be that which it is. It must do so without that knowledge of the self consequentially causing its isolation from the wholeness of creation, and that is why that ground is so dangerous. The analogy of attribution, when unjustified by analogy of proper proportionality, isolates the self, cutting awareness off from its kinship with the whole of creation in respect to *being*. For creation exists fundamentally at the level of *being* and not at the level of the discrete *ens*. To lose that sense of being is to become susceptible to reductionisms whereby all *ens* tend to become identities to intellect, losing their particularity. The inclination is various in intellects, the culmination of its extreme perhaps suitably described as a sentimentality that overwhelms the *ratio* through a perversion of the *intellectus*.

Intellect's initial encounter with being is through the discrete *ens*, in which it encounters the accidents accruing to *essence*, the accidents through which intellect touches *ens* through the senses. Here, we remember that the particular intellect's own incarnation is through an essence to which accidents accrue, as for instance in its own sensual extensions toward the rest of creation. Not to recognize the immediacy of accidents to its own being easily confuses intellect, and that confusion is perhaps the cause of a haunting duality, which encountered in the poet again and again separates the "I" from its sensual context, a partial separation of intellectual "soul" from its "body." Such is a metaphorical sign of duality which is as old almost as poets in the history of intellect. It was dissolving once more among intellectual poets at the turn of our century, as may be witnessed in Yeat's "Dialogue of Body and Soul." More important to one of our central "Romantic" poets, we might remember that Eliot wrote two "Dialogues of Body and Soul" (unpublished) before turning to a subtlety more appropriate to the complexity of the discrete person in his "Love Song of J. Alfred Prufrock."

We might consider the problematic effect of intellect's encounter with *ens*, and the temptation therefore to a reductionism wherein all *ens* become identities, each of the other. What becomes the problem to that procedure is the very instrumentality of reductionism, the intellect in its act of reduction. I take it that Walt Whitman clearly shows this problem in his poetry, the problem becoming that of the recessive "I" in that poetry. In Whitman, symbolic analogy is rampant, under the necessity of any incessant reduction of the thing itself when encountered intentionally by the "encompassing" intellect. Thus Whitman is committed to an interminable cataloguing of things encountered, and with each encounter the presumption is that the thing is incorporated to intellect. Whitman's intellect is an insatiable vampire feeding on being in this respect. He knows, of course, what men have said of the nature of man, that man was created in the image of God. What he undertakes is a reduction of the universe to himself. In "Song of Myself," that great epic of modernism, he says, "Why should I pray? why should I venerate and be ceremonious?" Why, that is, should I deport myself to existence in a way that suggests I relinquish my own power over being? For he is, he says, "Walt Whitman, a kosmos, of Manhattan the son." He is the All, descended into the flesh. A God made manifest by sign, by his word. Such is the fundamental position he assumes as intellect, through which he puts off the old man, man as created in the image of God, and puts on the new God, intellect as collective of existence, and therefore the cause of existence. "The Modern Man I sing." In the inversion under way, by the gnostic appropriation of being, there follows an attendant revelation: "Behold, the body includes and is the meaning, the main concern, and includes and is the soul."

I am quite aware that one may select other lines from the poem that speak a contrary. Few lines are more famous than those near the end of "Song of Myself": "Do I contradict myself?/ Very well then I contradict myself,/ (I am large, I contain multitudes.)" But the admission is a condescension to the "unknower," the critical reader, by the gnostic poet. In him alone (such is the promised mystery of his intellect in its incarceration of being) are opposites reconciled. This miracle is to be performed, however, only through the necessity of his intellect's incorporating within itself the whole of existence. But an irony here, almost humorous, is the necessity of the interminable cataloguing. It becomes a desperation of sign caused by a recessional "I" which is beyond any control of itself such as would be proper to a "God." One observes that once there is an amalgamation (or a supposed amalgamation) of the "I" and its incorporated *ens*, the thing announced as sucked into the intellect, there is always a falling back of an "I," which is distinct from, because intentionally comprehensive of, the late "I-*ens*." The new, separate "I" is forced to the abandonment by the willed incorporation. This operation is reflected in Whitman's point of view, in the technical sense of that term as applied to the literary text. What results is a pseudomystical climate in the poetry, much admired by some. But Whitman himself sees the difficulty: he is required, if he is to *be*, to "embrace" or to "contain" (a class of words we repeatedly encounter in the verses) all creation. One cannot live with Whitman's poetry long, I suspect, without gaining the impression of having encountered through that poetry a very hollow "god" insistently proclaimed by itself with the symbol *I* or *myself*, but equally insistent that this *I* is all men and all existence. It is that aspect of his poetry which leads to my epithet that, as poet, he is by intention a vampire of being.

To the contrary, in that intellectual ground wherein attribution is properly measured through a knowledge anterior to concept, in which knowledge there is incipient the other knowledge which blossoms from it—the knowledge of proper proportionality—symbolic analogy itself begins to flourish as a mode of knowing: concept governed by the reality of *being* as experienced. It properly flourishes in relation to intellect's recognition that, in the mode of the intuitive, intellect is properly oriented to the proportionality of existence. For when we speak of a Thomistic principle of proper proportionality, we must not suppose it a wistful theory advanced by an impressive intellect (Thomas's) out of desire unfulfilled. For Thomas certainly, and for any intellect in certain moments of its action, that "Principle" but articulates a reality about intellect's relation to being itself. In such a recognition, requiring no articulated principle as its justification, intellect comes to understand itself as governed, as limited by the inclusive gift of its own potency, wherein it is the thing it is. Because it is that thing, it is thus limited by the bounds of the gift of its potential, but discrete, being. That relationship of its own being and potency once recognized, intellect is prepared to order its knowledge with an understanding of the self larger than any mere "knowledge" of itself. As discrete intellect, therefore, it is prepared to venture once more abroad among things, aware of their own discrete existence as ordered by that fundamental cause in existences, proper proportionality whereby the specific thing encountered is the thing it is by the grace of the Cause of being. It is in this recognition that the poet will at last recognize the truth in St. Thomas's definition of beauty: beauty is that which when seen in its truth pleases through intellect's recognition of its beauty. (I have argued elsewhere, with playful seriousness, that it is thus that one must come at last to perceive the beauty even of a possum.)

It is in this ordering of the particular intellect toward things, including itself, that intellect may both know and love the particular thing. St.

Thomas's emphatic distinction between *diverse modes* and *diverse realities* of the "self-same reality" calls the poet's attention to what is crucial in his analogy: analogy properly taken is not a matter of accretion, nor of addition. It is not a *this* upon *that*, nor a *this* and *this* and *this*, as if analogy were a fine seine projected by discrete intellect whose end is to remove and collect particularities. Eliot makes this error, subsequently corrected, in his famous essay on "Tradition and the Individual Talent." In that essay he declares the poet's mind to be "a receptacle for seizing and storing up numberless feelings, phrases, images, which remain there until all the particles which can unite to form a new compound [the poem] are present together." In Eliot's metaphor of the poet's mind, he combines both the addition and accretion of particularities as if independent of proper proportionality. The unity and order and proportion he would establish is at the discretion of the autonomous intellect and not measured by proper proportionality. It is the same position which is dramatized, rather than argued, by Joyce in his *Portrait of the Artist*.

Analogy properly taken, then, is a means to vision of the whole through the particular seen in the truth of its being the thing that it is. One has a recognition of this in that mystical vision of Dame Julian of Norwich: God showed her "a little thing, the quantity of an hazel-nut, in the palm of my hand; and it was as round as a ball. I looked thereupon with eye of my understanding, and thought: "What may this be?" And it was generally answered thus: 'It is all that is made.' I marvelled how it might last, for methought it might suddenly have fallen to naught for little[ness]. And I was answered in my understanding: 'It lasteth, and ever shall for that God loveth it.' And so all thing hath the Being by the love of God." That is why, as Eliot came to see through Dame Julian, "All manner of thing shall be well." The incident from *Revelations of Divine Love* puts effectively the intellectual tension between analogy of attribution ("round as a ball") and analogy of proper proportionality, in which the hazelnut is sustained from the "naught" of oblivion despite its littleness by love, its cause, a love revealed in the proportionality to Being whereby it is the thing itself. Thus what is recognized is that the membership of discrete existences lies in the body of being itself. Not to see this prevents true vision, since the finite eye that would see on its own, through attribution, becomes entrapped by that surface with which corporeal intellect must plumb *ens* to *essence*, through the surfaces of particularity. The difference is revealed in poetry, as may be tested by comparing on this point Hopkins's "Windhover" and Whitman's "Out of the Cradle Endlessly Rocking."

One effect of that appropriation of particularity to poetic use, however the poet may attempt by empathy to conceal appropriation, is his disjunction from the things appropriated. There may be in that lonely address to the crowd of things constituting creation a distancing of a moral uncertainty. "Our meddling intellect," says Wordsworth, "Mis-shapes the beauteous forms of things:—We murder to dissect." That early indictment of intellect leads him to declare "Enough of Science and of Art," with his own version of the Husserlean preachment, "back to the things themselves." We must allow Nature to be our teacher, Wordsworth insists. Still, that may in the end prove only a strategy which fails of a recovery of community with being, leaving the heart living alone, "Housed in a dream, at distance from the Kind," to quote Wordsworth's later recognition of that possibility. For in the desire for a rescue of the self, the very effort may violate intellect's proper deportment as one of a kind among a diversity of kinds. It seems an inevitable consequence that thought may detach intellect from being, whether its mode be that of a subjective feeling or rational attempt at objectivity. What the Romantic poet comes to experience is that the separation of intellect unto itself is not necessarily overcome by a deliberate melting into the "kind" or into any object separate from the self if that action is at the expense of intellect's own particularity.

Keats spoke of this dilemma of the relation of intellect to being other than itself. For him a possible relation seems to focus in the problem of sign, of the word spoken of and toward a thing. What is necessary, he said, is a "negative capability," precedent to the use of sign. In good art one may come to that state through, and so beyond, the sign itself. It is thus that one reading the *Iliad* may find himself "shouting with Achilles in the trenches." Or by this empathy of the intellect's power of "negative capability" one may seem to enter into the sparrow pecking about the gravel, with a feeling for that creature, a sort of knowledge, that lies beyond empirical knowledge. But such a dissolving of the *self* into the *other* risks the self to a sympathetic dissolution perhaps, even as it obverse "Murders to dissect" in the rational syphoning off of particularity from the *other* into the *self* under the authority of the *ratio* declared decisive and ultimate in the full reaches of the intellect. In this species of "Romanticism" practiced on the full authority of the *ratio* one may think of John Milton or James Joyce, or of Eliot the critic who would have the poet's mind a storage tank of harvested particularities. This, in contrast to the ideal intellect whom Keats wanted most to emulate as poet, William Shakespeare. Or, closer to our own time, one might think of Walt Whitman or Ezra Pound in contrast to Gerard Manley Hopkins. Romantic rationalism and Romantic subjectivism through which the self dissolves into the other or dissolves the other into the self seem equally to sacrifice intellect, whether to an isolation of the self or to its obliteration.

4

Person in Suspense,
between Thought and Feeling

[A]s soon as consciousness makes its appearance, it reveals so much
to us that the infinite gulf between a science of consciousness and
consciousness itself leaps to the eye.

—Étienne Gilson, *Methodical Realism*

Eliot in his early poetry reflects an awareness of that burden of isolation
which is the inheritance of Cartesian Idealism, and because he most particularly engages the problem as philosopher, while writing poetry as a
secondary mode of dealing with philosophical difficulties, he becomes a
helpful subject to our concern for the difficulties in Western thought since
Descartes as those difficulties affect the poet. He is more conscious of the
difficulties in consequence of his analytical attention to them, as opposed
to the speculative address to them by such a particular discrete soul as
Wordsworth. Put another way, as philosopher, he attempts a perspective
upon the problems which is to us as "impersonal" as he can make it, and
it is no accident that when he turns to poetry as his primary concern,
ostensibly rejecting philosophy, he at first insists (rather naively as it
eventually transpires) upon the necessity to the poet of being impersonal,
of separating himself as intellectual poet from the actualities of his own
experience. It is a gnostic intention which is untenable, whether advanced
in relation to one's mode of address to reality as philosopher or as poet.
Still, that strategy is in support of what is in actuality a true philosophical
address to the problem, initially obscured even to him under the pressure
of his moment's argument. His argument is far more personal than he
would choose to have it. This is to say, siding with Gilson against Eliot,
that "the philosopher as such has only one duty: to put himself in accord
with himself and other things." In moving to such an accord, the "per-

sonal" becomes central, though in a sense more complex than the popular understanding of the personal as merely autobiographical, as autobiography is popularly understood to be principally a concern for the accidents of *person*. It is this motive in the philosopher as described by Gilson which eventually leads Eliot to an accord with that philosophical poet, William Wordsworth, of whom he is at first most scornful. That scornfulness he will come to regret as he discovers that his own supposed superior intellectual position in dealing with the problems of consciousness (as contrasted to Wordsworth's) is to be resolved only through engaging those problems very much as Wordsworth did. We shall find Eliot helpful, then, and indeed more helpful than he could himself have supposed at the time he is writing poetry as a secondary activity of intellect while pursuing philosophy as an academic discipline. In our examination of the disjunction between intellect and its inclusive context, the early Eliot is an inviting subject.

In Eliot's "Preludes," begun when an undergraduate at Harvard and labored over (despite its brevity) for some two years, Eliot advances as the theme intellect's isolation. In the poem he rather certainly has both Wordsworth and Keats in mind as representative of the Romantic poet against whom he is in revolt. They are held in mind, in relation to the making of the poem, by an intellect which is given to rationality in such a way that the *ratio* would repudiate the *intellectus* if it could but do so. Eliot was encouraged in such distortions, I believe, by the intellectual climate ascendant at Harvard in his undergraduate days. If the *intellectus* may be used to name an inclination of intellect under siege at that moment, it is not a very likely term to encounter at that time and in that place, the first decade of our century at Harvard. Still, the inclination is recognized as most dangerous, warranting the pejorative epithet, "Romanticism." Irving Babbitt will attempt some rescue of Romanticism from the denigration of intuitive intellect as implicit in the term in his *Rousseau and Romanticism* (1919).

Meanwhile, before that book is written, Eliot is struggling as undergraduate and then as graduate student to find intellect's bearings. Babbitt and Santayana, both Eliot's teachers, are evolving what becomes known as Humanism, a reaction to the dominant rationalism at Harvard as represented by the president, Charles W. Eliot. It was as well a reaction against the intellectually unsupported Fundamentalism that began to appear on the outskirts of the academy. This is to suggest that Humanism attempts to rescue intellect from the sterility of rationalism on the one hand and from what seemed to it an opening swamp of emotionalism into which Christianity seemed to be descending. If Santayana took refuge in a classical stoicism, Babbitt turned more to Eastern thought as a middle way between the antagonist forces beginning to develop, Rationalism and Fundamentalism. Eliot as student witnessed the engagement of those antagonists by Babbitt and Santayana. We might say that what they attempted was to heal a rupture in intellectual community which we know Eliot will speak of later, in respect to literature, as the "dissociation of sensibility," the separation of "thought and feeling." The grounds of that attempt would seem to lie in the domain of philosophy, though both Santayana and Babbitt would show certain consequences to the poet and to poetry. This is the point in America's intellectual history at which a divergence occurs, leading to intellectual factionalisms still very much with us. Leading for instance to that New Humanism, which Eliot came at last to reject, though he did not join the opposition to it that Fundamentalism made, Fundamentalism tending to be very suspicious of rational intellect. That war has been continuous between Fundamentalism and Humanism, even when the battle lines are only vaguely drawn. It is a war which at this present ending of our century continues the erosion of the fabric of community.

What Eliot was discovering in himself at a deeply "personal" level was the Romantic rationalism which left intellect isolated from Keats's sparrow pecking about the gravel. That rationalism reduced the sparrow to mere matter as attended by indifferent, deterministic forces in a conjunction which one might call "life," but not "life" as the poet would understand that term. The Romantic poet's alternative, however, seemed to serve only illusion. The illusion supposed that one might, by empathy, enter feelingly into the "feelings" of the sparrow as it pecked about the gravel, thereby allowing the poet to "see" into the life of the sparrow. The supposition here is nevertheless of a creatureliness of things that was quite contrary to the current deterministic, mechanistic suppositions about the sparrow and its fellow things advanced by the new sciences. The poet would contend against the charge of his excess of feeling that the rational application of deterministic readings of "life" was the real betrayal of intellect by rationalism's excessive reductionism. For, such a poet might insist, life is more than the disassembly of a sparrow into its constituent parts. Still, as the rationalist might at once object, man is not sparrow. Foolish pretensions to the contrary by Romantic poets could but subject the poet to derision whenever he might be required to muster "logical" argument to support his "feelings" as legitimate response to "reality." Such is the condition to intellect which Eliot dramatizes in his "Preludes," a poem in which our rationalist might delight, since it displays ironically the Romantic "feelings." But Eliot's poem is not without a sympathy for the Romantic, intuitive inclination. Sympathetic or not, however, the consciousness in Eliot's poem discovers that it is reduced to a colloquy with itself. It hears "the sparrows in the gutters" outside drawn window shades. But Eliot's speaker is capable only of "such a vision of the street" where that sparrow might be encountered "As the street hardly understands." *Vision* here is deliberate in its implicit ironic counterpoint to the traditional sense of *vision* meaning a seeing into the truth of things. Or to put that traditional sense as Wordsworth does, a seeing "into the life of things."

As for Eliot's consciousness, the protagonist of the poem, that speaker acknowledges a lingering, dying desire to bring the street and the fitfully held vision of the street (represented in the mind's "thousand sordid images") into an accord. But the very attempt seems, as best reason can decide, only a conjuring of illusion. There is no dancing of the heart in response to the sordid images projected against the ceiling of the seedy boarding house of Eliot's poem. The supposition that illusion is the consequence of a feeling turned toward existences is put with pathos in the final section of Eliot's brief poem. The words Eliot uses invite both our philosophical attention and our recognition that the philosophical implications rest in literary allusions.

> I am moved by fancies that are curled
> Around these images and cling:
> The notion of some infinitely gentle
> Infinitely suffering thing.

The only *thing* such *feeling* seems to attach to with any certainty is the consciousness itself as moved by dissociated images. In this respect, there is a sense of a unified world, but it is a world of isolated consciousness itself, unified only by its isolation, revolving by a centrifugal force as consciousness turns back upon itself. Any movement is interior to that world. The consciousness is moved by *fancies* that rather desperately *curl* about its own *images* and *cling*, such actions being the only certification it has of its own existence. That "self," though it exhibit a wistful desire for accord with some Other than itself, can only be granted that desire's intent as coming from a *notion*. It is a forlorn desire for perception effected. But perception as a potential to the intellect, if unsatisfied, leads awareness to conclude itself to be the "infinitely gentle/ Infinitely suffering thing." Thus there is available to that consciousness only the pathos of the desiring self cut off from any object for that desire, projecting itself upon a "world" that is an "Other" only insofar as it serves as a mirror reflecting the self upon itself. Thus the exacerbation in that turning inward to blackness of despair. A word like *infinitely*, then, gathers about it the sardonic irony of such earlier elements in the poem as *masquerades* and *vision* and turns it almost to self-pity, till the speaking voice regains its sardonic detachment. The recovery is not only from that mirroring world but from itself as mirrored:

> Wipe your hand across your mouth, and laugh;
> The worlds revolve like ancient women
> Gathering fuel in vacant lots.

In contrast, Wordsworth's "beauteous forms" of "Tintern Abbey" derive from a landscape abiding in memory through images, more comfortably connecting by echo the mind and an exterior reality. When remembered, vision is renewed and is real. What lingers in memory after an event is a knowledge of encounter by intellect with things beyond itself. And some of those encounters, realized out of memory, and made presently real by memory, rise to the level of a visionary still point when

> the breath of this corporeal frame
> And even the motion of our human blood
> Almost suspended, we are laid asleep
> In body, and become a living soul:
> While with an eye made quiet by the power
> Of harmony, and the deep power of joy,
> We see into the life of things.

One is led into that state, we should notice, through the body whose "affections" are turned toward the exterior world. It is in such a blessed mood, or so Wordsworth now argues in thought's defense against an old dream of unselfconscious affinity *in* and *with* creation, and he now feels

> A presence that disturbs me with the joy
> Of elevated thought; a sense sublime
> Of something far more deeply interfused

in all things, unifying both his own particular consciousness and all that creation which is separate from consciousness. He is assured of that *something* by an experience

> of all the mighty world
> Of eye and ear,—both what they half create
> And what perceive; well pleased to recognize

In nature and the language of the sense,
The anchor of my purest thoughts
                and soul
Of all my moral being.

That firm belief in Wordsworth, Eliot's poem suggests, is but belief in an illusion, a "notion" projected upon that "mighty world." Wordsworth's own new discovery in "Tintern Abbey," made through "thought," is of the "still, sad music of humanity" filling all that mighty world. Well enough, Eliot's poem suggests, but it is only the sad music in this instance of isolated consciousness, filling an "infinite" world, namely its own awareness, in the instance Wordsworth's consciousness.

We have already alluded to another poet who also responds to this "still, sad music of humanity" in a poem, in which poem that music resonates in a consciousness distinct from resonant creation—or such is that other poet's conclusion. In "Spring and Fall," Hopkins may be said to have expressed a version of Wordsworth's "Tintern Abbey." When different poets address the same question, the thing they make is necessarily a version of other inevitable attempts upon the question. That is what requires that our intellect be interested in what men have said *toward* the truth of things, which is an interest quite different from that too-pervasive concern for the *direct* influence of one mind upon another that for a while dominated academic criticism. In Hopkins's poem, the speaker understands a "something" *in* nature which is responsive to human sadness, and he understands it from a Christian perspective. Hopkins's words are, in their dramatic presentation, not spoken aloud, though presumably occurring in response to and in the presence of Margaret, "a young child." The dramatic mode of Wordsworth's "Tintern Abbey" appears to be that of monologue, but it is so personal and interior that is seems more nearly a soliloquy, up to a turning point in it, when we discover another person present. A dramatic virtue in both poems lies in the centering personae, who are not so much lecturing on the sad music of humanity, but exploring implications in their hearings of that music which in differing ways endanger the explorer. The tension lies in the threat that the speaker might discover a truth in his experience which might unsettle an underlying certitude in him.

There is between the two poems, however, a difference, accounting in my estimate of them for a better "making" by Hopkins than by Wordsworth. That is, "Spring and Fall" is I believe a better poem than "Tintern Abbey" when considered in itself, in respect to the good of the thing made. The difference one may detect perhaps through observing that in

Hopkins's poem Margaret's response to the sad music in herself is projected upon the world and that projection is the occasion of the poet's meditations. Dorothy Wordsworth, on the other hand, is more nearly an accidental presence to the Wordsworthean soliloquy. Wordsworth turns to her in what seems an excess of delight in the "truth" his thought has gained in the present experience, projecting upon her his "truth." There enters thereafter an excessive claim for that truth, namely the virtue of storing image in intellect in one's youth, and that projection is not convincing at last. In the resolution, one cannot fail to notice, as I suggest elsewhere, that the seeming attention to Dorothy, the encouragement to her about her future well-being, is given a curious twist. For the speaker does not say "When you no longer have me with you, I being dead," but

If *I* should be where *I* no more can hear
Thy voice, nor catch from thy wild eyes these gleams
Of past existence—[my italics]

In other words, the shadow of inevitable death intrudes, that inevitability being the one consideration not adequately addressed. The burden of the Wordsworthean meditation with the self has considered the past in relation to the present, only to have the future inevitability intrude. Indeed, read in the body of Wordsworth's poetry, one recognizes the inclusive question, the reality of human existence in relation to its beginning, middle, *and* end, as including (for brevity's sake) "Tintern Abbey," the "Lucy" poems, and the "Intimations Ode." Read together, one has evidence of a disordered address of intellect to the question of its own reality.

Let us suggest that the problem is the one Eliot became concerned with, but a problem seen by Wordsworth in a way differing from Eliot's initial understanding of it. It is the problem of the "personal" in relation to poetry. Eliot in a famous essay imputes a failure of *Hamlet* as play because, as he said, Shakespeare does not manage through proper "objective correlatives" a dissociation of Shakespeare's own "personality" and Hamlet's. "Hamlet (the man) is dominated by an emotion which is inexpressible, because it is in *excess* of the facts as they appear [in the play]. And the supposed identity of Hamlet with his author is genuine to this point: that Hamlet's bafflement at the absence of objective equivalent to his feelings is a prolongation of the bafflement of his creator in the face of his own creative problem." Such, I suggest, is the difficulty in Wordsworth's "Tintern Abbey," with an important distinction to be made. For the *creator* here is Wordsworth and the Hamlet is also Wordsworth. The poem is inescapably personal, its title anchoring the poet to the speaking voice of the poem. Eliot, should he agree with such criticism of Wordsworth's poem *as poem*, would no doubt, at least in 1920, attribute the failure to Wordsworth's inability to "depersonalize" himself as poet. But what I contend (and I believe that Eliot in 1930 would agree), is that the difficulty lies in its not being *personal* enough. That is, Wordsworth has not sufficiently come to terms with the mystery of his own person, being distracted by the accidents of events. He is quite aware of the necessity of coming to the nature of the self and to the reality of himself as *person*. His is the recognition that the initial problem is one of epistemology, of finding the ground in which knowledge unites the self-perceiving and the thing perceived in an understanding that is the intellect's fulfillment—that recognition he bears important witness to. And for this recognition Eliot will praise him at last.

Such is the depth of the *personal* necessary in the end to the making of a thing good in itself, beyond a dualism whereby the maker is not himself sufficiently accommodated to that intrinsic good to art. It is the problem which for Hopkins and Eliot as poets is resolved through their understanding that man, made in the image of God, differs as creator from God as Creator in this very necessity of accommodation, whereby man is understood as dependent *in* creation and not independent of creation. It is the poet's sense of a proportionality among existences, including the poet, as creator in relation to God as creator, determined in proportionality through being. This recognition accounts (or so I believe) for the relative superiority of "Spring and Fall" as a made thing over "Tintern Abbey" as a made thing. I say *relative*, since by this very aspect of the reality of existences, an absolute perfection of the poet as creator cannot be admitted. So then, Hopkins's poem has the virtue of being deeply personal, beyond any concern for the "biography" of the poet, the grounding in the nature of *person* underlying the utterance, in which the beginning, middle, and end of temporal-spacial life is recognized by bringing together in the common personhood of humanity this speaker and Margaret. We need not know or suppose our speaker to be approaching three score and ten in respect to his understanding. The tensional poles of the little drama nevertheless require our recognizing the speaker's depth of understanding, out of which proceeds his testing of that understanding. This means that the speaker at last is the dramatic center of the poem, not Margaret. And one evidence of the depths of his person as mature, as fulfilled, is that the poem must be understood as interior to the speaker, a soliloquy.

5

Person and the Personal, from Wordsworth to J. Alfred Prufrock

> . . . writing and speech only allow for the expression of a part of a word at a time. Thought not yet expressed is already there; thought already expressed is still there because the total thought (if the expression makes any sense) is always present to itself. It refuses to recognize itself in that which detaches itself from it, just as an animal refuses to recognize itself in its stillborn offspring. . . .
>
> Language is for thought a foreign body to which it has a hard time accommodating itself.
>
> —Étienne Gilson, *Linguistics and Philosophy*

If we return to Eliot and his problem with the "personal" as exhibited with ironic detachment in his "Preludes," we find him treating the "notion" of some "infinitely suffering thing," the alienated consciousness, with gentle pathos. The poem, too, is a self-lament, but in an impoverished understanding of personhood as compared to the self-lament of "Spring and Fall." In Eliot's poem as well there seems an intent to counter Wordsworth's easy enthusiasm of the moment out of his excess joy in an insufficiently examined experience. Wordsworth, such is the suggestion, is caught up by illusion, which he mistakes for vision. In Eliot's "Love Song of J. Alfred Prufrock," however, a poem contemporary to "Preludes," we encounter a more bitterly sardonic rejection of that Wordsworthian illusion. It is of interest, in respect to Eliot's artistry, that he as the maker sets his persona as an older intellect, or at least an intellect more weary with the world, than he himself. That is, Eliot as maker is younger than his protagonist, as Browning is younger than his dying Bishop.[6] Such is the obverse of Hopkins's position as maker in his poem. But having touched this point, a more interesting, as it is the more crucial, aspect of Eliot's protagonist in relation to his "creator" appears when we look at this speaker, or listen closely to him, not as a psychiatrist might—which is the more usual address to the poem—but as the philosopher might. Explicitly, let us look as the Thomistic philosopher might.

Here let us recall our suggestion that at Harvard in about 1910, as Eliot is writing "Prufrock," the *intellectus*, the intuitive mode of intellect, is held rather suspect. The decline in humanities as an academic responsibility is beginning to accelerate in the academy itself from that point in our history, despite Babbitt's and Santayana's best efforts. "Romanticism" is considered a dangerous infection in intellect, requiring at least a cautious, skeptical address to intuitive knowledge. Eliot, one may suspect, has something of this attitude about him, accounting for his scornful address to early nineteenth century literature for some years to come, and in his early letters we find him announcing his own skepticism as virtue. He lacks any sufficient intellectual justification of the intuition, though something of it, perhaps, accrues to him through his study of Sanscrit and his academic interest in Eastern literature. (Krishna continues with him as late as the *Four Quartets*.)

We are not surprised, given that context, to find Eliot's Prufrock a highly sophisticated intellect, who, knowing all the world is disillusioned through skeptical intellect, is forced to the defense of illusion in an interior battle between himself ("I") and a part of himself ("you"). The voice is interior to a consciousness that would take all else illusional, as acceptable only as reflecting mirror. But this is so for the "I," not for the "you," and between these poles the drama of the soliloquy is played out. It is usual to associate the "I" with intellect, the "you" with a sensual aspect impinging upon intellect and pulling it to the exterior world, against which "sensual" pull the "I" reacts. That is an acceptable reading, surely, and one which Eliot himself, at the time, would consent to. Such is the "psychological" ambience of the poem, in the wake of William James's growing influence. Eliot became more and more intent upon the psychological as at least designating *essence*, as earlier philosophers might have said it, though he would have been somewhat uncomfortable with such a term. In the years immediately ahead, under the influence of William's brother Henry James, Eliot turns with fascination to Hawthorne as America's first important "psychological" writer. But he was discomforted, as Henry James had been, by Hawthorne's insistence upon *sin* in man. Meanwhile, the psychological realism that was emerging as intellectual respectability proved suitable support to Eliot's poem, and he makes masterful uses of it.

If the poet (such is the reality of existence) is strictly attentive to the reality of things insofar as they prove available to him, what he makes may well prove larger in the end than he may have supposed possible in the making. That is why one says, as Flannery O'Connor observed, that the devoted naturalist by his very attention to detail may end by writing more largely than his naturalistic theory can accommodate. There may be metaphysical implications he could not know at the time of his making. It is for this reason that we may suggest a tenable proposition about the two presences in Eliot's poem, the *you* and the *I*: each may, at the deepest level of the *personal* which is inescapable to the maker of a thing since he is a person, reflect those modes of intellect we have been concerned with, the *you* as *intellectus*, the *I* as *ratio*. We have once more the advantage of hindsight, even as with our reading of Wordsworth's poetry whereby we treated the problem of the personal by suggesting its ranging through "Tintern Abbey," to the "Lucy" poems, to the "Intimations Ode." In respect to Eliot and his *I* and *you*, we observe Gerontion as, in this respect, a Prufrock at grave's edge. And we may observe a new attitude of "Prufrock's" *I* in the final section of *The Waste Land*, at the point where the speaking voice turns to its "friend," identified as "blood shaking my heart," in an ambiguous epiphany. It is as if there is occurring at that late point in *The Waste Land* a reassociation of the sensibilities, a recognition of intellect as a Siamese twin, a "female" aspect of intellect in the poet's usual metaphor, in relation to "male" aspect. The *ratio-intellectus* (that is, the *intellect*) has long been dissociated by modernist thought, and it affected Eliot in his quest. If one wishes a locus in which the *ratio* (male) recovers unity with the *intellectus* (female) in Eliot's poetry, I would suggest it in that moment of vision whose analogue is St. Augustine's vision at Ostia recorded in the *Confessions*: the third paragraph of Section III of "Ash-Wednesday." But that is far along in Eliot's journey, far from Prufrock's tea party and almost arrived at Eliot's accommodation of his own *person* to reality in *The Cocktail Party*.

Meanwhile, in the beginning there is Prufrock, who reluctantly consents to the journey declared in advance a sure disappointment. It will be made at a time when

> the evening is spread out against the sky
> Like a patient etherized upon a table.

Here Eliot's metaphor appears a deliberate ironic counterpoint to a Wordsworthian metaphor. On the beach at Calais, Wordsworth characterizes evening also. It is

> a beauteous evening, calm and free,
> The holy time is quiet as a Nun
> Breathless with adoration.

Prufrock promises himself just such a stroll along a beach, incidentally, though we know by his own witness that for him the beach, like the evening, signifies an empty world, suited only to reflecting himself to himself in that modernist self-justification, ennui. That is Prufrock's substitute for a spiritual state in relation to existence such as Wordsworth's metaphor suggests.

Not, of course, that Wordsworth could maintain such a moment's sense of a holy union in creation, nor will thought prove the salvation to that spirit in him which longs for such an estate as is promised in the earlier "Tintern Abbey." Another possibility out of thought, spoken by Wordsworth in another poem, recognizes the recent and seemingly mediate cause of a disjunction of thought and feeling that seems to doom such moments. The words we have already alluded to, spoken against what we have called the Romantic realist:

> Our meddling intellect
> Mis-shapes the beauteous forms of things:—
> We murder to dissect.

If such is the practice both of "Science and of Art," as Wordsworth charges in rejecting both, its origins are deeper than those disciplines themselves as tenuously joined in the academy, separate but equal, even as in past Freudian days a separate but equal consent is given *ratio* and *intellectus* secularized. (Still, though the academy in our day struggles to be all things to all minds, it is not easy to hold for a respiritualization of intellect.) As Wordsworth will discover, with devastating effect upon his spiritual state, the division is not truly localized when we set such external rallying poles as *arts* and *sciences*. The division, the polarity, is in truth internal to intellect, is always internal to this specific intellect in this moment of its action. Wordsworth, then, will come to a point, as we shall see, at which he believes very much as Eliot seems to believe on the evidence of "Preludes" and "Prufrock": that any *vision*, even though counter to the murdering, dissecting rational mind when it becomes aberrant, is but a *notion*, and so an illusion and not a reality. Prufrock enjoys some confidence in that conclusion, despite a moment or two in the poem's unfolding at which the actual exterior world threatens to draw him to an openness to reality. He speaks boldly until an encounter of arms downed with light brown hair. The immediacy of that encounter requires his retreat to images sterilized, put in detached objectivity. The arms become tolerable if seen "braceleted and white and bare."

For the Romantic poet, for Wordsworth and Keats as they become entangled in the problems of intellect as it attempts an accord with creation, it appears increasingly that image in the mind may itself be the very instrument to the mind's disjunction from reality which leaves consciousness isolated. That, as we have seen, is exactly the burden of Eliot's "Preludes," whose title reminds us that Eliot would probably have had in mind not only *preludes* in the musical sense but that ambitious attempt by Wordsworth to write a great epic whose protagonist would be Wordsworth, and more specifically the development of his own *mind* as poet. Wordsworth's attempt stands now a large unfinished cathedral to the mind, an incomplete monument to intellect, though its foyer, *The Prelude*, has a certain greatness of accomplishment in itself.

Prufrock, too, recognizes (such is his drama) that image is a sufficient weapon to dissociate himself as "I" from the rest of creation, and he practices a skillful surgery that sterilizes the "you" and makes any fruitfulness of intellect safely impossible. Consider, for instance, the famous "fog" paragraph, heavily sensual. The rhetorical development of its imagery imitates the sexual act. But the metaphor is deliberately deceptive, deliberately attributive, aimed at a confusion of the "you," that aspect of intellect which inclines *person* to an openness to the larger creation through the senses. Its final line, "Curled once about the house and fell asleep," suggests the languor after love, when we have only been talking about insubstantial fog. But the strategy allows the "I" his point unchallenged. After such action, what issue? And if no issue, why the hurry, for "indeed there will be time. . . ." With such delay, of course, thinning arms and balding head will eventually take care of the rest, will alleviate any inclination to an openness to the world which might possibly lead to an actual encounter with an actual woman. Gerontion's is an opposite tact, out of the same reading of existence and to the same end as Prufrock's. For Gerontion, like Marvell's lover, has "sported" himself, self-devoured along with his lovers, "like amorous birds of prey." When the body is decayed, given the version of existence held by Prufrock and Gerontion, the intellect goes out like a candle, as in the Shakespearean metaphor of flame that is prophetic of this modernist view of existence, "consumed with that which it was nourished by." (Shakespeare's sonnet characterizes the lover's self-pity devastatingly.)

The problem for the Romatic poet, whether we speak of Wordsworth or Keats or Eliot or Stevens, comes to center in the nature of image and metaphor in their relation to intellect on its first reflective encounter with the problem of reality. And that encounter will lead to a further problem: the uncertain origin of image and metaphor in respect to any initiating cause of image and uncertainty about the active intellectual participation with that cause in the life of image. The degree of power and authority in intellect itself is at issue. Where, and by what means, does experience leave intellect occupied by what Wordsworth describes as his intellect's possessions, those "beauteous forms" or at an opposite Eliot's possession of "sordid" images? These effects, registered somehow in the mind, seem to require a participation of intellect in their registration. But just how this should be yields little to a relational exploration of cause, other than a mere recognition of the image's presence to consciousness. The Lockean argument that image is written on the mind as words on a slate proves hardly acceptable, though Coleridge and Wordsworth toyed with the idea as they found it in David Hartley. Does it follow, then, that consciousness itself is the cause of what it knows as an effect? There is a paradox, forced by such questions but not easily resolved: it is that the mind seems both active and passive in respect to the knowledge it holds, as if (in Wordsworth's version) mind half creates and half perceives. Where then lies the authority to such knowledge, if mind is not completely passive receiver on the one hand nor active creator of perception on the other?

Further, is consciousness born *ex nihilo*, as if a clean slate? Or does it exist by a coincidence of image in consciousness? Image effects, therefore I am? However one poses the complex question, it still begs the question of agent cause of consciousness and most especially when put in relation to the closed cosmology of intellect with which modernism has burdened us. Consciousness cannot bring itself into existence out of itself as out of nothingness, for such a proposal already posits its prior existence as the bringer of itself. One seems forced more and more to a conclusion (at the level of the poet's concern with image) that consciousness is necessarily antecedent to its images. Consciousness, in some respect, *was* antecedently, and its reflections in relation to concepts are reflections not only *on* concept but also on its own existence as antecedent *to* concept. But what is that dark hiatus of consciousness that is so difficult to locate, between its beginning and its new beginning as evidenced by its conceptual actions?

We are speaking of image or metaphor, not as they may appear in the text of a poem on the page before our eyes, the poet's articulated sign such as *sparrow* or *nun*, but as they *are* in the mind independent of sign. Eliot, in "Preludes" speaks of them as the "images/Of which your soul is constituted," but whether images *constitute* mind or soul is the very question at issue. Signs, words on the page for instance, acknowledge image as already conceptualized and projected. But it is not only beneath or behind the word, the sign, that we are attempting to delve. We want to get beneath the concept independent of sign as well. That is the country of mind to which we are beckoned as to a mystery. Wordsworth, though reduced to sign, to a poem, as any witness to mystery must always be reduced, believed that at the moment of "Tintern Abbey" (noon, July 13, 1798) he had in certain moments now past entered "into the life of things" as an actuality of action in a present, which is now a past. There *had been* a sense of *presence* independent of time or place, what he will call in his *Prelude* a "spot of time." Furthermore, the things experienced in separate moments and as things separate among themselves one from another, somehow constituted a oneness. They were more fundamentally a *one* than the always feeble attempt to articulate the vision of oneness, the attempt made through concept and into signs and onto the page in black ink or into the air as sound. The mystery which intellect has such difficulty ratifying as vision lies not in the relation between concept and sign, but somehow at a level of perception and conception anterior to concept, even as concept is itself anterior to sign. It lies somehow in an experience of a community of the intellect with something not itself. That intuitive sense in intellect of having experienced a ground of reality beneath, or anterior to, rational engagement of intellectual experience makes the enlarging question of "cause" the more insistent.

Thomistic realism would approach this mystery, insofar as a rational approach is possible, by suggesting a *primal* knowledge as the consummation of intellect and thing, an event necessarily anterior to concept itself. It is an approach required by the nature of intellect itself, insofar as we can discover that nature. Thomas derives a principle from this experience from which to proceed reflectively (*Summa*, I 87, Resp 3):

> . . . the human intellect . . . is neither its own act of understanding, nor is it its own essence; the first object of its act of understanding is the nature of a material thing. And therefore that which is first known by human intellect is an object of this kind, and that which is known secondarily is the act by which that object is known; and through the act the intellect itself is known, the perfection of which is this act of understanding.

Such is an approach out of experience, not by the imposition of a principle upon experience. We discover the principle supportable as we observe not only our own actions of intellect but the actions of intellects about us. And we do so, despite Cartesian confusions that mistake Thomas's secondary act as primary. That, indeed, was Wordsworth's own procedure in "Tintern Abbey." He turns to his companion Dorothy for confirmation of his reflections on his own experience as valid, within their common, explicit circumstances. That, too, is Hopkins's procedure in "Spring and Fall."

And so I am myself brought to more immediate, personal experience, my observations of a small child coming to intellectual awareness. Confronted by a litter of young rabbits, for instance, what child at two years old does not display immediately an openness of love to the *things* as creatures, beyond any full capacity of response in the observer no doubt, who watches the child responding. The child's experience will be followed progressively by actions revealing a growing self-awareness, occasioned by this specific encounter and by like encounters with other things and under varying conditions. My example is quite specific. I have just observed my granddaughter, almost two, as she encountered new rabbits in a neighbor's hutch. My experience bears analogy to Wordsworth's in "Tintern Abbey," and to Hopkins's in "Spring and Fall," in that in each the speaker certifies his own thought by reference to the open response of Dorothy or Margaret in the present moment. Each reads his own earlier experiences of "thoughtless youth" more confidently thereby, seeing in the other, younger, person's eyes "shooting lights" of joy in the one instance and "tears for the things of man" in the other. Such experience is certified to me by my grandchild's own wild eyes, sparkling with a light which is a light not simply reflecting light's level in physics (as it must for my actual seeing). That is my seeing at the level of accident. But there is an interior light not yet accounted for, emerging into this world of accident out of the child's eyes and directed at the small creatures squirming in the hutch.

I suggest that one may certify this experience again and again, and in a variety of ways, both by memory and by observation of persons turning ten out of two, twenty out of both, and on even to the edge of our worldly nature that so oppresses Eliot's Gerontion. But at this moment, just past the initiating experience, I see my grandchild exhibiting more and more that secondary act Thomas speaks of, knowing both herself and the world about her as knowledge possessed consequent to her encounters. She does so in a new complexity: through the mystery of the continuing effects of experience borne by her intellect in its aspect as memory. For awhile yet, she insists on our revisiting the edge of the cage whenever we are near it, though she is not yet prepared to deal with a new mystery: the small creatures are at once the same, yet different with each encounter. At the level of the accidents of their being they change and grow daily, but that is merely a mystery at the level of accident, with which accidents science is quite adequate, are at least so to that point beyond change, death. But then, the same becomes noticeable in her, as I observe long before she can do so. She is and is not the same on my succeeding encounters. Her changes are more than changes at the level of accident, however, though those changes are not inconsequential. It is not so easy now to walk with her in arms over to the neighbor's cage. She has become an armful for an old man. But the more mysterious change is in her intellect, the sophistication of which change is daily advanced. The change is quite evident in the signs she deploys with a growing subtlety of her own intellect. At first, denied a visit to the small creatures, come tears, perhaps even the edge of a tantrum. But slowly there follows an emerging subtlety of the will, through which I am cajoled to make a visit to the rabbits. (Tea parties come later.) But always the growing complexity of intellect deploying sign. Very soon, no doubt, given the rapid accumulation of words at command I shall no longer be able to hear myself think in her presence.

We engage a mystery whose science is that of epistemology, and we are attempting to understand, not the relation of concept to sign but the mystery of an engendering *in* intellect, out of which intellect grows in its gifts of potentiality. We turn toward a relation within the initiating event, the encounter of intellect and thing, a relation which seems to require our resolving the intellect's perception in relation to concept formalized. It is an event, so to speak, of a *conception* as that term bears a biological analogy. Intellect conceives in response to an object encountered, in an action we sometimes designate in epistemology's language as *perception*. Now this event is anterior to that subsequent act by intellect whereby it knows itself as a consequence of that event which is anterior to its knowing itself—that event we might speak of as a union consummated between intellect and the thing itself. The seed in that consummation in Thomistic terms, is the *essence* of the thing so known. Such is a conception-perception event, out of which engagement intellect realizes—recognizes—a knowledge as already possessed, a knowledge which then issues as concept. In respect to our biological analogy, one might say that intellect is innocently pregnant with knowledge and growing toward a necessity to give that knowledge a name, concept.

But what is this process, what its cause? For analogy, even properly governed, fails at the brink of the reality that occasions it to intellect. By its best efforts, intellect seems again and again thwarted in its attempt to *certify* that action of intellect that is pre-self-conscious. In that failure, it finds itself haunted by sordid or lovely form, and that form seems divorced from substantiality. So entangling are the issues to intellect itself that Gilson is led to insist: "What we must do first of all . . . is free ourselves from the obsession with epistemology as the necessary pre-condition for philosophy." We must do so, he says, if we are to put ourselves in accord with ourselves and with other things.

Gilson is undoubtedly right that, in our post-Cartesian world, epistemology becomes an obsession. But epistemological questions must be not so much put aside as made ordinate, and I think St. Thomas's words which we have just cited show how that may be done. The *obsession* is the problem, and it occurs when truncated from experience of things. For, once one reaches that stage of intellectual development spoken of by Thomas as a secondary act, our knowing our own act of knowing, the fascination too easily comes to focus exclusively upon that secondary, and the primary is largely neglected. With that exclusiveness, the neglect of primary knowledge, a viable epistemology becomes impossible. Gilson does not reject epistemology, despite those words we quoted, for in the same work, *Methodical Realism*, he points to the corrective to our obsession: ". . . the object of epistemology is not *thought*, which is only the consciousness of an act of knowledge, but *knowledge* itself, which is the grasp of an object." It is in the failure to make this distinction that one becomes incapable of recovering the ground of thought in a primary knowledge, and so becomes incapable of a recovery through that knowledge of reality—including the reality of the action primary to self-awareness. One is thus trapped in Cartesian Idealism. But one is wrong, as Eliot was wrong, to conclude that philosophy is itself illusional. That shows just how thoroughly possessed his intellect had become by Cartesian Idealism.

We are concerned, then, with a consummation in intellect whereby it comes to bear, toward a possible fruition, a primal knowledge. The nature of its own participation is the problematic concern. Wordsworth tried an approach to it in speaking of the world of the senses, a world which the senses seemed to him to both half create and half perceive. Half conceive and half perceive. There is a metaphorical suggestiveness in these words, suggestive of the procreative acts of nature, and I wish to underline that analogy, suggesting that at some level beyond attribution we may discover the relation grounded in proper proportionality. One might well judge this approach to Thomistic epistemology, as here made by a mere poet. But it is supportable in Thomas himself, perhaps as explored philosophically by Louis-Marie Regis in *St. Thomas and Epistemology* (1946). Regis's concern is with the progress toward wisdom from the initiating experience of the *ens primum cognitum*, which is universal to an intellect, to that experience of *ens in quantum ens* and beyond, accessible to the philosopher as philosopher. It is that movement from rabbit, to the plural rabbits, and beyond to a unified vision holding the multiplicity of rabbits as it were. But our immediate concern is for that poet as Romantic, of consciousness encountering the rabbit and set thereby on a journey which, if the ground of that encounter be not understood, can but leave that "poet" coming to himself lost in a dark wood.

The issue sought—a release from intellectual exile from being—is through consummation in intellect, the seed in which is a primal knowledge to be accepted openly as gift. (The analogy that seems most appropriate to the point is the Annunciation.) What is present as a mystery is an inception of knowledge whereby a mutuality between the perceptive intellect and the thing as bearer of a truth (even the lowly rabbit of my granddaughter's encounter) makes intellect fecund, out of and around cause implicit. What is made possible in the event is the intellect's bearing of that effect to full term, issuing through image to concept, and from concept to sign. The knowledge born in sign to other intellects is afforded at best a manifestation, and indeed is as often but stillborn or retarded by sign as it is a vigorous presence beneath the sign. That is the presence St. Thomas speaks of as the "meanings of words" that "lie hidden under words." The uncertain state of intellect caused by its being possessed by Cartesian Idealism, a perversion of truth born as knowledge, lies in the inability to believe the miracle at the outset, the mystery of conception of knowledge in intellect as actual in itself and not as merely *thought*, for thought is a sort of morning sickness to intellect so to speak. That symptom, thought, though certain actually, seems to suggest a disease rather than sign of intellect's own nurturing creativity. It cannot believe it has *known* a thing (to which we are relating by allusion the biblical use of that term, whereby a virgin is said not to have *known* a man).

In relation to this somewhat audacious metaphor for the intellect's capacity to bear truth creatively, in a participation of the good both in respect to the thing borne and to its own good, it should be little surprising that the eighteenth century gave rise to metaphors of mind as virginal, or in another famous metaphor, as tabula rasa. Nor is it surprising to discover Coleridge and Wordsworth early in their thought attempting to deal with this mystery by recourse to David Hartley's psychology, whereby image in mind is not that ambiguously shifting creature Wordsworth later has it in "Tintern Abbey," his informing form, the suggestion in which is a companionable mutuality of intellect and object. It is rather to Hartley a seemingly material particle lodged in mind, a metaphor Wordsworth does not entirely escape. From such attempts at the mystery of intellect's conception of truth, little wonder that one is led, as Eliot was at first, to a sense of intellect as a thing somehow *known* by a deceiving incubus, the issue of which was a thousand *sordid* images. Wordsworth, of course, could not at last accept that essentially deterministic account of intellect, though it was a position already lending itself increasingly in his day to an environmentalism as cause of being. That was a circular logic which seemed ratified by Darwin a little later and which we are only now beginning to see as circular.

Within that climate of Cartesian Idealism where intellect discovers itself entrapped, little wonder that it fears that its desire for vision always must end in illusion. The locus of its encounter with itself is reality reduced, though reality reduced is still a reality. That is why Gilson says so effectively, "Evidently, it is because I am that I think, but it is not in the least evident that it is because things exist that I think of them. . . . So one must say: neither do things exist because I think, nor do I think because things exist." These alternatives deny necessary cause and so each leaves intellect trapped in a cloud of uncertain knowing. Or again, Gilson says, "*I think therefore I am* is a truth, but it is not a starting point." The *concluding* may not at the same time be the *initiating* principle.

And so Gilson is brought to put the position of Thomistic realism in terms such as the philosopher often enough must do in putting his position, that is, with the aid of, or in the manner of the poet:

> [T]he birth of the concept presupposes the fertilization of the intellect by the reality which it apprehends. Before truth comes the thing that is true; before judgment and reality are brought into accord, there is the living accord of the intellect with reality; it is because the intellect becomes the real thing that it can afterwards conceive its essence. . . . So first we have the immediate experience of the thing-in-itself, in which the self of the subject, by an effort of reflection [metaphorically, by a serenity of gestation following the un-self-conscious receptiveness of intellect, as of the wife in conjugal procreation], afterwards rediscovers itself. The realist method of reflection starts with the whole in order to distinguish the parts. It will not allow one of the parts, the last of these it reaches, to be posited as the pre-condition for the existence of everything else.[7]

6

The Pleasure of Notion, the Terror of Vision: Concerning Wallace Stevens and T. S. Eliot

[I]n the natural order there is a community of minds in as much as minds communicate in the love of truth and beauty, in the life and work of knowledge, art and poetry, and in the highest values of culture. . . . [T]he common good of the intellects is the intelligible treasure of culture in which minds communicate with one another.

—Jacques Maritain, *The Person and the Common Good*

If intellect find itself to be standing in the way of an enjoining which might yield image or metaphor as anchored in a dependable analogy of proper proportionality, what is it to do? Especially if that intellect is the poet? At best it seems to find itself standing in its own shadow. Out of that entrapment, to communicate with minds in the common love of truth and beauty seems impossible, and any pretense of communion of minds must be only a deepening of the shadow of self-illusion. In response to that dilemma, Wallace Stevens puts it in his "The Man with the Blue Guitar" that "The earth, for us, is flat and bare. There are no shadows." No shadows, that is, except those our imagination projects against that flat bare earth, against a plain glass jar in Tennessee as suggested in another poem. The imaginative act is unfounded by the earth's realities. And so, Stevens concludes, "Poetry/ Exceeding music must take the place/ Of empty heaven and its hymns,/ Ourselves in poetry must take their place," against the flat, bare earth as played upon imagination's blue guitar.

If one thus concedes as impossible any bringing together into an accord of Eliot's street and sparrow or Stevems's flat bare earth with the poets' vision of street or earth, there seem two possibilities open to the poet and his singing. For Eliot, lamentation, self-pity addressed to the self. For

Stevens, exultation of the self through new "hymns" to the self, replacing the God-centered hymns of the fathers. On either hand, exultation or lamentation is possible only through hymns of attribution centered in the self as cause. But we observe that even in Eliot's lamentations, at least a desire is kept alive directed beyond lamentation, if but fitfully. That desire wants still some issue or other to its faint hope of rescue, and that is already a promise of a turning from the self.

As for Stevens, he says in a letter about his "The Man with the Blue Guitar" that it "deals with the relation or balance between imagined things and real things which . . . is a constant source of trouble to me. . . . I have been trying to see the world about me both as I see it and as it is." The poem puts it somewhat less hopefully:

> Here I inhale profounder strength
> And as I am, I speak and move
> And things are as I think they are
> And say they are on the blue guitar.

What he cannot pierce with understanding is the meaning of that "profounder strength" as somehow inhaled into intellect from the seemingly flat earth. To set about that concern would be to undertake lamentation, and Stevens would bypass lamentation to sing delight. So there is that other way: the way of the "blue guitar," the way of that "necessary angel," the imagination, through whose actions "Things as they are/ Are changed upon the blue guitar," justifying a conclusion that "things are as I think they are/ And say they are."

Thus Stevens would seize upon uncertainty as a certainty sufficient to the play of attributive metaphor, for "What is there in life except one's ideas,/ Good air, good friend, what is there in life?" Given only the certainty of illusion, one may set about making, through the attributive power of imagination, "A Supreme Fiction," as one of his extended poems sets out to do. The flat world has imposed upon it a greenness by attributive act. The accident of *green* is in the eye, not in the grass. For insects and animals do not see the flat world as man does; analytical science demonstrates as much, even providing us pictures of the way the world would look were we fly or fox. Our imagination, the instrument to attribution, makes us content with the blueness of imposed attribution upon a flat, bare earth, requiring only the consent of our will. Why then lament Grandfather Wordsworth's difficulties with the problem? Why even bother with the strain upon will and imagination in an indictment of Grandfather Wordsworth such as Eliot introduces into his early poetry and criticism? One can instead play fictions of blue upon a green guitar, turning it blue. As Stevens says, in objecting to a particular critic's imaginative attribution of likeness between Stevens and Eliot, in a letter to that critic: "Eliot and I are dead opposites and I have been doing about everything that he would not be likely to do" (*Letters*, April 25, 1950). On another occasion, considering the sort of person who might occupy a poetry chair at Harvard (the letter is dated October 15, 1940), Stevens says of Eliot, "I regard him as a negative rather than a positive force." For Eliot has by then professed himself Christian, and that position is necessarily counter to the attributive freedom Stevens would require for the poet. Stevens says, in aphorisms collected under the title "Adagia" in *Opus Posthumous* (the juxtaposition is mine): "We live in the mind. . . . God is a postulate of the ego. . . . It is the belief and not the god that counts. . . . After one has abandoned a belief in God, poetry is that essence which takes its place as life's redemption. . . . Poetry is a means of redemption." Poetry is *a* means, there being others, but ways dependent on how one lives *in* the mind. If one chooses to live intellectually through poetry, then "poetry must resist the intelligence almost successfully," being "a pheasant disappearing in the bush." It is out of this tension in mind of poetry's *almost* escape and the mind's almost capturing it that makes poetry the agent of salvation.[8]

As for the timid Eliot (as seen from Stevens's point of view), Wordsworth's insistence that there is a "something" deeply interfused in differentiated creation is not answered by concluding that Wordsworth's *something* is merely a "notion" projected by discomfited intellect. One cannot let it go at that. Such a conclusion not acted upon can only checkmate imagination's desire to create. Against Eliot, Stevens insists that to make "Notes toward a Supreme Fiction" is sufficient to that hunger in intellect to create, by accepting this condition to imaginative creation as the point of departure rather than its end. Nor is one agitated by a concern on the part of that activated imagination for any other imagination to receive or value the thing made, the poem. As set down in "Adagia" and repeated elsewhere, "One does not write for any reader except one," namely oneself. Thus a plurality of uncertainties are laid to rest. One has solved the dilemma of object in relation to the particular intellect. One merely accepts without question whatever intellect inhales. It is "profounder strength" from "good air." But more important, one has solved the nagging sense of responsibility of intellect to other intellects, by writing for oneself only. For Stevens, there is no longer the attendant problem so nagging to the Romantic poet: his relation to other men, the question of whether as poet he differs accidentally or essentially in respect to his intellect as compared to theirs. If, essentially, that might justify hierarchial superiority to other intellects, a persuasion not uncommon among Romantic poets. But it also introduces a multitude of questions about his responsibility to a community with mankind, whether he sets himself high or low at the common table.

Given his beliefs about his own existence, Stevens finds little need to justify the poet as a peculiar instance of intellect, freely granting that there are other ways of living in one's mind—the ways of politician or philosopher perhaps. He is aware, as his poetry shows, of thus breaking with a tradition. For poets have seemed driven to justify the Poet as at once different from and yet like other men, since Sir Philip Sidney at least. Witness the unhousable volume of apologies for poet and poetry since Sidney. That genre of apology gives way, with an acceleration in the eighteenth century, to criticism of poetry itself, much of it by the poet as apologetic critic. And that has been a trend conspicuous in our own century. Stevens would demure from poets' or poetry's defense, though he finds himself pressed to some apology beyond himself as sole audience. Though reluctant, there are those few pieces of his "criticism," published as *The Necessary Angel,* in which many of the "essays" are presented as poems. But then that witty strategy might remind us how much of his *Collected Poems* is essay, usually argumentative. His poetry is heavily a justification of his intellectual position, deliberate in its dialectical stance, which is insistent that he holds no intellectual position save that of a devotee to the imagination. Considering his sometime public insistence that "one writes for one," then, there is that further suggestion in the argumentative poetry that he must repeatedly convince himself of the rightness of his position. In "The Auroras of Autumn" imagination speaks, defining itself by epithet and operation: "I am the necessary angel of earth,/ Since, in my sight, you see the earth again." It is at least ambiguous—or so Stevens might well contend, though he is not much concerned with consistency in the logic of his position—whether the *you* here is anyone other than the poet himself. So this poem, too, may be read as internal colloquy with the self, as one reads Eliot's "Prufrock" or Stevens's own "Idea of Order at Key West." Indeed, much of Stevens's poetry teasingly invites the accidental reader to just that conclusion, for in the drama whereby one writes for one, any other "reader" is accidental, even random, presence to the poem he happens to encounter.

We must add, however, that Wallace Stevens as Romantic poet is a rarity, though in his rejection of the poet as possibly Christian (his rejection of Eliot), he shares with William Carlos Williams and with Ezra Pound a belief that God is a projection by a race of egoists. That being accepted as true, what then? Williams or Pound embarks from that conclusion upon rescue operations the rest of humanity, where Stevens practices an indifference. It is this differing response to the conclusion that God does not exist that makes him rare among Romantics. Many Romantics insist on God's existence. Many deny it. But few build their work on an indifference to either conclusion, deist and atheist alike usually actively evangelical for his own conclusions. Stevens is, in the context of our argument, a poet who seizes upon Cartesian Idealism with delight. For in that Idealism, appropriated and not examined too closely, it becomes possible to justify to oneself metaphors of attribution. One may then, at least for the moment of the imaginative attribution, practiced against the backdrop of the flat gray world, enjoy an exhilaration of intellect as if it were freed of all prior restraint. As always, it is the *as if* that proves destructive to the position if examined too closely, as is true of the same position we see in Stevens as defended by Robert Frost. (On this coincidence of belief, Frost and Stevens are much closer than usually recognized.) Narcissus, says Stevens in *The Necessary Angel*, did not expect to discover snakes as hair in his reflected image, or hate in his own eyes as reflected from the pool: "he sought out his image everywhere because it was the principle of his nature to do so and . . . because it was the principle of his nature . . . to expect to find pleasure in what he found."

There is a considerable attention in our criticism to Stevens in relation to Wordsworth, the unsuitableness of which is evident when we compare these words of Stevens to Wordsworth's attempt in "Tintern Abbey." For there is a radical difference between Stevens's deliberately seeking his own image in the flat bare world and Wordsworth's seeking of that image in a world he is convinced is anything but flat and bare. It is with a considerable shock, then, that Wordsworth comes to an arrest in his looking, precipatated by the death of "Lucy," at which point he is consumed by despair. That despair is precisely because of the sudden dark shadow of Stevens's conclusion that one lives in the mind. The sudden possibility that the action of mind is only a projection of fanciful intent against a flat bare world shocks Wordsworth deeply. Eliot's own lamented inadequacy of *notion* as merely precipitating the illusion of *vision* becomes a principle in which Stevens delights, but he may do so only by denying in advance the possibility of vision. Wordsworth's expectations of his visionary moments, insufficiently grounded in his own experiences of reality, result in a simplification through that desire for the complexity of reality. And so his vision into "the life of things" so transports him in his conviction that he does not consider, let alone account for, the death of things. Thus his faith is left resting solely in "beauteous form" untrammeled by any shadow. Eliot to the contrary, in his early poetry, embraces a proposition differing from Wordsworth's: the mind is constituted of ugly forms, and Eliot can only end up dejected in that he does not believe in any "life" in things. Stevens solves these two extremes, of course, by denying either life or death in things. Life and death are merely concepts suited to the mind's existence as mind. The life giver is the imagination, whose operative sign touches a principle of belief about the nature of mind's existence as mind. The life giver is the imagination, whose operative sign touches a principle of belief about the nature of mind's existence is *as if*. That is the sign that reminds intellect constantly that it is engaged in making a *fiction*, not in pursuing a vision of existence itself.

But there is a problem that will in the end have its way with Stevens, a problem implicit in the principle of *as if*. The very principle implies not only the conditional, whereby intellect withholds consent, but a necessity of an *is* as well, without which the *as if* can but raise a continuous doubt, and doubt requires a *possible*, against which doubt is registered. The earth *is*, even if it is flat and bare. It is this doubt to which Descartes supposed his resulation sufficient, his *cogito ergo sum*. But that *as if* depends, we are saying, upon some *is*, since it cannot be *as if* except consequent to its *being*, whether as idea or palpable thing or gradations between these extremes of being. Narcissus cannot escape the intrusive subversiveness of the *as if*, which is made subversive by its dependence in reality. This intrusive subversiveness appears first as a doubt in intellect before it becomes a sign expressing doubt as held conceptually. And Narcissus must be always turning from that doubt, seeking his reflection as renewed. He must be always turning to the flat, bare world, while repeatedly required to insist that it is flat and bare, with the constant possibility of a recognition that his is an illusion of the world, a fiction preceding his intended fiction, and thus an illusion of himself. The world as flat and bare will in the end suggest that it is only Narcissus himself who is flat and bare. And that is a terror difficult to bear, however strongly he finds the reflection of his hair beautiful and his eyes reflecting love, not hate. For in such a faith as his, love is that of the self, which forces upon the mind a hate of the world. The hate is a reductionism of that world to flat and bare. In the moment when that illusion collapses, what Narcissus will be left with is the recognition that his self-love has proved effectively self-hate, but that his hate for the flat gray neutral earth is reciprocated by a love out of that world beyond his imagination's reductionist powers. That, at last, is what Eliot comes to see in affirming the Word in the desert. It is what, in the end, Stevens himself came to see, a point to which we shall turn later.

Meanwhile, Narcissus as Narcissus (to echo an essay by Alan Tate) must be always seeking his reflection. He must be unvarying in his imaginative action because that limited action alone can keep reality at bay. He must be constantly projecting expectation of a pleasure of self-revelation. There must be an uninterrupted poem of the mind, but necessarily the sequential notes as poems reflect discursive action. There is an inescapable labor of discursiveness to intellect by its very nature. And it is precisely here that reality is most insistently intrusive. For such is the reality of the nature of the would-be Narcissus. Alas, even the angel imagination, for all its powers, allows no *continuous* supreme fiction, for that angel exists only in relation to its finite mind, even in Stevens's hopeful view of imagination. That relation makes inevitable a dualism in mind, constantly at war, never more disturbing than in the pause from the poem or between the lines of a particular poem. One might make this point clearer, perhaps, by reference to that most influential poet upon the modernist mind as it struggles with this same dualism. Mallarme bears some influence on Stevens's mind, as on Eliot's in those early years. We look at Mallarme from the Thomistic realist's position, for which position Gilson is such a clear spokesman.

The difficulty to the poet's imagination as saving angel lies in the necessity of discursiveness, in both thought and speech, and that discursiveness complicates the immediacy of idea or the immediacy of vision as translated in any mind into concept beyond any simple experiences of the vision or the ideal. In *Linguistics and Philosophy*, in addressing the difficulty, Gilson considers Mallarme:

> Mallarme, intoxicated by speech, had wanted to be able to think words directly, words which were no more than signs of their own signification without reference to any real object.
>
> He therefore obstinately struggled to sanctify language by imposing on it that nearly total poetic purification. But to push this operation to its term would have been a disaster, since that would have necessitated the elimination from poetry of language itself, which is the matter upon which the act of the poet exercises itself. . . . [He would] try to create poetry out of his own substance and out of that alone. In order truly to create, he create *ex nihilo creaturae* and through the efficacy of his creativity alone. Thus understood, the poetic act is that of an intellect which owes its work only to itself and, in order to assure itself of that, discards everything else in order to possess itself as totally unconditional, therefore anterior to its own expression.

The result, in Mallerme's own words: "nothingness having gone away, the castle of purity remains." The affinity between Mallerme and Stevens is most evident here. But one must note a difference. Mallerme is fanatically serious, from which there results a sense of desperation in him which Stevens avoids. Stevens does not present himself as poet as the profound savior of purity. Poetry as savior for Stevens is Savior of his own intellect. Mallerme insists on being heard, an insistence which is itself a contradiction of his position, for such purity as he proposes must be finally indifferent, purged of all impurities, which means in one respect purged of any concern for audience. It is in this respect, perhaps, that Stevens is more Mallerme than Mallerme, in spite of the rich excessiveness of his own poems in contrast to the sterile "castle of purity" which Mallerme would build.

And so one might, whether Mallerme or Stevens as Narcissus, imagine as an ideal condition to Narcissistic intellect a continuous imaginative act separate from its articulation into "notes," into a supreme fiction or a dream castle of purity. But that moment of imagination can never itself be continuous, as it must be if its dream fiction or its castle mirage is to be sustained to the comfort of the imagining intellect. As a creature built *ex nihilo*, it collapses as merely *nihilo* when the necessary angel is forced to nod by the inescapable human dimension of intellect. What we witness in such an attempt is the poet's presumption of his power that it is the same as that power we usually attribute only to God. Such are the principles of reality, exercised upon even the Narcissistic nature, that the presumption leads first to intellectual and then to spiritual collapse. From Steven's reading of the reality of his mind as maker, requiring nothing anterior to its actions, the very survival of that mind increasingly depends upon the imagination's continuously sustaining that mind, though from a position removed from the discursive entrapment of imagination. The imagination's necessary distance is not from the human "kind" in this instance such as Wordsworth felt himself guilty of. (Wordsworth, with an anecdote as near humor as one is likely to come in him, remembers that "Nine-tenths of my verses have been murmured out in the open air. . . . After a long absence from home it has more than once happened that one of my cottage neighbors has said: 'Well, there he is; we are glad to hear him booing about again.' ") Stevens's imagination must stand off from the reality of his own mind by poetic actions called *fictions*. The dualism must, if reflected upon, become intolerable under the pressures of reality, those pressures of what things are in themselves, mind included.

In Stevens's deliberate and contradictory reduction of reality to a separateness from the imagination, which requires a separateness from the reality of intellect itself, we should not overlook his own deliberate appropriation of Genesis to metaphorical fiction, a mischevious appropriation which contradicts his supposed indifference, for he intends at least to tease any who may encounter him who yet believe in God as Creator. Stevens appropriates *in the beginning* to the imagination as agent. One is struck by echos in parts of what we have quoted from him as we remember Genesis: "In the beginning the earth was without form, and void; and darkness was upon the face of the deep. And the Spirit of God moved upon the face of the water." It is the Imagination as the spirit of Stevens's own mind that moves upon the flat bare earth. Or again, remembering Stevens and Eliot as "dead opposites," we might recall the opening words of *John* that Eliot comes to embrace: "In the beginning was the Word." Stevens's imaginative appropriation of that text is quite evident in "The Idea of Order at Key West." For it is the Imagination, and not Eliot's or John's Word in the desert, which is that "Blessed rage to order words of the sea." The imagination, presented as a "she" in the poem, means that "there never was a world for her/ Except the one she sang and, singing, made." For "She was the single artificer of the world/ In which she sang."

But the principle is one thing, its exercise quite another. The "green" world has its vengeance upon the poet: he cannot *be*, by an act of his own imagination, a self-divinized existence beyond the reach of that flat, bare earth he must acknowledge. The body itself is of that world and, as Plato suggested long ago, always interrupting the pretense of intellect to autonomy, let alone the pretense to existence through continuous self-creation by intellection. That means that the imagination as the holy spirit to Narcissus must always be laboring at its play, for the moment it ceases its labor, both it and Narcissus fall in some manner into the clutches of that "green" world in which all along the greenness has been devouring action, denying intellect's pretense to greenness as merely attributive. For that green as accident in the Aristotelean sense accrues to the things of the world in their particularity, as opposed to its being an attributed accident whose source is the seeing eye. This is true, despite the difference of that color to the insect's eye or to man's.

The labor of a blueness as forced upon the "green" world seems the only possible opening for the imagination in the Stevensonian understanding of imagination and its power. The attempt of such an escape rouses sleeping dragons, with which intellect through concept must struggle to contain. They sleep in the depths of intellect itself, though somehow to be related to the green world as engaged by intellect. One of those dragons we have already encountered, and no small one, lurking in that subversive ally to intellect, *as if*. Narcissus arrested before a word, when that word is taken only as mirror, finds his arrest possible only through a labor more like that of Sisiphus than at first supposed. The rescue of intellect to its comforts of self-love repeatedly collapses, requiring that it be lifted back into place before an object redeclared a mirror. Those dragons were roused by Eliot in his own intellect through his lamentation of his intellect as isolated. His dissatisfaction with the conditions of Narcissus, as he sees his reflection dwindling, becomes more suggestive of a lean and hungry condition in the self, even though seemingly seen as a reflection in a shadow world of a shadow self. What that "vision" of the self turns out to be for Eliot is an actual, if lean and hungry, soul accusing the disordered self of its attempt to maintain a false *stillness*; the false stillness of self-love.

Those waking dragons, necessary to the soul in its hunger, we speak of in attempting to tame them to our service through the discipline of philosophy, the discipline whereby we seek to know the truth of things, dragons included. We give them formal names toward their domestication, such sciences as Ontology or Epistemology. But the most frightening dragon of the soul-borne litter, as Wordsworth encountered it after "Tintern Abbey" and as Stevens encountered it near the end of his life, is that one wakened in intellect by uncertainty. Sometimes it leads to desperate attempts of self-creation as a defense. It is named Teleology, a seemingly gentle beast on first encounter, even amenable to the illusions intellect builds by attributive imposition. Teleology increasingly reveals itself, however kindly in its ferocity, as infused in things by their substantial reality beyond all expectation, drawing intellect with the aid of a variety of other waking dragons to the mystery of last things. That is the kindly ferocious dragon discovered as always lurking in intellects, always drawing us through our becoming toward Teleology: the drawing of becoming to perfected being as end. A dragon friendly to its mates such as Ethics, Epistemology, even Psychology. And devoted in its service to Metaphysics. And all are concerned to draw intellect toward ends that are Good. That is the Good, in our view. As for the poet, he must contend with those waking dragons as interior to his thought, his fascination as "maker" with order, proportion, unity and the like—with beginnings, middles, and ends. And he finds these ultimately in Teleology's keep. The poet as "maker" labors in his creating a thing (the poem) in which these aspects of *thingness* are present under the rubric of "beauty." If he labors under the allusion that order, proportion, unity and the like are present in the poem by sole virtue of his attributive action, he will be confounded in his own end. For, since art as an action of intellect is an imitation of action (a point we shall engage *passim*), the attributes of being in the thing made whose effect we call the thing's beauty reflect by art's indirection the attributes of the creating soul itself in its own nature. It is here that one discovers the impossibility of the poet's removing the "personal" from his act of making, for in the sense we are concerned with the merely autobiographical accidents giving the poet a spectacle and a name are not the fundamental issue. What his act of making reflects is the actual in relation to the potential of the soul itself as that soul by its nature exists beyond historical demarcations such as the details of the poet's "autobiography." Order, proportion, and unity are aspects of perfection possible to a nature by virtue of its given nature, whether we speak of the poem or of the poet.

Which brings us to reflect that, since the nature of a particular thing is a given (since a thing cannot give itself its own nature), the gift of actual and potent being of the thing is the circumscription of finitudes. Because it *is*, it is limited by its finitudes. And this being so, its finitudes include those we think of as related to beginnings, middles, and ends. Modernist determinism attempted to shift the implications that lie here. Mechanistic explanations of being would explain the present and future as determined by the past, in a rigid deterministic cause-effect, whose patron saint is History (as we suggested) and whose theology is called Historicism. But, again the old dragon Teleology, who is always fed by the reality of being as encountered in this present moment. For Teleology would give account of the past and present, not merely in relation to the future, but to an end, which in its profound indications is not a concern easily resolved in temporal terms. The difficulties raised are ever present to intellect in relation to its nature. For intellect discovers its finitudes through its becoming, its movement from the state of the actual to its acquiring its potential as actual. Now *becoming* has to do with *beginning*, and beginning and becoming inescapably with *ending*. Teleology, then, has in its keep the poet's abiding concern, Beauty, which is the aspect of perfection St. Thomas defines in saying that beauty is that which when seen pleases. And so that subtle dragon Teleology, though ever so quietly and however subtly by indirections, turns intellect toward Beauty as Perfection. The shock to intellect is that perfection speaks an end.

If such be true, as I believe, then the soul finds itself inclined through its peculiar gifts of being, by its "nature," to ends, and the question raised to its potential is that of ends in relation to *the* end. The perfection implicit in becoming: is its final end oblivion? Or beatitude? That is the agitating thought in intellect. Not that it may not be possible to that soul to delay the question somewhat. We have been considering Wordsworth's "Tintern Abbey" as a representative thing reflecting the "Romantic" poet. And we might observe in it that Wordworth is very much aware, on his revisiting the banks of the Wye, of that river's "inland murmurs," which resonate for him those inland intellectual murmurs, in relation to

its own beginnings to this present moment. The poem is heavily concerned with a middleness, and with an attempt to understand this middleness in relation to beginnings. So that it is most surprising to us, as it
will prove shocking to Wordsworth, that he avoids the implications in
beginningness, and middleness of endingness—of death. When, after the
shock of necessity to consider death, he writes his "Intimations Ode," he
will advance a Platonic abstraction to cover that progress of the soul,
against the fear of the end as oblivion. A much more wiley poet, resisting
the necessity of coming to terms with the implications of Teleology as to
an end, stages a constancy of resistence to that inclination to ends, as if
thereby to make middleness the only immortality. I have in mind Robert
Frost, and the poem which dramatizes the position here described is his
"West-Running Brook." It is, his speaker insists, the "backward motion"
against nature's pull to ends that "we are from." Put as a reaction to
nature's flux as the characterization of creation, order as a backward motion avoids the teleological problems, more or less.

Let us not leave this exploration of dragons in the intellect without,
first, observing their presence in Eliot's intellect, and then remarking
them somewhat more largely, since our intention is not primarily to define and exhibit those dragons in themselves but to make note of their
presence as complications to the poet in his attempt to find a way through
his own portion of the dark woods of existence. As it turns out, teleology
lay in wait for Stevens as for Eliot, though Eliot is early in coming to
terms with it. Stevens, in his last days embraced an end far other than that
endless end of supreme fictions he had thought sufficient unto his end.
Eliot finds the teleological creature in his thought amenable to the harness
of concept at last, though concept to such a poet is fashioned from paradox. Eliot says, for instance, "In my end is my beginning," a statement
firmly woven in paradox as are the accommodations to teleology by intellect in the whole of the *Four Quartets*. In these poems, as in the sentence
just quoted, there is a position much advanced beyond the uncertain encounter of that paradox as dramatized in "The Journey of the Magi":

> I had seen birth and death,
> But had thought they were different; this Birth was
> Hard and bitter agony for us, like Death, our death.

My attention to such dragons as teleology or epistemology in these
pages may appear more cursory than perhaps they are. Gilson says, in
Methodical Realism, that the realist takes as his starting point for his reflections *being*, which in effect is for us the beginning of knowledge: *res*

sunt. "If we go deeper into the nature of the object given us, we direct ourselves towards one of the sciences, which will be completed by a metaphysics of nature. If we go deeper into the conditions under which the object is given us, we shall be turning towards a psychology, which will reach completion in a metaphysics of knowledge. The two methods are ... complementary, because they rest on the primitive unity of the subject and object in the act of knowledge, and any complete philosophy implies an awareness of their unity." It is evident that, on the one hand, I have not undertaken either of the metaphysical completions nor any complete philosophy. I hope that it will be evident, however, that I am somewhat familiar with the importance to that philosophy of the sciences of nature and the sciences of psychology. In respect to the problem of epistemology, then, I am aware of the considerable attention to the sciences of nature as focused upon the brain and the sciences of psychology that focus upon the mind, even as I am aware of the considerable attempts to bring those sciences into conjunction as a science. The necessity of metaphysics to that endeavor, however, I think too much neglected, so that I am intending to recall us to that necessity. The several sciences focused upon human intellect are certainly necessary prelude to such metaphysical attempt, as is nowhere more evident I think than in those attempts to create intelligence out of that physics which takes being mechanically.

I remarked ealier Roger Penrose's recent *The Emperor's New Mind: Concerning Computers, Minds, and the Laws of Physics*, noting both his contribution to the proper question to be put to the advocates of artificial intelligence and its inadequacy at last, since it rests its case in physics no less than do the proponents of artificial intelligence. One finds a considerable literature in that genre, which might be spoken of collectively by reference to Julian Jaynes's *The Origin of Consciousness in the Breakdown of the Bicameral Mind*. In those works, the biology of mind attempts to raise the concern beyond physics and its mechanisms only, though still resting in that ground and so not touching the metaphysical necessity except by implication. By implication: one must be struck by the suggestive parallel, out of the exhaustive explorations of the actions of thought as differently influenced according to their origin in the left or right hemisphere, to the metaphysical concern Thomas speaks of as modes of intellection, the *ratio* and the *intellectus*. And since thought first became aware of the self as a thinking creature, there have been recognitions of distinctions of rational actions of the mind and intuitive actions of mind, about which distinction we have had much to say already. That the several sciences of the nature of mind are necessary prelude to a concern for a metaphysics of mind is fundamental. What we must insist upon, however, is that those preludes, while necessary, are inadequate to a full account of intellect. Intellect, like Shakespeare's star, may yield its height to us, through science, but its worth requires even for the partial *understanding* vouchsafed intellect (as opposed to our *knowledge*) a metaphysics. The mystery of teleology fascinates us out of, beyond, mere science, prompting ever new attempts upon height and breadth and depth. The plant, its growing end cut, adapts in itself to provide a growing end, as a red oak in my front yard always reminds me. A lateral limb is now transformed as a continuation of the trunk and has produced its own lateral limbs over the years. And the mystery of compensation in intellect itself reminds us that teleology speaks toward a fullness of being beyond the limits of physics. One need only read that account by Oliver Sacks, *The Man Who Mistook His Wife for a Hat*, to be reminded first of the mystery of *knowing* and then of that deeper mystery in intellect, the desire to *understand*, which are quite different aspects of intellect's possible perfection. That careful realist Étienne Gilson, observes a gift in our being crucial to our proper ends: Preceding any philosophical attempt to explain knowledge is the fact, not only of knowledge itself, but of man's burning desire to understand. It is a precedent no less to science than to philosophy.

7

Beauty, toward Beatitude

[B]eautiful things are those which please when seen. Hence beauty consists in due proportion . . . . Now, since knowledge is by assimilation, and similarity relates to form, beauty properly belongs to the nature of a formal cause. *(Summa Theologica,* I, 5, 5, ad. 1) [Beauty in relation to the nature of a formal cause is reflected in beautiful things and] includes three conditions, *integrity* or *perfection*, since those things which are impaired are by the very fact ugly; due *proportion* or *harmony*; and lastly, *brightness* or *clarity*. [*Integrity* or *perfection*, has likeness to the Son who] has in Himself truly and perfectly the nature of the Father . . . .[*Proportion* or *harmony* echoes the Son's property whereby He] is the express Image of the Father. Hence we see that an image is said to be beautiful, if it perfectly represents even an ugly thing . . . . [*Brightness*, or *clarity*] agrees with the property of the Son as the Word which is the light and splendor of the intellect. *(Summa Theologica,* I, 39, 8)

In arguing the inadequacy of Wallace Stevens's jerry-built philosophy, which he makes to justify his poetry, we need not deny our own fascination with his achievement as poet, nor feel guilty about rejecting his argument while yet valuing a certain beauty in certain things he has made. The imagination as the creator of intellect's "only world" is nonsense, as intellect's response to complex existences repeatedly demonstrates. But who, having insisted on this point, would deny Stevens the title poet, or deny that certain of his poems are good in themselves, in respect to their perfection or proportion or clarity? By his craft as maker, he has accomplished the poem's intrinsic potential, which is not to say that it does not fall short of intellect's desire for perfect truth since it is enabled by its imperfect conception to bear but a partial truth. As a partial truth, it is witness to the possible or probable in relation to reality. And it may, indeed, bear a true witness thereby to that which is actual in reality, in the sense Thomas speaks of in our epigraph. For a poem may be beautiful in itself in that it perfectly represents the nature of an imperfect thing. Though we might thereby conclude the poem perfect, it does not follow that one need subscribe to the imperfect truth which it truly represents by its own nature as a thing called art, called a poem. Such a distinction is important to our *understanding* of the *knowledge* allowed intellect through art, and for that reason we pursue the distinction somewhat further.

If art is, as St. Thomas argues, an imitation of the *actions* of "nature" and not an imitation of natural things—as if art were intellect's candid camera—then art must inevitably reflect, not the actual things, but the possible or probable actions of things. That is the problem which the modern novelist has had to deal with again and again, from Joyce's direct imitations of his own actions as poet in *Portrait of the Artist as a Young Man* to Robert Penn Warren's imitations of the actions of Huey Long as politician in his Willie Stark, in *All the King's Men*. A weak acknowledgement of this problem, though not restricted to the artist as artist but artist as historian, is found in the disclaimer at the beginning of novels or plays or movies: "any resemblance to actual persons living or dead is purely coincidental."

Having remarked the possible or probable as art's province, we must observe a corollary. For if art reflects what are possible or probable actions of human nature, we shall no doubt on occasion perceive the possible or probable action as itself actual in reality. That is why we are amused to remark, on occasion, that life imitates art. But what we are concerned to discover here is a sense in which it might be said that art inescapably imitates the action of life, when we take life at its most fundamental level: in the nature of the artist himself. For his nature in not that of the "artist," but that of man, as the philosopher's is not the nature of the "philosopher," but the nature of man. One's calling does not make him specific, however much the poet (or philosopher) might want us to be content with his person as specific with his calling. One is "born" to be a poet or philosopher pretty much as one is "born" to hang. This is to say that the gift of one's calling is a grace to one's personhood and is not the *essence* of his personhood. To make that distinction does not in the least suggest that anyone can be whatever he would be—philosopher or poet or scientist. It is rather to distinguish between those effects of grace, whereby in one aspect of grace's action one is a person by the gifts of being, and in another possibly a poet or philosopher by the grace of one's calling. One's calling complements his nature as person but it is not the essence of personhood. If we could ever get that point clear as a principle governing order in society, we should alleviate most of the intellectual misery accompanying the pretended "formal" order of education in our age, which destructively insists to the young that they can *be* whatever they *want to be*. And so, in the light of distinctions so far advanced, we may recognize a poem as good if it *is* good, even though it may be built out of, or upon, bad principles. And with that distinction we may become concerned with the false principles as truly witnessed by the art, without declaring the art itself false. What this will mean, again and again, is that we are turned to consider the inadequacy in the poet, the maker, in respect to his personhood, as it inescapably affects his art through the limited vision that is his as measured by the truth of things. Insofar as we can make and maintain that distinction, we will avoid the confusion that grows out of our intuitive recognitions of what is the false as that false is truly witnessed by art. We shall then be less inclined to burn books. What is required is that fortitude of intellect which dislodges false understanding from intellect, our own intellect most centrally. But there is an additional obligation to explore and either expose or confirm understanding in intellects not our own, in the interest of intellectual community. Knowledge, as opposed to understanding, is rather more simple to deal with, being more immediately available to exposure by critical intellect, if false. The false "knowledge" upon which Stalin allowed the USSR's agricultural concerns to be built decayed with more immediate spectacles of failure than the collapse of Marxist "understanding" of the nature of man. The collapse of Marxist ideology is only now reaching the level of spectacle in Eastern Europe in 1990 and will continue sporadic explosions in various regions of the world for some time to come. The point: we are required to exercise critical attention upon an established *understanding*, which by its distinction from *knowledge* is not amenable to falsification as scientific theories of knowledge are. Still, we must move with resolution to put understanding to the test, within the governance of humility, required of us precisely because of intellectual finitude. Intellectual finitude is one of those limits in our nature, and through that limit alone we *are*. Through that limit alone, we are *enabled* to move, resolutely or otherwise.

If we say that the sign (in our concern, the poem) may bear true witness to a false thing, we do not exonerate the false thing thereby. This is a distinction to be made in that cloudy debate over the meaning of pornography. Pornography is a practiced deception, aimed at appetites that are not in themselves evil. It is an evil counsel, in that by a pretense to the immediacy of art it attempts to bypass the reason that is proper to art. Its interest is not the truth of things, especially those things we call appetite in relation to the soul. Rather, where intellect by its address to the truth of things maintains a perspective on truth submissive to truth as independent of intellect, pornography intends a violation of such truth through excess—through appetite rampant in relation to being. It is, indeed, one of the manifestations of that gnosticism which, at the larger spectrum of social order, depends also on an appropriation of sign to a devious end, namely to a subversion of being in relation to that truth of being expressed in the principle of proper proportionality. Whether one speaks of the actions of the political or social gnostic or of the entrepreneurial pornographer, the instrument each seizes in his manipulation of being is the sign, through which he attempts a subversive principle that Eliot remembers in his own discovery of his first responsibility as poet: "to purify the dialect of the tribe."

Pornography, then, is that pseudo-art whose intent is to imitate, not the actions of human nature *proportionately* in respect to the complexity of the soul, as is necessary to the good of the poet in his actions as maker. That is the struggle, including those struggles with appetites upon which pornography feeds, and it is properly toward a perfection, toward that good which is proper to the soul. That such is a difficult task requires only our remembering that first great autobiographical novel-like memoir, St. Augustine's *Confessions*, that portrait of the saint as a young man. *The Confessions* has been so important to many souls in progress, and in many centuries, and especially to those souls whose calling is to be artist. Instead of art's motive and formal matter lying in the tensional complexity of our *personhood*, however, pornography "specializes," rejecting the complexity in favor of the violation, of the excessiveness, divorcing appetite from any temperate pole. In such a restructuring of the actuality of personhood toward the ends pornography seeks, appetite is established as the criterion of personhood. By this operative principle, pornography must deny good as an end desired, though it may play upon residual remembrance of such good. (Are fallen "preachers" popular figures as protagonists for this reason?) *Pornography* as we are using the term may be operative as a means in social or political programs, of course, and indeed has been particularly useful to the general social and political upheavals of the past hundred years. For, once the good of the person is dislocated from any transcendent reference, some substitute will be sought in the immanent world and that is a world which, once secularized, can only be taken as materialistic in its nature, which means that the appetites become more and more central. The dreamed-of worker's paradise is necessarily a world centering in appetite. Various versions of a "new morality," exciting envy, have been used to further the social or political agenda of gnostic intent. It is a topic of a considerable history, affecting Western culture particularly through its art. The Marxist invasion of cultural media in the late 1920s and 1930s, demanding art's service to social and political ends, is sufficiently established as a part of art's history in this century and in its baldness is now less threatening to art. But what is increasingly at issue is that continuing impetus which with the collapse of communism and socialism as economic structures, leave no clearly defined social or political ends. The battle now seems to be reduced locally, turning upon art in relation to family and individual morality. Indeed, this is precisely where the question should center at last, in questions having to do with ends proper to persons as persons. But in our present circumstances the local arena is in confused disarray. Community is seen as resting in principles incompatible to community, such has been the modernist victory. The uses of pornography, in this situation, exacerbates the anarchy destined from the triumph of intellect as autonomous. Democratized to an extreme pluralism, each intellect is its own state. Its desires are localized, increasingly focused in the appetites.

The denial of good as a perfection beyond mere satisfaction of appetite in its animal dimension, or of appetite as a refined gnostic power over being, is the principle most difficult to corner in our concerns for community and its dissolution. Perhaps that is why pornography as a topic is so current with us. But the battle as joined in judicial debate is hardly likely to resolve the continuing spiritual erosion. For if a principle which denies the existence of the good as a spiritual end advances itself in the name of art and lays claim to art's integrity, it seems supported by a conditioned reflex, especially apparent in the intellectual community, which must carry the day for it. That good which is art's according to its nature is subverted in the name of art. That such an intellectual shell-game is pervasive needs only our closer attention to current legal squabbles over pornography, as presented in the actual court debates. Even more indicative is the manner in which the several media treat the debate, for the "enlightened" position advocated by the media is in support of pornography, though the media call it art. There is, in the intellectual community for the most part, a thoroughly established sentimentality about "Art," in which one's feeling is rationalized through clichés to justify whatever appetite desires. There is an accompanying body of support among those who, though less inclined, nevertheless feel guilty about not knowing what art is, about not "feeling" as they are told they are supposed to "feel" by the experts in such matters. What we may learn in the confusion is that *Art* is currently a shibboleth—as *motherhood* used to be, or *apple pie*. But it is not so easily ridiculed as those others. Whatever finds sanctuary in the temple of Art must be accepted as sanctified in the magic name of Art. For there must be, such is the vague inclination of intellectual community, somewhere a principle, an idea, rescuing vague desire from the buffetings of chaos in this world now secularized.

We could pursue this further, and the topic has been, as in Bryan F. Griffin's *Panic Among the Philistines* (1985). But here we are interested to consider how pornography attempts to advance the *shadow* of being as if it were being. It is the *absence* of significant *perfection, proportion*, and *clarity* that pornography treats as if it were *substance* of being. And yet it does so in the name of perfection, proportion, and clarity—in the name, that is, of art. If we urge this distinction, as we must, we must not then fall into an old error of denying the shadow, denying the absence of good as intricate to the concerns of art for perfection, proportion, and clarity. For we have insisted that art is by its nature an imitation of the action of nature, and since that action of nature is, though various in manifestation, the action of a coming-to-be whose complexity is such that a merely mechanistic account is insufficient, then the shadow falls in fallen nature itself. Therefore it is a shadow which art must necessarily reflect in some aspect, even though it might seem desirable not to do so to the discomfited Puritan Gnostic. We know a species of non-art which purports to be art, a species analogous in this respect to pornography. It might be called "Sunday School Tract," aimed at children, though not exclusively, as if to counter its avowed antagonist pornography, or humanism, or secularism. The point, of course, is that these are proper antagonists to be met and defeated intellectually, but that art is not itself directly an instrument of that defeat. The difficulty with this shadow is as ancient as Adam, but we remember it in philosophical and theological dimensions conspicuously present in ancient Gnostic heresies. In attempting to rid the soul of that shadow, to rid the soul of evil, the old Gnostic established its cause in material existence. It therefore, on the authority of this gnosis, rejected the world in attempting to reject the shadow. It established a sort of transcendentalism on its own intellectual authority which we find re-emerging in Puritanism, on the continent and in England and in a pronounced manifestation in the American northeast.

One might put it, in a metaphorical summary, as a translation of the Orthodox understanding of *temperance*, to a militant *abstinence*. The development of the intellectual and historical context of this metaphor I have attempted in *Why Hawthorne Was Melancholy*, and the present argument depends in part upon that development. But neither the ancient Christian Gnostic (a contradiction in terms in respect to the heresy, though a title assumed by the practitioners) nor the Puritan Gnostic cannot reject the world, short of a preemptory suicide. Origin's self-castration is too partial a solution as that descendant of Puritan Gnosticism, T. S. Eliot, remarks wryly in his "Mr. Eliot's Sunday Morning Service." The constancy of existence in the Puritan Gnostic will eventually, therefore, erode Gnostic intent upon Heaven, as Hawthorne saw clearly. To reject sin by denying oneself as sinful and to whitewash one's exterior as sign of cleanliness will lead to such spiritual convolutions as Hawthorne treats in his "Young Goodman Brown." But we must observe that Puritan Gnosticism is one of the possible deportments of the soul to existence which is not determined by time or place but by the deportment. It is not, therefore, a historical phenomenon located in the New England states in the seventeenth and eighteenth centuries. It is a deportment sometimes discovered in the current nemesis to Modernism—Fundamentalism—and is now seen as having shifted south, that shift first noticed with delighted alarm by H. L. Mencken.

Wherever that deportment reveals itself, and whenever, it allows the skeptic, the iconoclast, the pragmatic gnostic ample illustrations to discredit the spiritual nature of man. It is one of the ironies in the present battle over pornography, for instance, that one has the remnants of Puritan Gnosticism contending with secular gnosticism over the definition of art. Both, so is our contention, tend to pervert art itself to ends insupportable by art. For only art abused is instrument to structuring the world by gnostic power. There is an added irony when we look at the uses of art made by one of the fallen Puritan Gnostics, Jimmy Bakker. His spectacular career, as brought into every living room by the evening news, reveals a "life style" which is not adequately accounted for as merely "bad taste," though that tended to be the level of ridicule practiced by the delighted media in its repeated updates on Jimmy's houses and dog houses and the like, with the added moral justification of such intrusion, being that his supporters were, as we like to say now, "ripped off." On the other hand, a similar running account of the trials of that photographer elevated to supreme Artist, Robert Mapplethorpe, presented what is at least bad taste as high art. Appetite denied will have its revenge. But then appetite as the definitive principle in human nature will do so as well. Abuse becomes its own punishment to the spiritual creature, as Dante understood so well, though it is not easy to maintain that perspective in the midst of spiritual disintegrations of the community.

To the Puritan Gnostic, art came to be considered suspect in relation to religious, social, and political order. Under the new dispensation of modernist gnosticism, however, it became rather an instrument to be used in establishing the disorder of Eden secularized. Both violate the truth of art, which in its nature is suited to the making of things by a person. The collateral aspect of art lies in this: through the actions of making, the person moves toward the perfection of his own gifts as person. We must recover an understanding of art as that action of making which is possible to the created soul, whereby it shares creative actions with its cause, though its actions are distinct in nature from the creative actions of its cause. That is, by nature, the person is created in the image of God. This is the position to be held, and we recall Maritain's words to this point, from his *Creative Intuition in Art and Poetry*:

> . . . let us observe that if it is true that art is a creative virtue of the [prac-
> tice] intellect, which tends to engender in beauty, and that it catches hold, in
> the created world, of the secret workings of nature in order to produce its
> own work—a new creature [i.e., the poem]—the consequence is that art con-
> tinues in its own way the labor of divine creation. It is therefore true to say
> with Dante that our human art is, as it were, the grandchild of God—

What we are underlining as we go along, in our concern for the recovery of the "Romantic" poet, is the difficulty the artist has in distinguishing art's "own way" from God's way. The most ready instance of this difficulty is that already alluded to: Joyce's young artist Stephen, who would make his art his own child independent of God through the presumption of his intellect as autonomous. To deny art's dependence in the artist as implying as well a dependence of the artist himself in being is to attempt an elevation of the artist to Godhead. And if we see in such a gifted artist as Joyce himself the operation of this attempt, at such high art, as I think we must, we may equally see pornography as a low extension of that presumption, in which the made thing would be the soul as merely appetitive—a bundle of appetites served by stimulus to appetite, though the stimulus purport to be art. It must make such self-defense, because there is a common sense still resident in intellect, even in the artist as pornographer, despite the long process of deconstructions of the soul by modernism. That common sense recognizes a distortion of reality, though it may not be able to articulate the distortion persuasively to itself. There is also a subtle sophistication serving the deliberate distortion of art, against which an unsophisticated common sense (the usual audience for pornography), in its attempt to reject the distortion, appears confused and naive. That is why it becomes even more crucial that the good artist recognize his responsibility to "purify the dialect of the tribe."

The shadows, the failure from being or the failure of advancing through potential being that are the conditions to the soul, are aspects of the soul's actuality proper to art, though such shadow be seized as the whole of art's concern in a distortion of the soul's reality. Concerning the possible and probable as the province of art, as distinct from the actualities of created souls, it is the recognition of the shadow which again and again we concern ourselves with as critics, when we attempt to distinguish between comedy and tragedy, between tragic effect and that lesser effect, pathos, for instance. The tension between good and evil of which we speak in ethics and morality, distinguishing virtues and vices, are real to the nature of intellect. And it is the reality of intellect which most immediately, because it is mediate, orients art.

It is here that art "in its own way" is a continuation of that divine labor whereby the *all* is. Art's principle is an imitation of the action of that divine labor. And that is why Thomas says that art imitates, not nature, but the *action* of nature. That is the discovery made and celebrated by Hopkins in his attempt to relate the *inscape* of art to the *instress* of the actual. It is through the recognition, as Maritain points out, that art "engenders *in* beauty, it does not *produce* beauty as an object of making or as a thing contained in a genus." (My italics.) That is, beauty is not itself a genus created by art. One can only bemoan the academic confusion of our day, which pretends it possible to produce beauty, a pretense (says Maritain) which is a "perversion of the fine arts" as well as of the literary arts. Flannery O'Connor has this point in mind when she says that there is a sort of "creative" writing that can be taught, but that it is the kind that one must then teach people "not to read." In the artist's address to the concern for beauty, as with any soul's concern for "happiness," it is worth recalling (given our having been created in the image of God) that God as creator *made*, after which He saw that what He had made was good. (The discursiveness speaks to the limits of discursive intellect, not to the simple action whereby God's making and seeing are *simultaneous*, that term being metaphorical as the only approximation possible to discursive intellect in its intimation of the Divine Simplicity.) It is only after the making, only after the thing that is made in its own goodness exists, that we perceive it engendering a "beauty" such as Hopkins sees shining forth like "shook foil." Hopkins's perspective upon a furrow turned by the plow is accidental to his finitude, but the beauty so encountered is not, being a "fathering forth" which he would celebrate by the "instress" of such images dedicated to that *action* of being.

The poem—the new creature—may bear true witness not only of a true vision, as in Hopkins, but of a false vision, a failed visionary nature in the artist who is its maker. The failed nature is undeniably actual in reality, in a particular *thing* (the poet himself as intellectual creature) in relation to the potency of that intellectual creature: the gift whereby *he* is insofar as he *is*.

What follows from that truth about things inclusive of the maker, the poet, and especially relevant to our concern for the poem as good in itself, is that art's possible or probable as an imitation of the actions of the nature of things may be, as art, also properly of those actions of failure in things. Here is the intriguing locus to speculative intellect in its concern for the nature of tragedy or comedy in literature. It is here that an Aeschylus or Sophocles locates his tragic hero. It is the same locus, however, for the whole range of literary art, significant to the lyric as well as to the tragedy or the epic. And we have already seen an interesting aspect of this center to the poet's making, in relation to the poet as the reflected agent, the efficient cause, of his own poetry: the discovery of a unity to the body of his poetry is made through seeing him as the protagonist maker. That is why we will, at last, find it necessary to read Wordsworth's "Tintern Abbey" in relation to his "Intimations Ode" or Eliot's "Prufrock" or "Gerontion" in relation to "Ash-Wednesday" and the *Four Quartets*. Pound's sequence of *Cantos*, in which he is the pilgrim in a progress to those fragmentary conclusions of his journey, yields interesting analogue to Dante's control of his own journey as poet, in which he dramatizes Dante the pilgrim in relation to Dante who in the end is the visionary poet. From his *Comedy* there emerges an aesthetic unity to the *Divine Comedy* differing sharply from the attempt at such a unity in Pound's *Cantos*, or Eliot's *Collected Poems* for that matter.

The point which we have been gradually introducing into our reflections is that the poet as maker (as opposed to the entrepreneur of intemperate appetite as being, the pornographer) insofar as he imitates the action of human nature (which, when all is said, is the artist's only "subject") most immediately imitates the action of his own nature as created soul. For just as we say that God as Maker is implicit in creation as made, so too is the poet implicit in his poem. And in that maker, in his actuality, are implicit the possibilities of his nature, ranging from the edge of his absolute failure of being (never absolute so long as in any respect he *is*) to the edge of perfection (never absolute so long as he is not yet arrived at Beatitude). That is why Goethe says, for instance, that anything man is capable of doing, even the dark things, he is himself capable of. Anyone who has ever been party to the academic teaching of "creative art" knows how often this question is raised. The shibboleth given to initiates is to "write about what you know." Write about what you have actually experienced, which is why there is a plethora, not only of "autobiographical" art, but also of that species of "fiction" that usually struggles with the first person point of view.

On such academic occasion, I recall an anecdote told of Dostoevski (the text is not to hand). At a sort of literary tea he attended as guest "writer," one of the ladies who come and go at such events expressed a delighted horror at the grotesque events in his fictions, raising that question about whether one can write of such matters if one has not experienced them. For surely Dostoevski had not actually experienced such events as he sometimes puts into his fictions! Whereupon, the story says, Dostoevski launched into an account of his having participated in horrible events, including his catching Turkish infants on a bayonet point. It was rather a desperate response, and to one not very likely to understand as Dostoevski does so deeply. For what he understands is the *possible*, even probable, that is contingent to his own nature as person. That is the heart of the artist's "experience" which is indeed necessary to art. Nor is it a relation which necessarily excludes actual events in the "life" of the artist, though Dostoevski's biography records nothing of his having actually slaughtered the innocent, save perhaps as one may speak figuratively of his treatment of his hostess at the literary tea. Dostoevski understood, better than most writers, that the proper ground to art lies deep in the nature of *person*, most immediately his own, in relation to that soul's actual being as contingent to its potential being. (Hawthorne is an American writer very like Dostoevski in this respect.) It is here that the possibility of a failure of being is always actual in some degree, since no soul is perfect, is *perfected*, short of Beatitude. If this were not so, the hope of grace would be unnecessary to the soul and intellect, as the modern gnostic or the modern Pelagian fervently wishes to be so. For what these wish for is an autonomy whereby *person* supercedes God. When one has become disoriented from reality, of course, one has no longer a recourse to prayer and must settle for wishful thinking.

Such then are the complications to our concerns when we would judge the work of art, not in respect to whether it is good in itself, but with a concern for its potential to bring to actuality in discrete persons the error whose reflection it truly witnesses. Such is not art's responsibility, for those concerns are proper to ethics, not art. It does not however follow that pornography, for instance, does not exist, any more than that it is art because it shows with art the use of signs. Signs turned to an intentional deconstruction of being is not art but counter to art. Those ends, and not art in itself, are at issue. From which we might well say that pornography is distinct in its nature in that it depends upon a manipulation of signs in a reductionist distortion of the actuality resident in its manipulated subject, its patron. It conspicuously lacks a grounding in that patron at the depths of *person* such as the grounding Wordsworth pursued. The mys-

tery of memory's role is that it effects a real presence of past event, beyond the event as merely the sensually remembered, though it does so to
such a degree of presence that the sensual body itself participates. Wordsworth is awed by the participation of his own body in its sensual aspect
in response to event remembered. And it is this actuality in relation to
memory which the pornographer seizes upon and manipulates. We might
well observe as an instance the deliberately "pornographic" use Prufrock
makes of this truth in his "Fog" personification, a metaphor developed in
an imitation of the sexual act, intending to put the "you" off from its
attempt to respond openly to reality beyond the "I's" psychological defenses against such encounter. (Could a poet other than Eliot, with his
"Puritan" background, have managed the passage so effectively?)

We hear, again and again, a defense against this truth that the image
remembered has an actual relation to intellect affecting the whole of one's
being. The defense is intended to obviate the intellect's responsibility to
come to an understanding of this mystery through turning to creation in
an ordinate openness. It is a defense against that necessary reflective journey into understanding, for that defense would make beauty merely Pav-
lovian, thus freeing the gnostic manipulator of the defense to pursue
whatever ends he intends, whether the making of pornography or the
making of a state in his own image. The defense? "Beauty," it is said, "is
in the eye of the beholder." That is a truth, but only a partial truth, and
it intends to violate that witness to truth which good art bears. The
"beauty" in art is contingent upon the work's truth, the truth as witnessed by its own good (the *good* of *art* in relation to its own *nature*, as
Thomas says). It is good insofar as it is the thing it is. The truth of art,
the truth of the poem, results from its own internal witness to its own
existence by virtue of its nature as a made thing. But that nature of which
it bears true witness, as we must repeat, may be of a nature which we
are obligated to judge false in its actual manifestation as opposed to art's
imitation of the action of that actual manifestation. Consider with what
difficulty, if we do not make these distinctions, we are able to respond
proportionately to the true witness in Milton's art of his Satan in *Paradise
Lost*. So persuasive that art that Satan has been taken as the hero of the
epic, leading C. S. Lewis to attack that false position in his famous *Preface
to Paradise Lost*. It is, of course, significant that Milton's Satan is taken as
hero in proportion to the "taker's" embrace of modernism.

8

The Poet, Speaking like a Child

If I ask for a pound of bread, I could do so in a study on linguistics, in which case *bread* is a noun which signifies the idea of bread. But if I pose the same question to a grocer, *bread* does not signify the idea of bread; it signifies bread, and it does not signify through the idea of bread. That is its meaning directly and immediately.

—Étienne Gilson, *Linguistics and Philosophy*

". . . what man is there of you, whom if his son ask bread, will give him a stone? Or if he ask a fish, will he give him a serpent?" . . . [H]e taught them as one having authority, and not as the scribes.

—The Sermon on the Mount, Matthew 7

It may seem too radical a shift to move from Milton's Satan as hero to Wallace Stevens's poet as hero, as Stevens's poetry would have it. For one thing, Milton's Satan is deadly serious, and so resolute that his destructiveness, made in the name of mankind against God's authority, tends to obscure both the destruction and its nature. Stevens, on the other hand, does not seem to take his poet too seriously. Consider, for instance, his treatment of that hero in "The Comedian as the Letter C." His wit and good humor, however, obscure a witness in that poetry to a truth which, when actual to the soul, is destructive, and not only destructive to that soul but destructive in the same way as Satan's false counsel is. We may be easily seduced to the theory about the nature of intellect which supports Stevens's poetry, a theory intolerable in its actual truth, though effective as art. And that is to be reminded once more that, in dealing with the question of the social or political effects of art, we must be continually attentive to our intellectual responsibility, or else we confuse ethical and moral concerns with aesthetic concerns.

It is intellect's responsibility to make such distinctions, lest it be led into an intolerable relation to reality itself. Indeed, we have been suggesting that Stevens makes himself as person more and more susceptible to exactly this disorientation, by the habit of his own intellect's submission to, and advocacy of, a false principle of the nature of intellect. This, despite his playful deportment toward the principle, by which he himself (in his own person) intends not to take the principle very seriously. Not too seriously: that is, not in itself definitive of the whole of his nature, symptoms of which nature are his professional life as insurance executive and his love of gardening and other deportments of his life. His is a tendency to life as departmental which disposes him to the dangers in his poetic principle. Upon that principle he develops his "habit" as poet, but it becomes more and more his principal habit. One is reminded here of the anecdote, told by a poet friend, who accompanied Stevens to lunch with some of Stevens's professional peers. It was the occasion when the peers learned that Stevens was a poet and the poet friend learned that Stevens was an insurance executive.

If good poetry may be good even when its "goodness" lies in its precise capture of that which if actual would be "bad," the paradox here forces a responding intellect to its responsibilities to itself in respect to its own good or failure from good. Nor need we deny that there is in the "good" poem a certain "reality." Indeed, we speak of it when we acknowledge a "shock of recognition" in such a poem. Surely we recognize, for instance, that Eliot's "Prufrock" catches something of our own actual nature, our own relation of our actual being to our potential. Or, in another instance, what devout Christian may not be sorely tempted by Stevens's pagan poem, "Sunday Morning"? On a dark and rainy Sunday morning or on a bright and sunny Sunday morning, we may surely find our appetitive natures inclined to sleep or to gamboling in the green wood. Remembering Stevens's delightful poem, one may be tempted to take it as acceptable scripture supporting the moment's desire, rather than take it as the marvelous poem it is. Most surely, such poems have as one effect a reminding of our past experiences, points in our personal history, even experiences in this present moment despite our confidence in having moved, by the rightness of intellect, beyond such temptation as too easily accepted. Given this in our nature, of course, the world's body no less than art's "body" may tempt our violation of the good of the world or of art itself.

This point put another way, we must—if truth be told—have been susceptible to what we have called Cartesian Idealism, which I have argued but a particular manifestation of a contingency in our nature, spoken to by the theologian in such terms as *free will* or *sin* or *original sin*. Such is the contingency always at that point where actual intellect meets potential intellect. It is that point in intellect where reality itself supplies contingency to the will, and as such is always transhistorical, though always a present. That is why this transhistorical dimension to *person* is so crucial to the possible or probable which concerns art. It is the locus of art's drama, wherein art imitates intellect at intellect's point of contingent becoming. In art this is not actuality, but a *possible* or *probable* issue from contingency. Poets from Chaucer to Hawthorne, aware of this most dangerous country to the poet, have again and again felt uncomfortable as artist, as "creator." The discomfort lies in a sense of presumption in art's *possible* or *probable* resolution of contingent potency in the actual intellect. It is as if to suppose that art could thereby *determine* the actual. This is the confusion which, in the good artist such as Chaucer, leads to deathbed retractions of art, repudiations of what the artist has made lest it not be just to the inherent good of that art.

The *as if* of art in this context is not actual, though art reflects, and the artist must engage, the distinction if he is not to confuse the one with the other. In the actual there is the always contingent state of will, moving intellect, and though this is the *essential* action in intellect which art imitates, art always falls short of that actuality. (Here it perhaps becomes somewhat clearer what St. Thomas means when he says that art is an imitation, not of *nature*, but of the *action* of nature.) To recognize such distinctions will, perhaps, clarify the problem of the personal in art which so concerned Eliot. For if we have here suggested the local in the actual upon which art's drama depends—the point of contingency in intellect itself at which its actuality touches its potentiality under the purview of will—such a relation to this reality affects the poet's made thing. It is here that art joins the actual and at the level of the "personal" in respect to the poet himself. It is surely sufficiently clear by now that we are not speaking of the personal as if it were the accidents of person, the history of the particular person who is the poet. But nevertheless, this is a point of disquiet, to Hawthorne no less than to Eliot. And the poet as maker must distinguish the actual from the accidents of the actual, his *person* from the *accidents* of his personhood, lest in the confusion he confound his own making. For he may not find sufficient "objective correlatives" to his person if on the one hand they are but his own accidents employed to his convenience, as Eliot feared of the poet's "personality" used in art. But neither is he likely, save by coincidence, to employ adequate objective correlatives if they are so rigorously purged of personality as to sterilize the person as well by the severity of his intellectual detachment from himself as person. What is required, and I think Eliot came to this recognition by the time of "Ash-Wednesday," is an accommodation of the poet's person to the realities of his personhood, whereby the accidental ("personality") is controlled in relation to the essential. The *essential* is personhood. It is no accident, then, that sound critics remark that man alone among the creatures of creation is artist, despite beaver or bower-bird.

We are prepared, then, to acknowledge Wallace Stevens an impressive poet on the evidence of his poetry, not only in respect to its technical virtues as verse, but also in respect to that "vision" which the poems witness. But, once more, this is something quite different from giving assent to the principles he advances in support of that poetry, any more than he gives assent himself unwaveringly. One cannot read his poetry without recognizing, for instance, that his assertion of the earth as flat and void save for the imagination is spoken in defense of attributive metaphor. But one notes as well that he does not abandon thereby the actual green world as if it were shadowless to the senses. He is much given to good paintings and to good wine and to the roses he grows in his garden, those devotions speaking much of his surrender to the good of things in themselves beyond a mere gluttony for being such as we have charged to Walt Whitman's account. One would no doubt find similar evidences of Whitman's consent to things extraneous to his poems, but Stevens evidences that recognition of the good in things themselves in his poetry, though intent on commanding the accidents of things to his metaphors.

Stevens's stance as artist is made dependent upon a principle asserted as a fundamental truth of the existence of intellect. And what follows from that principle, in the realm of the actuality of intellect in opposition to the principle, is the necessity of *play*, which is a contradiction in the realities designated by *necessity* and *play*. An unceasing, uninterrupted labor of intellect at play, which the principle dictates as cause to intellectual being as maker—Stevens as poet—can but prove inadequate to his own experiences of becoming out of his own being, whatever he may decree as the cause of his being. Here reality erodes principle steadily. To see this is to see the foreshadowing of that end to which Stevens comes at death. For all the witty and entertaining sophistications supporting his position, indeed because of them, he is required to make poetry such a play as we see among children, who pretend that one thing is another through imaginative attribution, but with the important distinction we have made which gives the laurel to children. For they are insistent on a distinction between actual and imagined. How popular this idea, that we are all "born poets," losing our imaginative powers as we become adult. It is a major source of adult sentimentality which robs children of their childhood, while making the adult more child than adult. One can hardly avoid here St. Paul's admonishment: "When I was a child, I spake as a child, I understood as a child, I thought as a child; but when I became a man I put away childish things." For if we examine the child at play in relation to his speaking and thinking and understanding, I think we find the child more nearly adult in his understanding of child's play than adults in their childish view of his play.

Not that the distance between child as poet and adult as failed poet isn't easily supportable as we observe the child at play. That is the ploy Wordsworth used in attempting a Platonic transcendence of the world as a solution to his despair over having lost his visionary power through the unsettling visitations of death, both that of "Lucy" and of his brother John in a sea storm. In watching Hartley Coleridge at play about his feet in springtime, Wordsworth fears the child's turning to imitations of adult-hood as play. The child, through his "newly-learned art" of play, imitates "A wedding or a festival,/ A mourning or a funeral." But what Words-worth seems not to notice, we must: the child is more closely aware of the present realities of the green world than is comfortable to the disquieted adult Wordsworth, who is having such difficulty himself coming to terms with weddings and festivals no doubt (he seems seldom comfortable in such circumstances), but even more difficulty in coming to terms with mourning his lost vision or dealing with the question of death in those funereal ceremonies that somewhat alleviate the grief attendant upon the inevitable intrusion upon consciousness of the spectre of death, that final thing which teleological science speaks toward. The child, at least often, is more acutely aware of the encroaching reality when at play than the discomforted adult watching him at play. Indeed, the adult may long nos-talgically for his own lost childhood estate, having by the distortion of that very longing obscured or quite forgotten the actualities of life at five or ten years old. We have only to look now, or to remember without nostalgic distortion, to see the point reflected conspicuously by the child at play. In this recovered understanding of "play," we may see how the child's play differs from Stevens's.

Such a child, by an imaginative act of attribution, *pretends* that one thing is another—that an old broom is a horse or a stick a sword. At play with his fellows, by mutual agreement to play, children set their minds in a common recognition of a reality which governs their play by limiting imaginative act in respect to possibility or probability. This does not mean that they are incapable of fantasy, but that their sense of fantasy is itself touched at points by a reality they do not deny. Without an agreement of play in the context of reality, indeed, there would be more numerous casualties among our children than we now record. Those casualties grow, one suspects, in proportion to the intrusion of adults upon children's play. Such intrusion feeds an incredible entrepreneurial industry in "toys." The making of toys is taken from the child in the interest of a saleable product, but the product is made saleable as often as not in respect to either its fantastic nature (being removed from the controlling influence of reality) or by making the toy as "real" as it can be short of being actually the thing itself. We know, for instance, the traffic in dolls, who are supplied with biographies, along with bodily functions, certified by name as if on a civil register (for we have more or less abandoned the old certification of baptism and entry in church record). The old broom as horse, the stick as sword may be far less dangerous at the level of its reality as broom or stick than those things made more "realistic" by appropriating the child's imaginative vision from the broom or stick and applying it to the thing made in this species of art, in plastic often enough, and often enough, stamped made in Hong Kong or Taiwan or Seoul. Among the necessities that follow in the social community is the existence of watchdog committees concerned with child safety.

As for fantasy divorced of reality, the loss of the child's imaginative tying of the *supposed* to the *real*, that is increasingly accomplished through technological efficiencies, another adult intrusion into child's play which conditions play for disaster. Consider, for instance, the recently vocal concern of parents for the effect of television upon the growing child, those shades of a fantasy world closing upon the growing child as Wordsworth might put it. Specifically, consider the Saturday morning cartoon fare which has raised a storm of protests from parents. The character-hero, or even the villain of the brief narrative in picture frames, moves in a world voided of physics, while pretending to the three-dimensional. Not that physics exaggerated beyond its realities are not borrowed in the interest of spectacle, for we know that spectacle is exciting to the child. (War, where is thy sting?) Cartoon characters caught up in violent acts do not consequently bear reflections of the action in violent event. But it is not violence per se which is reprehensible, though parents tend to object on this ground, themselves responding to spectacle—to accident—instead of to the essence of the violations.

It is rather that, freed of reality, this cartoon art's violence ignores the limits prescribed by the proper proportionality of reality, as for instance those designated in the science of physics and biology. When a cartoon character is run over by a steam roller and shown as if actually flattened, or is forced through machine gears and issues as if a sheet of paper, the child very soon comes to expect an appearance of the figure restored to its "reality" in the next frames. The objection, then, is not to violence per se but to a more destructive intellectual violence: the suggestion that violence is inconsequential to being. William Carlos Williams writes his little poem, "The Term," against such violation of reality at the level of physics and biology: a paper sack rolling like a man, run over by a vehicle, *unlike* a man, rises with the wind. The poem is aimed at the danger in metaphors of attribution, reminding of a maturity required to our response such is not available to the child. The child can but be awed by the technology whereby colored figures seem possessed of life, a life their imaginative action participates in giving, but only in a very limited degree.

In such programs manipulating intellect, the child is isolated into a cell of attention much more restricted than Keats's visiting a Greek urn in a museum. The child sits on the floor with his bowl of vitamin-added cereal, absorbed as intellect in the flickering colored shadows from the tube. Still, there is in that child a common sense operative, sometimes revealed in his testing of the impossible. That is why when several children are so held, if there is not the dictating presence of an adult, very often they become violent with each other. Such a reaction may not be so terrible as it may seem to the adult, who is distracted from his adult Saturday mornings by the commotion. For whether violence in practice is good or bad will be determined perhaps by the degree to which the children recover reality against the cartoons' distortions. In their immediate arena of reality, the family den, violence is consequential, though one pray it fall short of terminal consequence, which does not always seem probable to an adult who is at some distance from that play which is testing the pretense to reality that has been shown on the tube.

Our concern is not with "policing" Saturday cartoons any more than with policing high school or college athletics as "play." We are rather concerned to notice the child as realist at his play, to our own health. He is not that Romantic realist we have been talking about, but more nearly the Thomistic realist. His play is set by his growing recognition of the limits of play, the limits prescribed by reality. Indeed, early in his play, he is likely to describe play by his running verbal account. He makes a contemporaneous epic of his fanciful pretense. His sentences describing fanciful action follow from his enunciated "play like." That phrase in the heat of his play, at least in this part of the world, becomes "plaque." His is that same *as if* we spoke of earlier, but with a difference. For what is to be accepted through his verbal formulae is a common recognition among the children at play of the *actual* as distinct from the *pretend*. Pretend, "play like," I am Achilles shouting in the trenches. Pretend that you are Hector. Or pretend that I am Custer and you are Crazy Horse, at this juncture of history more likely to be "pretend I am Crazy Horse and *you* are Custer." Pretend this stick is a revolver or a rifle, upon which may be accrued through pretense the stick's transformation, subsequently even from revolver to machine gun. It is of interest to the point that such transformations sometimes require negotiations of the limits of accretion. For the game does not hold if one has a machine gun suddenly, the other only a spear. Unless . . . unless. . . . . And so the game develops. But always as prescribed, as measured, by a common consent to reality as reflecting some measure of fantasy. For the realities of spear and machine gun are circumscriptive of the play. That circumscription yields at higher levels of play the established "Rules of the Game."

Children at play make an order of their play through agreed recognitions of the disparity between the actual and the pretended. The agreed recognitions, the "rules," are established by practical necessities in the particular games as dependant in reality. Of course children, at least initially, require no formal term, so close are they to the reality of the circumstances of their play. That complex play appeared distant from Wordsworth as he watches Hartley at his feet. It is when one is encouraged to accept the rules of play by ignoring the limits prescribed by reality that the imagination becomes wildly random to an unsettling degree. Any parent as arbitrator of a squabble will discover with few exceptions that the squabble is a consequence of one child's having accidentally or deliberately ignored the rules as agreed upon within the circumstances of reality, within the arena where the play develops. It is almost irresistible to transform one's own spear into a machine gun in the heat of play, in the context of the current rules. The imagination, active beyond the limits prescribed, leaves that player himself disoriented and increasingly forlorn, in an exile imposed either by the judgment "Go to your room!" or by a self-imposed judgment to loneness, "I'm going to my room" or "I'm not going to play anymore." The latter response intends to dissolve the rules of play back into circumstantial reality.

Such a dissolution, the action of a "bad sport" it is sometimes said, is often spoken as if in revenge upon those demanding justice in relation to the common contract understood as the rules of play. The aggrieved child, of course, has by now concluded that the "rules" are raw injustice. Lingering in one's room, like Prufrock's lingering in the chambers of the sea of his consciousness in a self-exile, is a form of revenge against not only rules to imagination, but tends as well to be a reaction against reality itself, as the child's bill of particulars—his analysis of the character in his erstwhile playmates may demonstrate. Such revenge toward reality on the part of a revenge-bent intellect is not peculiar to the child, as our allusion to Prufrock suggests. For whatever the actual years of one's residence in reality, one is susceptible to that escape. And so it is not a question of imaginative action in relation to reality as such that is of ultimate concern. It is the concern, in St. Paul's words, that one put away "childish things."

9

Words and Tinker Toys

[E]xcept for man, we know of no dialectical, sophistic, rhetorical, oratorical animal who is concerned with judicial, political, or formal eloquence. Nothing of all that could exist without language, and language includes all that.

—Étienne Gilson, *Linguistics and Philosophy*

We have been saying that the child *knows* actually, at the level of elementary physics though beyond his articulation, the limits of the things he constructs with a Tinker Toy set or Lincoln Logs or Lego set. As I write, a nine-year-old is busy at construction with the latest of these, called "Constructs," with which one "builds" a seemingly infinite number of distinct machines, vaguely reminiscent of carts or trucks or trains or bull-dozers or planes or rocket ships—or, in a surprise twisting of parts, a robot somewhat reminiscent of the figure of a man. The *whole* of the thing this child is making seems to require his constant explication of his making, as if to me but more certainly to himself in a refinement of the concept emerging in his own intellect. There is, at least secondarily, however, a concern that I be able to "follow" what he is doing, since in doing so I may anticipate the end, which is to recognize that which is in the made thing's beginning, his concept of it, resting immaterially at the moment in his immaterial mind, which itself seems somehow to be associated with his material brain, though just "how" is problematic. The problematic seems to generate in concept itself, as if idea fecundates idea, as apparently it may, listening to the contemporary epic of this making at my feet. For at any moment the form, more or less held in intellect and to be executed upon the "Construct" in hand, may vary by concept's decree from being a tank to being a plane. And so one necessity for this uninterrupted explication of concept as epic, lest I (a mere adult) lose my bearing by seeing this thing being remade only in relation to its own nature, independent of the present action of making. Not to see the imagined is to lose a dimension of this present moment of reality in which an imaginative act is in operation, whose memorial epic invites me to an imaginative participation through the signs spoken.

Those signs, it turns out, in a limited sense incorporate the actualities which one might enumerate were he to step just outside the room to look in upon the material arena of the room. However appointed, in that room are two presences, two bodies, one small and somewhat loud, as if singing an accompaniment to the motions his hands make with some object. The other larger body, silent, seemingly attentive, looking at the boy and his motions, listening to his words. What is clear from this detached perspective is that the object in the boy's hand centers the arena. The room at large seems to fade into inconsequentiality, though it may prove a larger trap laid by reality perhaps than supposed in the moment's concentration upon the developing object in the child's hands. But that aspect of reality aside for the moment, what emerges to detached reflection, if one be leaning against the doorjamb looking in unobtrusively, is that the object under construction is but the moment's focus to a larger action in progress, a communion of the man and boy, not simply through the object in the boy's hand but through that object as perceived imaginatively, an object through which the boy's intellect is opening upon reality in such a way as to begin to stir, unknown to himself, some of those sleeping dragons we spoke of earlier. For he is at once scientist and philosopher, aware of the present limits of reality in relation to a visionary end. He is poet, singing that vision as it were, but with words anchored in immediate reality by his knowing and his limited understanding, and by his desire to share what he knows and understands in relation to what he is making *out* of them and so *upon* the thing changing under his hands.

There is here, in this child's serious play, an imitation in respect to the actions of nature—the actuality of the stealth bomber, which this child knows consciously in more detail than one might suppose, including its failure to escape radar detection as had been imagined of it by its designers. And that reflection underscores a reality beyond the accidents of play with which we are concerned in their varying aspects in child and adult: it is through actual action of intellect that the object actual and imagined emerges as an accident of that play action. What is most real is the present intellectual becoming. We might take Wordsworth's famous line, "The Child is father of the Man," and turn it to a truth freed of Wordsworth's Platonic dislocation of that truth.

Wordsworth's reflections on his own line, used as epigraph to his "Intimations Ode," leads him to conclude that the child is "best philosopher" because so recently come from heaven streaming clouds of glory, a small perfection of man which he will grow away from. One might well be disturbed by such implications of initial perfection in Wordsworth's reading, insofar as this idea borrows from the Christian doctrine of the Incarnation. One is, so I believe, in much sounder ground than Wordsworth to see the child as father of the man in relation to the Aristotelian and Thomistic principle of being in relation to becoming. Otherwise, and such is the darkness of Wordsworth's Platonism, death as a rebirth of the soul becomes a mechanistic inevitability and robs that soul of those virtues possible to it as image of its creator. It becomes doomed to a most dark shadow world, those years of its falling away from being during which the "prison house" of temporal existence closes more and more upon it. That is what Wordsworth, in his late Platonism exercised against despair, would have as the soul's earthly state. Eliot's "Journey of the Magi" speaks to this confusion in Wordsworth, if one supposes Eliot's speaker a Wordsworthian Platonist encountering the actual Incarnation. It is through that encounter that the "ways deep and the weather sharp" in the dead winter of that journey, but also the "summer palaces" and "the silken girls bringing sherbet," can be reconciled beyond the state in which Wordsworth seems to find himself (as Eliot's poem describes that state): "no longer at ease here, in the old dispensations,/ With an alien people clutching their gods." Little wonder that in that state one should say "I should be glad of another death." That is, for both Eliot's speaker and for Wordsworth of "Intimations Ode," a desire as yet insufficiently understood. One must remember, for instance, that the Crucifixion and Resurrection are events still to be encountered in their realities by Eliot's magus. The concluding line of Eliot's poem is spoken in an advance upon Prufrock's moment of pathos. But it expresses pathos nevertheless, and from an incomplete encounter of the death desired. It is no accident that, considered in the body of Eliot's poetry, this line echoes Prufrock. "I should be glad of another death" is nevertheless a move beyond "I should have been a pair of ragged claws."

How far we have come from that nine-year-old who, a few minutes ago, was busily engaged with his own Christmas toy, a "Construct." But really not, as the accidents to his play on the occasion of the gift suggests. Both are "Christmas" occasions. And our becoming out of being is a sort of constant dying to be reborn as well. What is lost in that transformation is something of the potential, since it becomes an actual, so that what we may conclude is that one is in some way (we put it metaphorically), reducing what as thing we *might* be to our *isness* realized, a progress toward perfection which is to be understood beyond the limits allowed by "Romantic" rationalism. To see it more particularly, we return to the child as poet-philosopher, playing with his "Construct," a toy most aptly named for our interests. He knows that as poet, imitating the actions of nature, he must supply the friction of intellect to reality if he would *enforce* the imitation: an infusion of "life" into the toy by "the noise of his mouth," to quote St. Augustine on the imagination's relation to vision. And beyond the weakness of his words, there is an introduction of the elementary physics as it were, at the level of accident whereby the precedent *person* participant, the child, takes on the burdens of the accidents of person in his life-giving act. And behold: the toy flys, held by the child's hand as he runs—no doubt into the doorjamb to which we have withdrawn to observe. In the moment he is at last oblivious of our presence as observer as he is of the reality of the doorjamb.

Or in another scenario to this epic: overcome by fancy, by the seductions of attribution, he may withdraw his hand in the expectations that it will indeed fly, having first (in deference to the reality of gravity) given it a starting heave. That is, he may launch it against lamp or the observer in the doorway, those concurrent accidents of reality having been ignored. The debris of his made thing or of the lamp or of the protesting adult will, of course, recall him to known but forgotten things, and so to the limits of his imagination. A moment of sadness, touched by distress, responding first to the rebuke of physics and then to that of his parent. And from this context of prophetic encounter with reality comes his remembering of known but forgotten things, a recovery through a new beginning to yet another creature of imagination's attribution. Perhaps more acutely aware of the limits of attribution, at least initially so in this new beginning. So it is for us all, moving from the known to the imagined, from encounter with the way a thing is to reflection upon what it might be. In that movement of intellect, we may become disoriented by a subscription to what we have called Cartesian Idealism, a moment in which we suppose ourselves as person exempted from reality by the inclination of any will and a sense of power in the imagination in its address to being.

Gilson remarks, in *Linguistics and Philosophy*, that "infants think before speaking. Every parent knows this, and, moreover, no linguist contests the issue. But can we imagine thought devoid of words . . . ?" Can we imagine *"in-fans*, the nonspeaking" as by nature *thinking*, as intellect in action, intellect itself as infant Word unable to speak a word? Can we imagine person as created in the image of God? To begin to do so is to move toward a vision of reality, to discover at least perhaps that the life of intellect is an unending sentence punctuated by reality. Reality's arresting the action of intellect—at a point (reality's punctuation) on the banks of the Wye, or in a Boston tenement, or in a neglected English garden at Burnt Norton: these recall us to temporary ends which are always temporary beginnings. They recall us to that mystery of our existence that is our *becoming* out of *being*. And with that recognition there will likely follow a shouting across the moment's seeming chaos which separates intellects as witnessed by the small child's insistent *"rabbits,"* of which we spoke earlier. That child means let us go then, you and I, and recover the reality of that past moment into a present moment. Or the growing boy's continuous shouting, which at the level of physics is only a continuous chatter over and about plane or rocket a-making. Or it is the shout as witnessed in Wordsworth's famous preface to *Lyrical Ballads*, when he insists that the poet is "a man speaking to men." Or even as witnessed, with a certain petulance, intending at once to reserve a separation and to bridge it, when Stevens insists that "Eliot and I are dead opposites."

However the poet's deportment—which is to say in its largest sense, the intellect's deportment—in reality, as "Romantic" his cry reflects a desire for a recovery of a community of intellect within the prescriptions of reality. And it is through those prescriptions alone that recovery is possible, such is the nature of finite intellect. That recovery seems somehow necessarily associated with a recovery of image to its cause, if there is to be any recovery of that reality which justifies—which punctuates—not just the sign but thought itself. The punctuation of thought by reality makes possible, through sign, companionable intellects in community. It is to this mystery of intellect as thought punctuated by reality that Gilson speaks. Thought before language, before sign, we know as a reality to mind. It is "the experience of a presence whose nature escapes us and whose reality is attested to only by its effects, which are however material, audible, visible, and objects of a particular science, phonology." Yet thought becoming language is already language, though possible only "on the condition of proceeding by means of a sort of parcelling out of thought." And yet we know that the thought that speech expresses, the very meaning of speech, does not lend itself to division.

It is no good to explain the necessity of "parcelling out" thought at the level of mere physics or biology, the limits of the material medium of sign—paper, pencil; throat, nose, ear. The parcelling necessity lies deeper, in the very nature of intellect itself, whereby we conclude of that nature that it is discursive out of the necessities of its finitude. One who would "begin to speak," says Gilson, "has the sense of the presence in his mind of something that he wants to say or that wants to be said." But that something is most peculiar in its immateriality, differing from those desires in that aspect of our nature which we classify as appetitive, such as hunger or sexual desire. And the response to the necessity of "saying" that "something" through the body is likewise peculiar. For, again Gilson, "One sees with the eyes, one smells with the nose, one hears with the ear, one walks with the legs, but one speaks with the mouth, teeth, nose, and many another organ no one of which has as its specific function to speak." The play of intellect with image, exhibited to other intellects necessarily through the senses, as best we may through organs not specific to sign, must in some way be understood as a play within the bounds of reality, the most elemental reality being that of the nature of intellect itself. To order intellect is to order that reality and thereby make possible an ordered play as contingent to reality itself. Reality as sheer chaos will not serve. Reality, whether of the intellect as *tabula rasa* or the earth as *flat*, *bare* and *shadowless* will not do. Intellect unpunctuated by reality would itself be a continuous flat, bare, shadowless void. And so we make a new beginning of our concern for the poet as intellect in relation to his concern for image.

Image, stirred in consciousness, stirs intuition, which will not be content at last with analogy of attribution. It is in this recognition, the Thomistic realist will insist, that intellect possesses a knowledge already as it turns through an image of that knowledge toward reality, aided in that turning by concept. That is, aided by intellectual order dependant upon a knowledge of the order of reality: that order of reality *inclusive* of its own order. Such seems the process of a coming-to-be out of potential being, by a grace of knowing anterior to any realization by intellect that it possesses that knowledge. It is here that the inseparable simplicity of body and soul is founded, as in that moment of arrest which seems palpable when the child sees the bunny for the first time. The known which stirs intuition stirs imagination as well, both focused in image, which if it does not become opaque—that is, become a reflecting pool for intellect as Narcissus—begins to rouse those interior dragons which as yet and perhaps never require formal naming. For first, the wonder at likeness in unlike things, which raises at once a question: unlikeness in like things. And so intellect enters that journey to possible ends, imminent and transcendent.

If that now-questing intellect is diligent, if it is capable of putting the right questions to its own desire for suitable ends—and if it is further graced beyond its own reductionist accounting for its existence as willed accident—one suspects it will discover the quest leading toward a recovery of metaphor understood as intrinsic to the order of reality, beyond its convenient imputations. Beyond attribution. Having so come to itself in its dark wood, intellect may recognize the distinction of metaphor as attribution and as governed by proper proportionality, which is not to

abandon attribution so much as to know that, though it is an initial inclination in our use of signs under the influence of that emotional wonder
stirred in us by intuitive recognitions *in* existences, *beneath* the level of
accident. Reason will bring such metaphor to its limits in sign when,
through such distinction, it both recognizes and consents to the truth that
reason's analogy is in its structure independent of intellect as the primary
cause of intellect. The inevitable play of intellect in response to intuitive
seeing and reason's justifying that seeing are in a field of play pointed at
one extreme by "fancy" at the other by "imagination," if we may borrow
Coleridge's terms to prescribe the boundaries of that play. It is in this
field of play that intellect prepares its capacity for a vision of reality. Intellect prepares itself to depend on analogy, as it must, because analogy is
itself dependent on being through the structure of creation as designated
by the multiplicity of discrete beings. We say this, not only remembering
Coleridge's attempt at ordering intellect in relation to reality, but even
more remembering Wordsworth and Keats as intellectual pilgrims, fore-
runners in this concern of Eliot and Stevens.

And so we turn to that mystery of likeness in unlike things, believing
analogy consequent upon the structure of reality. We note that Wordsworth in his preface explicitly cites Aristotle as authority in asserting the
poet's interest in "similitude in dissimilitude." Given such hints and given
what we have seen in some of his early poetry, we might consider Wordsworth, up to the time of his preface at least (1802), as an incipient Thomistic realist, but one who does not recognize the questions his reason must
put to his intuition. The complication for Wordsworth, as it will prove
for Keats, lies in whether he *makes* or only *discovers* metaphor. Whether
he structures through image—an act of intellect determining proportion
in his pursuit of likeness in unlike things. Or whether there is a precedent
structure in the source of image, in things themselves. That he desires the
second possibility to be the true principle of being is reflected in his insistent conclusion that it is so, an insistence we have located in "Tintern
Abbey." But that insistence, however, lacks the firmness of rational support, so that when he must deal with the problem of evil in its effect
called death, he is not able to do so. He recognizes well enough that one
encounters within the "dreary intercourse of daily life" the problems of
"evil tongues,/ Rash judgments, . . . the sneers of selfish men,/ . . . greet-
ings where no kindness is." But blessed by an attunement of intellect
only to "beauteous forms," he is confident of an innoculation against the
infectious virus on that unreal world, the city.

It is as if Wordsworth's error, in spite of his intuitive vision of the truth
of things, is an environmentalism very like the one that will sweep scien-

tific thought a few decades later. Browning's question, "What porridge had John Keats?" intends defense against that modernist intrusion into our thought which will issue in mechanistic determinism out of Darwinian theory a little later. But the error lies incipient in Wordsworth's thought already, only waiting occasion. From that failure of firm rational ground to support his intuitive knowledge of being, and so mistaking the mind as essentially affected by environment, Wordsworth does not notice that the city is necessarily a part of reality not to be set aside from "nature." It is nature established by man's art, and so nature transformed by man's will, and so inescapably a consequence of human nature. The recognition is very close on occasion, as when on one quiet morning (September 3, 1802, he tells us) he looked out over London from Westminster Bridge at the "city" which wears "like a garment" the "beauty of the morning."

The prospect is equal to any "splendour" of "valley, rock, or hill" such as perhaps one might experience along the banks of the Wye, and he rebukes himself, at least indirectly, for such imputations upon London as he has made elsewhere. For "Dull would he be of soul who could pass by/ A sight so touching in its majesty." So lovely that he personifies London as a beautiful woman, by attributive metaphor, whose "mighty heart is lying still." It is an experience of the "City" placed in perfect harmony with the enveloping natural world of fields and sky. But the harmony lies in the eye of the beholder, an eye little troubled by thought. That is, the city as Wordsworth sees it is void of humanity, thereby returned to a state of nature untroubled by man's presence. It is, as Eliot will suggest by implication in his famous phrase from Baudelaire's view of Paris, an "Unreal City," even when asleep, for what is asleep is not the city itself but the disoriented people in the city.

We shall see London in another contingency of morning, and at another London bridge, falling down from the realities of being:

> Under the brown fog of a winter dawn,
> A crowd flowed over London Bridge, so many,
> I had not thought death had undone so many.

Judging from Eliot's peopling of his London, it is less lady than whore. Or, put another way, what Eliot sees that Wordsworth does not is that the city is out of the corruptible heart of man, common and so an aspect of Wordsworth's own which "beauteous form" is insufficient to anneal. Most conveniently, Wordsworth's apostrophe to London ignores the nature of man, for "the very houses seem asleep;/ And all that mighty heart is lying still!" The catalyst to vision for Eliot as he reflects upon London will lie in the mighty heart as well, but it is man's heart, capable of transgressions through the nature of its own freedom to transgress. We have been reminded of Eliot's significant turning in his unsettling poem, in the final section, to "blood shaking" his own heart. That is a turning in Eliot lessoned at least in part by Hawthorne, and counter to Wordsworth. In the years leading up to his writing *The Waste Land*, Eliot had been reading Hawthorne and writing about him and had learned from this Romantic poet something of the relation of the psychological mind to the sinful heart.[9] That was a lesson not sufficiently studied by Wordsworth, too easily content with man's being set aside through the attributive metaphor whereby London as beautiful woman, touched by morning sun and not yet quite awake, prolonged for a moment his confidence in "beauteous form" as rescuing intellect beyond destruction by "evil tongues" or "rash judgments" or "sneers of selfish men."

Wordsworth's is an intuitive vision unaided by rational intellect. It follows from his failure to establish firm rational ground in support of his vision that when the teleological dragon comes ravenously alive in his intellect, he is shocked into taking as true a metaphor out of "form" accepted as inevitably beauteous. But it is attributive, out of wishful thinking. The earlier belief, affirmed by a faith in his having experienced the order in things, acknowledged in "Tintern Abbey," is thus seen to have been but a "slumber" of his spirit, sealing that spirit off from reality. He is, he now believes (*vide* the "Lucy" poems and "Elegiac Stanzas Suggested by a Picture of Peele Castle, in a Storm . . .") of a sudden wakened from his slumber. As for Beaumont's painting of Peele Castle in storm, had Wordsworth been the artist during that slumber, intending to express what then he saw in slumber, he would have added (he says) "the gleam,/ The light that never was, on sea or land,/ The consecration, and the Poet's dream," and he would have done so "in the fond illusion of my heart."

Is likeness and unlikeness *in* the things, or only *in* the intellect, or in *both*? And if *in* either or both, how so? We have seen Eliot's growing distress over the problem, as disturbing to him no less than it was to Wordsworth. We have seen Wallace Stevens cutting with the sword of his will this tangled philosophical question, declaring metaphor simply the power of intellect, executed by the authority of the will through imaginative actions of intellect. The signs of that power are his poems, in which images are juxtaposed attributively in metaphors to delight the intellect in its momentary stay against confusion. Eliot, out of his distress in finding no philosophical resolution, turns from philosophy to poetry, because philosophy seems always destined (as he says) to become "preposterous."

Poetry, and even criticism of poetry as a slight acknowledgment to the philosophical cast of his mind: perhaps that is the way out. Thus, not entirely freed of the necessity to philosophize, he announces an event in Western thought which occurred after Dante and Donne, dislocating poetry decisively: the "dissociation of sensibility," the intellectually fatal blow to poetry of the separation of thought and feeling. It occurred at about the time of Milton and Dryden, and because thus located as an event in history, the theory seemed to allow his attention to its history and so a turning away, somewhat, from the philosophical dimension of dissolution from reality which is at the center of his own thought.

To make that dissociation an event in literary history obscures for the moment the truth about the inclination to dissociation: it is a separation occurring in the discrete intellect always, and so is not accountable to history. One need only look at some of that criticism Eliot himself was writing to discover how cautiously he sets "feeling" aside from the intellectual control he insists is necessary to the poet's mind. Feeling becomes, indeed, but "matter" to be turned to poetic account just as the actual person of the poet is to be. Thus does Eliot as intellect set his own immediate "history" aside. The inconsistency operative in this early criticism, contradicted by the poetry itself, will bring him to that traumatic encounter of the problem as at last undeniably in himself, out of which issues *The Waste Land*. Meanwhile, there is a buried Hegelian address to history he has not yet overcome. We have already implied that the end of Hegelian history for Eliot is memorialized in "Ash-Wednesday." If Hegel is more sophisticated than Hobbes, and so more appealing to the poet as Romantic rationalist, there is nevertheless a simplistic dimension to that sophisticated argument. Actual experience, responded to initially by common sense, puts that argument to flight. Hegel and his "time," in this respect, is not unlike Hobbes and his suggestion that one is as one eats. One is as one thinks about time or porridge, so that Browning's almost Swiftian caricature serves well for both, as he puts it in "Popularity":

> Hobbes hints blue,—straight he turtle eats:
> Nobbs prints blue,—claret crowns his cup:
>   Nokes outdares Stokes in azure feats,—
> Both gorge. Who fished the murex up?
>   What porridge had John Keats?

10

Hobbes Hints Blue, Poets Blue the World

> Thomistic personalism stresses the metaphysical distinction between
> individuality and personality. . . . [T]he metaphysical tradition of the
> West defines person in terms of independence, as a reality which,
> subsisting spiritually, constitutes a universe unto itself. . . . Personal-
> ity is the subsistence of the spiritual soul communicated to the human
> composite. . . . Man finds himself by subordinating himself to the
> group, and the group attains its goal only by serving man and realiz-
> ing that man has secrets which escape the group and a vocation which
> the group does not encompass.
>
> —Jacques Maritain, *The Person and the Common Good*

When as member of an intellectual community one is caught up by the
general acceptance of an intellectual fad, there may appear no necessity to
examine too closely the premises upon which the general consent is given.
There is a sort of intellectual euphoria of rational rightness, even righ-
teousness, to the consent. Confident and generous patrons of the position
bear themselves as if the principles they bear are not only self-evident,
but also have been adequately examined long since, and justified by intellectual rigor. The position thus appears to have, not only a viable cur-
rency, but a tradition of assent as well. What intellectual fare had Tom
Eliot? we asked, and suggested it the rather pervasive unsustaining air of
modernism as one encountered it at Harvard at the turn of our century.
It was as generously present as the smoke hanging over an industrial
town, though some fresh winds stirred, through Babbitt and Santayana
and their questioning of President Charles W. Eliot's attempt to institu-
tionalize modernism on the authority of nineteenth-century science, at
the expense of the humanities as more anciently understood.

When Eliot took leave of Harvard for Paris, encountering Bergson
there, the intellectual climate was more volatile, his fellow intellectuals
more passionate about abstractions. When a little later he went to En-

gland, to Oxford to study Aristotle and Greek philosophy more thoroughly, he found Oxford rather provincial, "much like *New* England,"
and London became a welcomed distraction from his serious pursuit of
philosophy. But, himself increasingly a part of the London literary scene,
he increasingly encountered the brittleness of an acidic skepticism. If university towns and university people "are the same everywhere," as he had
written Conrad Aiken, London seemed different, as it first seemed to be
to Pound as well. It was in London that he met Pound, whom he found
"rather intelligent as a talker," he wrote Aiken, though his verse while
"well-meaning" is "touchingly incompetent." Thus the triumvirate of
Americans in London, Aiken, Pound, and Eliot. But then there were all
those others, the English intelligentsia in and out of the literary capital of
Western civilization, as Pound would have London. Perhaps the brittleness of skepticism experienced in this milieu began to erode Eliot's comfort in the old dispensation, manifestations of which he encountered at
Harvard, then at Paris, then at Oxford.

What he was beginning to experience was the playing out of that old
dispensation in the lives and words of the intelligentsia which had grown
out of modernism, and it made him uncomfortable. Slowly he began to
wonder at the will's consent to ideas that seemed more stylish than intrinsically vital to the maintenance of his seriously skeptical address to existence. That skepticism he had begun to value as the necessary balance to
his intellect in its encounter with meaningless existence. There begins to
appear, though slowly, an aspect in Eliot's irony beyond its earlier sardonic defense of self-pity. Irony begins to turn outward upon other intellects, as if he would distance himself from his intellectual kind. He pays
his respects to that decaying fad of Cartesian Idealism which leaves the
particular intellect centered helplessly in self-love, in that dissociation of
sensibilities which he will represent presently in the "Game of Chess":
on the one hand by the sterile relation of the man and woman surrounded
by the burnt out ends of Western culture, the "withered stumps of time"
that appoint the arena of their futile encounter. And on the other, a London version of Sweeney's Boston world, the pub scene—all feeling and
no thought. There is a sufficient spectacle and witty mimicry in the pub
scene that may overshadow the devastating rebuke to pseudo-intellectual-
ism. Pound will have by then also paid his respects to that decay, in *Hugh
Selwyn Mauberley*. It is in his portrait of Lady Valentine two years before
The Waste Land. But Pound's concern sees more as if with the intent of
Hercules in the Augean stables than Eliot's more subtle, analytical surgery. Eliot's approach means for him a certain distancing without an
abandonment, where Pound's tribute to the London cultural center in

collapse is a leave taking. (When he includes *Hugh Selwyn Mauberley* in his *Personae*, his prefatory note says, "The sequence is so distinctly a farewell to London that the reader who chooses to regard this as an exclusively American edition may as well omit it and turn at once to page 205.")

Eliot dramatizes in "The Game of Chess" a late Belinda, circa 1920 (for he had learned of Alexander Pope). A character surrounded by fragments shored against his futility, the signs residual of a tradition, now more trinket than sign, more artifact than art. And then there is that Shakespearean harridan, indifferent to the rules of order, of the manners attendant upon those rules in any civilized dispensation of order, who hears not at all the increasingly insistent "Hurry up please it's time." On the one hand; on the other. The dissociation of sensibilities raises both pathos and laughter in one who is safely detached, in the reader. And to some degree, the poet himself is detached, as if these are the conditions to life as he must accommodate those conditions, unwilling to leave London either for Harvard and academic position or for Paris and the life of the artist pure, as Joyce and Pound had done. But Eliot's could not be an accommodation to London as Unreal City such as Pound's Lady Valentine supposed possible. For her, poetry is "a means of blending/ With other strata/ Where the lower and higher have ending." Art so taken is art as social device, whose intent is to preserve separation, not effect a community of sensibility. Eliot's male presence, if we may so designate it, in whose head rattles the "Shakespherian Rag," seems to anticipate an evening slumming among the pubs, the sort of social condescension as entertainment which Aldous Huxley had treated with devastating wit in his "Lady" Viveash in *Antic Hay*. Eliot, however, had discovered something in those working-class students he taught literature that his social peers had forgotten, if they'd ever known it. But how may art anneal the dissociation so palpable in the social fabric unraveling? And is the separation merely a cultural phenomenon, an effect of history—especially economic history? Surely something more fundamental is at issue. And so there follows Eliot's arrest, shoring fragments against his ruin.

From our safe remove, we might delight in imagining an encounter between Eliot's Lady Belinda and the pub denizen, expert in procreation and its expense to the body. It makes the sort of imagined drama in which each gets what we safely suppose is deserved by each. But that would be a social drama which would resolve none of that questions beginning to disturb Eliot, particularly about the nature of existence in relation to the person experiencing his own and existence in general. And if *person* is somehow the crucial aspect of the encounter to be resolved, then social comedy or satire cannot advance much toward resolution, since its effect must largely be that of calling attention to absurdity of the social disparateness in conflict, the social turmoil of the moment, which is being addressed on Hegel's stage far removed from London by the new Marxist saviors of social order. Those are the "hooded hoards swarming/ Over endless plains" that must be acknowledged, as Eliot does in referring the passage to Hesse's comments on the Russian Revolution in *A Glimpse into Chaos*. But what purchase is there upon any permanent things in replacing a decayed social aristocracy with a decaying proletariate, since both are made impertinent by Hegelian history?[10]

Long after Eliot's concern with the question of the relation of the permanent things to the uses of art, a young poet far removed from Paris, London, and New York engaged the question, herself influenced somewhat by Eliot's quest. And we might even say she takes a mischievous delight in confronting Eliot's intellectual with his Sweeney. It is through an art that, at its surface, is rich with social satire. But that is a camouflage whereby to stalk the modernist as pseudointellectual and to turn such a captive toward the insistent questions about the permanent things. Flannery O'Connor in her story "Good Country People" has her antagonist, a diabolic Bible salesman, deliver a shocking rebuke to her protagonist Hulga, a pseudointellectual. It is one of those stories of hers in which, as she acknowledges, the devil proves in service to the Lord, leaving Hulga a somewhat collapsed intellectual. Hulga, through her academic labors in recent intellectual history, has become disciple to Jean-Paul Sartre, after much long labor having arrived at a faith in *nothingness*, as opposed to *being*. Nothingness is the ground of the latest sophisticated metaphysics of attribution upon the green world. But "You ain't so smart," the roving Bible salesman says on learning her labored view of existence. By revealing it to him, she has been trying to shock him out of what she supposes his intellectual innocence. "I been believing in nothing ever since I was born!" In her state of shock, watching his retreat from the hayloft, she sees his "blue figure struggling successfully over the green speckled lake" of the country landscape, the choice of colors here very possibly echoing Stevens's famous uses of those colors, for she knew Stevens's poetry. But whether or not an intentional echo, the details fall helpfully to our present consideration.

The question raised by the separation of thought and feeling is precisely the dependability of metaphor, whether we mean this in respect to the articulation in signs—"my love is like a red, red rose"—or in the correspondences of image held by intellect in its attempt at some identity of sign and thing—"a rose is a rose is a rose." It is a question spoken to the poet through the accidents with which he must first attempt to solve the question of metaphor. We touch Flannery O'Connor's *blue* in relation to *green* at her story's resolution. We see those same colors in Stevens's "Man with the Blue Guitar," or "The Comedian as the Letter C," as we see them also in the "blue and white" of that woman going "in Mary's colors" in "Ash-Wednesday." We find it in the delight of Wordsworth's response to a prospect of the world in which that world is clad in "one green hue" under a blue sky. Or Keats's melancholy turning of an April green into the sharpness of black death, where Melancholy "hides the green hill in an April shroud," dwelling with the beauty of the morning rose which is already decaying in its moment of perfection, making April a month more cruel ever than the tender Autumn with its "last oozings" of Beauty. And underlying this difficulty of metaphor to the poet, reflected in his use of colors, is the growing suspicion that image taken as independent of articulation, as somehow a disturbing presence already housed in intellect itself, intrudes upon our intellectual independence which might otherwise be free in its attribution.

The inescapable effect seems to be that image, discovered by thought as already resident in the intellect, certifies a separation of consciousness from that of which it is conscious. In the most desperate moments of awareness, image seems to effect an insurmountable separation of awareness even from itself, with a recessive descent of consciousness, a falling away from its own awareness of itself which brings forth the pained cry: *cogito ergo sum.* Such a poet as Whitman, we observed, attempts to make of this descent a virtue, that of the "receding *I*," which at a moment of its awareness of a something becomes aware of the "I" as already separated from the observing, the now detached, thought-full "I," requiring an assimilation whereby like the phoenix bird, the "I" is reborn out of the ashes of the moment's conscious assimilation. The "I" that is aware of the "I" that is aware . . . and so on and on. The insistence on this discovery as the reality of consciousness is played out in "Song of Myself," in which poem the "I" contains, with a charitable largesse of condescension to existences, the "multitude" of existences other than the "I."

Such is Whitman's acting out of what Eliot in his early state puts another way and without Whitman's enthusiasm: consciousness is the receptacle of the "thousand sordid images" constituting consciousness in its agony of separation from reality, exacerbated by the images themselves. Neither Whitman nor Eliot arrests the difficulty as Stevens does, for both have—Whitman recognizing the intent and Eliot not—a compulsion to rescue not only the self but all mankind through that self. Stevens is content with his own entertainment, his metaphors intended to the pleasure of "one," as opposed to Whitman's One as receptacle of, and so rescue, of the Many. Eliot, at this point, is incapable of moving in either direction, though in *The Waste Land* we shall hear him biding ado to the Whitman who has somewhat drawn him to a sympathy. For instance, compare those lines in "What the Thunder Said," 346–366, to Whitman's "When Lilacs Last in the Dooryard Bloomed," especially sections 9, 13, 14, 15, and 16 of Whitman's poem. The thrush in Eliot begins to signify a quite different vision of the actual creatures as perceived through the senses than appears in Whitman's thrush. Eliot's echo of the Journey to Emmaus, from *Luke*, turns aside Whitman's figuring of Lincoln as saviour as well as Whitman's "I" as the rescue of the "We," humanity in general.

Is metaphor then—the poet asks himself, usually in a poem—merely attributive, the "I's" prerogative independent of reality, whatever "reality" may be? Is metaphor at best subjective in its origin, made by will out of enigmatic image already resident in consciousness, though consciousness knows not how? As such it may touch reality, even Stevens's flat bare earth, through correspondences. But it effects not a union with reality beyond intellect but only a chimera, a "fiction." Is the poem creature of fancy, rather than an action of imagination grounded in a reality accepted as independent of intellect? If so, then analogy, in which lies intellect's pursuit of the structural order it finds necessary to its desire, is called in question as signifying no actual but only an "imagined" order. Consciousness itself will next be called in question, requiring that desperate Cartesian assertion of its existence. Any metaphorical sign, any assertion of likeness in unlike "things," whether made directly or implicitly, serves only to undermine any confidence of intellect in its kinship to other beings at the level of being itself. For what is most desired, whether recognized as the object of desire or not, is some anchor in such kinship, in what the Thomistic realist would call the common ground of being itself. That is the ground of *essence* suborning particularities, independent of intellect. For the Thomistic realist that is more comforting vision, a solution to the nagging "modernist" assertion of particularities as imposed, as projected, by intellect. Put another way, intellect seems not comfortable at last when it must assume the responsibility as the First Cause of being, for that is the office of God, however much intellect may delay a recognition of its discomfort by an ever-escalating activism to hide discomfort.

Thus the fear in intellect: not only metaphor, but even image, is most tenuous. Is image itself somehow merely attributive? Is Plato's position only partially right, in that image—idea—has no transcendent source but is only a futile action of entrapped consciousness as Plato would not admit? If one is Eric Voegelin's modern gnostic who desires power over being, that is an acceptable conclusion, since it justifies whatever actions of consciousness necessary to command power. If one is that other Romantic, if one is yet inclined to lament the entrapment, one may conclude with a dark pathos, as Edgar Allen Poe does, "All that we see and all we seem/ Is but a dream within a dream." As for any help from consciousness other than its futile struggling, that is forlorn hope. For it must follow, from rational argument severed from intuition, that all other attempts to the contrary are merely illusional attempts by intellect to rescue itself from its closed world. Separate worlds, other consciousnesses, Eliot concludes, revolve upon themselves to no end. Constellated community is at best a *notion*.

What one wants to point out at once to this indulgence in despair is that somehow other consciousnesses have already spoken to this supposedly isolated awareness, and on this very point concerning consciousness itself. For as it speaks of futility, it reflects in its signs, in the words uttered, ample evidence that it has already heard what other men have thought on the question. It is not as if this isolated intellect has arrived at an original position, which it must necessarily be if indeed intellect were hopelessly isolated from other worlds. By allusion, the words now used are the words others used, inescapably certified as a common property now possessed by the uttering intellect by its recognition of allusion. Ideas have been borne into that intellect by signs discretely, particularly made by quite other intellects. Signs used with such conscious recognition of their allusiveness undermines the presumption of intellect as exclusive in its isolation. The response of Eliot's peers to his early poetry emphasizes the point. His discomfort at their charging him with plagiarism leads him to append those extensive notes to *The Waste Land*, in one of his explanations a matter of "spiking the guns" of those who would accuse him of stealing other men's words.

There is a point of some importance here, which Eliot did not at first take so healthfully as he might: in the dramatic context—in the poem made by the craftiness (in several senses) of this new individual talent, T. S. Eliot, there is an imitation of the action of an intellect which at once knows but does not understand the significance of its knowledge: it bears the arguments of "what others have said" as a first movement toward learning "how the truth of things stands," as intellect must do in recovering potency to its actuality. In the very act of accepting or rejecting that burden, or parts of it, on the ground of its desperate isolation, accepted as if an absolute isolation, intellect contradicts itself. Nor may it escape, as Whitman attempts to do, its responsibility to reality by retreating behind that culprit sign by saying: "I contradict myself. Very well, then, I contradict myself." Nor as with Emerson, who attempts to avoid intellect's responsibility to the truth of things, which demands at least a consistent deportment toward truth. For in declaring that a foolish consistency is the hobgoblin of little minds, Emerson would license intellect to the freedom of a foolish inconsistency.

Although Eliot's chief intellectual protagonists at the moment, say between 1910 and 1920, were minds such as Descartes's and Leibniz's and Kant's among recent European giants, one must remember as well that, while he is entangled with the problem of consciousness as "monad," he is as well in a somewhat violent revolt against a more immediate antagonist holding him in clutches reason alone seems incapable of breaking: his origins in American Transcendentalism. He attempts to exorcise a residue inherited at a local, family level, a residue which includes not only Emersonian thought, but the Puritan thought antecedent to Emerson which Emerson adapted to his own ends. Eliot's attempt to come to terms with that inheritance bears affinity to Hawthorne's own attempt, as Eliot no doubt recognized. (This is a point I have pursued at length in *Why Hawthorne was Melancholy*.) One might put it that Eliot was attempting to break free of an epistemological trap built out of Descartes and Bacon, and refined through Locke, which had already claimed his New England forebears of whom his family was proud. Consider to the point "The Boston Evening Transcript," "Aunt Helen," and "Cousin Nancy," remembering also that Sweeney is Boston born.

In this respect Eliot is somewhat akin to Pound, who more openly and decisively rejected, not the epistemological trap itself, but those of his forebears who had not managed that mechanism to the intellect's advantage. Pound rejects Whitman on the grounds of Whitman's shallow cultural understanding, his isolation from the sweep of Western culture. But he embraces Whitman's principle that it is the poet's discrete intellect that is the source of order, whether in respect to the interior order to which Confucius speaks or that exterior order of the given world which the poet must command and reconstitute. He made "A Pact" with Whitman, whom he has "detested" long enough as "a pig-headed father." For it was Whitman who "broke the new wood," making it available to Pound "for carving." Pound's acceptance of an epistemology derived to the uses of modernism is dictated by his intention: to elevate the poet-king as the supreme director of a world yet to be made. It was perhaps Confucius who clarified for Pound what is incipient in the "great ywap" Whitman, suggesting a mutual advantage in ordering internally (Whitman's gulping of multitudes) and a projection of such order upon the external world.

One may well understand such reactions as Pound's and William Carlos Williams's, then, to the shocking beliefs that begin to emerge from Eliot's poetry beginning with *The Waste Land*. For in his prosody, Eliot had seemed at first one of the sons of Whitman. In respect to the *uses* of poetry, Eliot will not, it seems, take a stand. He cannot act effectively, whether to advance proletarian concerns as Williams would do out of his reading of Whitman, or Pound's sense that in Whitman lies a possibility to the poet's power beyond any proletarian concerns. Even the dependence upon allusiveness up through *The Waste Land* suggests that inability, and with the publication of that famous poem Williams declared at once and maintained thereafter that Eliot had betrayed poetry back to the academy. Pound sees somewhat more clearly just what is afoot, after that poem, beginning to refer to Eliot with the epithet "Parson Eliot." Thus Eliot, celebrated as the great modern poet, the principal among peers by Pound, seemed to refuse the responsibility of his leadership to Williams, but Pound rather saw that instead Eliot was leading toward an end he, Pound, could not approve. The striking out into a desert where there seemed no water, the hunkering down at the end in order to shore fragments of history against ruin, promised one issue, if any: that which Eliot comes to in "Ash-Wednesday."

In relation to this emerging disappointment in Pound and Williams, let us make another observation concerning Eliot's own fate in the academy, to which he seemed to have delivered poetry as hostage in Williams's view. His poetry has proved most popular, academically, because it is convenient to academic exercises, given the richness of its allusiveness and the complexity of the prosody. The emerging center of that interest, as Pound sees it, lies in the later poetry, which has never enjoyed the reputation in the academy that the earlier poetry did. And so one might suggest that the ambivalence in his own mind, whereby Eliot attempted to remove the personal from poetry's province, left sufficient vacuum to explicators of various persuasion. If "just for academic respectability he left us," as Williams might have put it if paraphrasing Browning on Wordsworth, to the academy Eliot's desertion was actually somewhat later. He surrendered his "intellectual independence" in a submission to what the emerging academic mind (after World War II) would see as a benighted, reactionary declaration of a consent to existence as created, not evolved out of the black and utter chaos of history and nature.

Our address to Eliot differs from either the academy's as here characterized or Williams's and Pound's reading of Eliot's ambivalence of mind and his resolution of it. One has a mind, we have been saying, that is indeed ambivalent, but disquieted by that condition. It was a state necessary to it no doubt in view of its sense that knowledge pertinent to his taking decisive action was not yet available to him. This is to say that out of such hesitation there comes about a slowly-blossoming recognition of hope in Eliot, at the very center of his more obvious despair. Eliot will stumble upon the implications of contradiction in his intellect's judgment of its knowledge as determining intellectual isolation. It will at last seem to him that the knowledge possessed is dependent in a cause separate from intellect's own action. If ironic detachment is the deportment of that intellect governing the early poetry, somewhat mitigating the inclination to self-pity whose proximate cause seems to lie in the mystery of memory itself, Eliot will move beyond the tensional relation of *desire* to *memory* as governed by ironic detachment. He will enter into the country of paradox, in which the poles of contention will become *hope* and *despair*. The thematic center of that early poetry is focused in the opening lines of *The Waste Land*: "April" is said to be "breeding . . . mixing/ Memory and desire, stirring/ Dull roots." The announcement of his having crossed into the quite different country of paradox lies in "Ash-Wednesday," as we shall see more fully along the way.

Through his growing discovery of the collapse of irony occasioned by the contentions of hope and despair, Eliot was at last able to come to terms with his American intellectual origins. He has already encountered them in their more sophisticated European manifestations, those species of thought developed out of the same intellectual error as that home-grown. Gilson and Maritain call it Cartesian Idealism, to which they counter St. Thomas's intellectual realism. The truth of things stands against the failed intellectual attempts to manipulate that truth. And with a shock of recognition, Eliot recovers realism to intellect. Such was not to be the lot of his contemporary Romantic poets, Pound and Williams and Stevens and Frost, or at least their recovery is not significantly a resolution in their poetry. One might except Williams from that generalization perhaps. That is, if we look closely at Williams's *Paterson* as analogous in reflecting his journey to Eliot's *Waste Land* journey, and look at the poetry following *Paterson*, we see a change in progress in Williams. An immediate sign of that change is his coming to terms with prosody through his triadic verse as built on the variable foot. The poems in *Journey to Love* (1955) show how far he has come since his first fascination with and imitation of John Keats. One reads "Asphodel, That Greeny Flower" to this end. Or "The Sparrow." In these poems we discover, despite the disparity of diction and prosody, a spirit more nearly tuned to that "inscape" of things that Hopkins tuned to. Or perhaps we might read these poems in relation to *Little Gidding* and discover the late Williams and late Eliot more nearly in accord in their vision of the truth of things than either might have supposed possible. That is a matter for reflection in considering the whole of each poet's work as the map of each journey through the dark woods, though Williams nowhere gives so clear an evidence of terror as Eliot at his outset.

The terror in Romantic consciousness over its isolation as the only world in which it may sing appears at first in Eliot less a terror than an occasion for ironic ennui in Eliot's representation of it in his early poetry. In Section III of "Preludes," the time is a dusk of morning, a twilight world of consciousness which is neither day nor night, and in the act of projecting a "vision" which by the very term is denied to be true vision but is rather an illusion of the street such as the street cannot understand: in that entrapment what is one to do? One seems able only to "wipe your hand across your mouth, and laugh" sardonically (Sect. IV). This irony, turning in upon consciousness, yet takes a sort of revenge upon the body that distracts and confuses consciousness. For the body is reduced to parts in the poem, making it a decaying robot manipulated by a will to defeat. One's own body is no doubt like those of others, the "muddy feet," the "hands" raising shades and lifting coffee cups as "morning comes to consciousness," that nicely ambiguous characterization of consciousness (*nicely* in its root sense).

But even sardonic irony, even the pose through ennui as of the *poeté maudit* which Eliot learned of Baudelair and his successors, speaks deeper than pose. The (then) popular sophisticated pretense of indifference, the ambience in those social circles in which Eliot moved in London at the time of World War I, speaks nostalgia as well. Thus in its earlier capture by his art in "Preludes," but more impressively in "The Love Song of J. Alfred Prufrock," Eliot proved prophetic, since those poems were made before his sojourn to London. He has, before Joyce, drawn a portrait of the artist as a young man pretending to be an old man in his "Prufrock." And the perceptiveness in that poetry is a reflection of a truth about that world to which Eliot himself is drawn, though he feels uncomfortable in it. It is, in this respect, a self-portrait, and one which Pound will castigate in his own portrait of the artist coming to himself in the dark entanglements of English intellectualism as focused in London. I mean *Hugh Selwyn Mauberley*, as we have suggested, in which the women who come and go in that environment are represented by Lady Valentine, for whom poetry is "the border of ideas," whose edge is "uncertain but a means of blending/ With other strata." Pound's acidic judgment of the London he knows is echoed with some puzzlement by Eliot in his early letters. He is moved by and drawn to a serious engagement with literature, but surprisingly, more through the attitude of his working-class students in the course he taught to keep bread on his own table than through the brittle indifference of his intellectual peers with whom he spent his social life. To his discomfort, he could neither embrace nor extricate himself from that social milieu, as his early letters reveal. We see Eliot at this period, between the publication of *Prufrock and Other Observations* and *The Waste Land*, in an arrested intellectual state, that state captured so persuasively in "The Love Song of J. Alfred Prufrock." If we compare a poem we might propose as Wallace Stevens's version of Prufrock's alternatives, we may better appreciate, see more clearly, something of Eliot's own arrest in relation to Stevens's welcome of those circumstances to consciousness perceived by Eliot to his growing distress.

The fear that intellect is isolated unto itself smolders as a controlled terror in Eliot, until his "nervous breakdown" in the early 1920s. Wallace Stevens, however, responds to that possibility with delight, as witnessed by his "Idea of Order at Key West." There he celebrates by projecting an image of the poet as empowered by isolated consciousness. His imagined Beatrice is a woman singing on empty sands, oblivious to sand and sea and sky, and of the projecting agent, the speaker of the words, as well. She is "the maker of the song she sang," a past tense which allows a projection of that singing figure with something of an illusion of her actual existence. For we are required to suppose no actuality in the experience of the poet who here sings the woman who sings. She is the *maker*, and all else is "merely the place by which she walked to sing." The conclusion: "there never was a world for her/ Except the one she sang and, singing, made." Little wonder then that Stevens, in remarking the poet's office, asserts elsewhere that "one writes for one," namely for himself alone. One has in the early Eliot and in Wallace Stevens almost to his death-bed conversion the same conclusion about the nature of, and the limits of, consciousness. Consciousness, awareness, stands in an existence which is isolated from other existences, insofar as intellect can discover that relationship. What intellect must deal with in attempting to discover the extent of isolation is image in intellect. What it may do with image toward recovering a union, or so it seems to the poet, is to build bridges of metaphor for its passage out of itself. What it is uncertain of is the anchor for such bridges in solid ground beyond the shifting sands of its own desire. Eliot in these circumstances laments isolation. But Stevens celebrates the isolation as autonomy which allows unhampered freedom, so that intellect may do as it will with metaphor.

Perhaps we may take it as an irony, though Eliot and no doubt Stevens himself at the end would more likely see it the action of grace: in a curious way, Wallace Stevens seems forced to an encounter with the nature of his own existence through his deliberate strategy of assuming a Cartesian dualism. That seemed the address appropriate to his gift as poet. Putting aside for the moment his last days, that early embrace of contradiction in his approach to poetry, his consent to poetry as fiction divorced of reality, does not seem in accord with his general conduct. For he is a pragmatist at heart, and such a pragmatist would call himself a realist no doubt. But there is no contradiction in the pragmatist's appropriation of idealism as device, for one is not thereby committed to a belief in the thing appropriated. When one becomes tempted to such a belief, as Keats was tempted, one is defeated as pragmatist. Indeed, that is the argument in that very famous poem by Stevens, "Sunday Morning," which he says in retrospect "is simply an expression of of paganism, although, of course, I did not think that I was expressing paganism when I wrote it." (*Letters,* 250) One resting faith in illusion will only be able to give "bounty to the dead," and nowhere more sadly, in Stevens view, than as the Christian does. We may affirm only, he argues, that "We live in an old chaos of the sun," and so must declare that "The tomb in Palestine/ Is not the porch of spirits lingering." And in "A High-Toned Old Christian Woman" one finds Stevens again a "dead opposite" to the Eliot of "Ash-Wednesday," declaring "Poetry is the supreme fiction, madam," and "fictive things/ Wink as they will." And so the pragmatist will use such fictive things as he will, including the *as if* of Cartesian Idealism.

Eliot himself saw this same possibility of using idealism pragmatically. In the letter we have cited already, to Norbert Wiener on Epiphany 1915, he declares himself a relativist, asserting that "One can . . . be a relative idealist or a relative realist." But as was true for Eliot, so for Stevens: such presumption has a way of turning upon the presumer. If Stevens is capable of presenting "Thirteen Ways of Looking at a Blackbird," the implication in that baker's dozen of ways seen from the position of power now assumed by will is that the measure is but an earnest of infinite ways, dependent in intellect. But there is also another possibility implicit, the Thomistic realist might counter: not simply that intellect's ways are inexhaustible, as Stevens must suppose in his rational appropriation of things to gnostic use; for things in themselves are inexhaustible to finite intellect because they are anchored in the fullness of creation. It is in the nature of reality itself that one discovers so singular a creature as a particular blackbird and in that singular creature all the world is made implicit. Such a recognition comes slowly and most gradually to Stevens, in contrast to that bursting recognition which Hopkins celebrates in "The Windhover," a bird in which there lie myriad revelations. Hopkins's discovery in such a little world shows how the *little* becomes *all* the world, or more properly is *becoming to* all the world, in the moment of vision. Dame Julian of Norwich, reflecting on the hazel nut in her hand, finds that all of creation is dependent in a common ground, and dependent from the common Cause to any and each thing, and so to all things, through the common effect of being itself from that Cause. Nor is that Cause, her vision tells her, the actuality of finite mind, though the Cause is present to it as that finite mind beholds blackbird or windhover or even the lowly hazel nut: the Cause of the possible ways of being is not in the beholding intellect as itself the cause of those possible ways.

Dame Julian remarks, in the fifth chapter of her *Revelations of Divine Love*, that God "shewed me a little thing, the quantity of an hazel-nut, in the palm of my hand; and it was as round as a ball. I looked thereupon with eye of my understanding, and thought: 'What may this be?' And it was generally answered thus: 'It is all that is made.' I marvelled how it might last, for methought it might suddenly have fallen to naught for little[ness]. And I was answered in my understanding: 'It lasteth, and ever shall for that God loveth it.' And so all thing hath the Being of the love of God." Such recognition, late or soon, may come through the understanding soon for Dame Julian, late for Stevens. To Fr. Arthur Hanley, who received Stevens into the Church in his last days, Stevens remarked, "Everything . . . has been created. There is only one uncreated." This after a long history of private meditations in St. Patrick's Cathedral over his late years. His lingering problem is the ancient one, which among others occasioned *The Divine Comedy* and *Paradise Lost*: how does a good God allow evil to exist. That is an old charge which Dame Julian herself had difficulty with, resolved for her by a vision in which Christ tells her that sin is "behovely" and that all manner of thing shall be well, through the encompassing love of God. It is also the knotty problem haunting Eliot, to which he becomes reconciled in *Little Gidding*, concluding that last of his poems with this passage from Dame Julian. One need not insist that Stevens came to accept fully that sin is behovely in his final days, but Fr. Hanley reports how comfortable he became when he could declare himself at last "in the fold" after Fr. Henley baptized him. (See Peter Brazeau, *Parts of a World: Wallace Stevens Remembered, an Oral Biography*, 294–96.)

In relation to our theme, exploring the problem of metaphor at this point, we might consider that Stevens, given his calling as poet and his early adoption to Cartesian Idealism, came at last (through his manipulations of poetry to willful analogy of attribution) to the borders of vision. There occurs a glimmer of that fundamentally sound sort of analogy, the

analogy of proper proportionality. It is in that recognition that one declares, "Everything . . . has been created." As myth for Eliot at first
seemed merely a device to order chaos in the interest of art but proved in
the end not fiction but the beginning of vision, so Stevens's metaphor, a
weaving of likenesses under the supposed autonomy of intellectual imagination, proved in the end more deeply anchored in reality than merely a
projection of fancy upon words by intellect. As Dame Julian with her
hazel nut, or Hopkins with his clod of turned earth, or Eliot with his
roses that suddenly have the look of roses that are looked at independent
of his own intellect, so Stevens may have recognized a glowing of transcendent implication out of a blackbird and discovered thereby why that
creature is so rich in its feeding of analogy.

Meanwhile, there are those more spectacular poets, activists in reaction
to isolation who remain adamant to the end. Like Shelley in reaction to
Wordsworth. Like Ezra Pound in reaction to Eliot. With *Hugh Selwyn
Mauberley*, Pound bid "a farewell to London." As Poet Prophet, he
shook its dust from his shoes. But from our perspective, such poets appear rather as if at a child's play, having too quickly lost the limits of play
in reality. Whether by setting tracts adrift in the Irish Sea (Shelley) or
assuming dominance of the estate of letters in the new capital of intellect,
Paris (Pound), to thus blink reality as proper context to intellect must lead
only back to intellect's self-entrapment. Shelley's seems less spectacular at
this distance, but we have Pound's sad account of that same sad past age
in the *Pisan Cantos*, reflected in the details out of his literal encagement
at Pisa.

Ezra Pound refused to submit to consciousness as a closed world
doomed to revolve helplessly like ancient women in vacant lots. He would
restructure a world beyond consciousness. The position from which he
moves does not differ in its premise from that in the early Eliot or Stevens.
But for Pound in his assumption of power over being, that instrument of
power (the sign) must be recognized as dangerous to the operator of it if
not carefully controlled, and to use metaphor is to begin to lose control.
Metaphor too easily introduces subjective response by the isolated intellect, with a consequent reduction of imaginative action to merely fanciful
action. We see at once why Pound would quarrel with Stevens. Power
must be focused through the sign. That focus seems possible if sign is
used as the instrument to restructure existence as separate from intellect.
It is not accident that such an activist poet as Ezra Pound, therefore, is
highly suspicious of metaphor as tending to reinforce the isolation of intellect from its power over being. For a plurality of meaning in words,
introduced through metaphor, allows no concentration of disparate ener-

gies of disparate intellects, to be managed through the poet's authority over the acceptable word. The word must be purified to this end by the poet as engineer, and here we see as well the great distance between Eliot and Pound as to the intended issue of "purifying the dialect of the tribe."

One puzzled by Pound's celebration of Mussoline will find the reason here I think. For it is not the philosopher king who must rule Pound's version of Plato's *Republic*, but the poet king. It is the poet who projects an image of a desirable world, however necessary it might be to expedite that image with the king's forces. That all the king's horses and men cannot put Pound's desired world together seems rather obvious to most of us now, demonstrated by our recent experiences of social reality both in the West and in Eastern Europe, but it did not yet seem so impossible to Romantic realists or Romantic intuitionists—to scientific kings or poetic kings—from the time of the Encyclopedists at least up to the present collapse of the communist world. It is of interest to our point that "poets" are now presidents in Eastern Europe, Vaclav Havel in Czechoslovakia and Arpad Gontz in Hungary. As far as the poet may be supposed the unacknowledged legislator of mankind, as Shelley would have it, we seem rather to have regressed than advanced since Shelley's declaring the poet into that office. But to come too easily to that conclusion is to submit too quickly to the modernist spirit of our age: to the illusion of progress possible in the city of man at its most fundamental level of reality. Our intellectual state is still, and likely always to be, that of Wordsworth and Keats. Which is to say, it is the state of Eliot and Stevens and Pound and Frost and Williams in its aspect which we have called "Romantic." Let us then, given our advantage of perspective through hindsight, look somewhat more closely at the Romantic poet as seen in Wordsworth and Keats, and Shelley. We are not concerned to discover a paradigm for that Romantic mind, or a figure of that mind as a retrospective vision. We are rather concerned to recover the common circumstance to intellect that is as old as Adam and as new as our address to our local, personal experience of the world as that world will meet us tomorrow when we wake from whatever slumbers.

11

Floating Transcendentals out of "Finite Centers"

For the realist, whose thought is concerned with being, the Good, the True and the Beautiful are in the fullest sense real, since they are simply being itself as desired, known and admired. But as soon as thought substitutes itself for knowledge, these transcendentals begin to float in the air without knowing where to perch themselves. This is why idealism spends its time "grounding" morality, knowledge and art, as though the way men should act were not written in the nature of man, the manner of knowing in the very structure of our intellect, and the arts in the practical activity of the artist himself.

—Étienne Gilson, *Methodical Realism*

John Keats concludes his "Ode on a Grecian Urn" with highly debatable lines:

> "Beauty is truth, truth beauty"—That is all
> Ye know on earth, and all ye need to know.

The lines are debatable as a proposition, of course, but there is a question preliminary to that debate, though a part of it. Keats punctuates the lines differently in two manuscripts, raising the question whether there is one speaker or two. Whether the urn is to be understood as "saying" the whole of the two lines, or whether the last line and a half are the poet's own response, his turning upon the urn as it were, saying that such a proposition is well and good if one happens to be an urn or a poem, but is cold comfort if one happens to be an urn maker or a poet.

You will also have recognized in my epigraph from Gilson a clear, precise putting of a central Thomistic point about "being itself" as the pivotal recognition separating the Thomistic realist from the Cartesian idealist. What interests me in putting these texts together is the light Gilson sheds on that large and amorphous intellectual movement in Western thought we speak of as "Romanticism," and particularly that movement as reflected in literature in English. Gilson makes his observation in the early 1930s, just as a very significant modern "Romantic" poet, T. S. Eliot, is becoming a realist—or rather is recognizing that almost unknown to himself, so sophisticated a Romantic has he been, that he has metamorphosed from secular idealist into a Christian realist. And it is at this time that Eliot as critic begins to praise John Keats, after long disdain of the English Romantics. His praise, at heart, is for Keats's Cartesian ambience of thought that dislocated the poet increasingly from his desired position in community after the sixteenth century. To have recognized the difficulties is not, of course, to have overcome them, being only the first step necessary to a recovery from intellectual confusions. Much stumbling may, and does, follow for Keats and to an extent for Eliot before he at least (unlike Keats) comes to rest in what is essentially a Thomistic realism.

When Gilson in our epigraph says that "as soon as thought substitutes itself for knowledge," those trancendentals—the Good, the True, and the Beautiful—"begin to float in the air without knowing where to perch themselves," he puts the Romantic's dilemma rather clearly. The proximate perch of those transcendent realities is in the intellect, as the poet knows intuitively. Intellect is but a visitation site for the transcendent, for finite intellect is at best an uncertain roosting place, save through grace. Losing sight of this truth about the limits of finite intellect, modern philosophy, aided and abetted by the emerging empirical sciences, has since the Renaissance increasingly insisted that the desired, the known, and the admired are causally occasioned by finite intellect: that the Good, the True, and the Beautiful exist by and through the operation of a finite intellect. The poet, intuitively disturbed by such a position, should he extend metaphor out of Gilson's figure of the floating transcendentals might well liken his own circumstances in this confused age to those of the falconer whose birds remain leashed, though circling near his outstretched but carefully gloved hand—that controlling perch of his own intellect. Such a violation of the reality of intellect through metaphorical *attribution* (in its Thomistic sense) will call forth at last an eruption, perhaps such a one as William Butler Yeats cries in famous lines:

> Turning and turning in the widening gyre
> The falcon cannot hear the falconer;
> Things fall apart; the center cannot hold;
> Mere anarchy is loosed upon the world . . . .

So apt are Yeats's words to the breaking asunder of intellect and reality in our century that they are his most quoted ones, characterizing as they do our centripetal intellectual chaos. Few philosophers dealing with that chaos can resist this very Romantic poet, whose work is a rich source of epigraphs to the explorations of our age's malaise in which intellects gasp as order dissipates—order being the intellect's necessary medium.

We have been concerned to explore this confusion as signaled by our Romantic poets generally, in order to rescue what has been too casually called the "Romantic" impulse. I rather take that impulse to be in its actuality a Thomistic intuition unrealized as such. It is a gift of intellect through its very nature, and so timeless, though in certain times and places more highly visible in the arts as an intellectual community begins to lose its common consent to the necessity of particular and communal order. In a recovery of the intuitive as legitimately real lies the significant future of Thomistic realism: in its clarification and then restoration to an ordinate service of intellect's complementary gift, the rational. Still, I am uncomfortable in speaking of a "future" of Thomism, even as I am restive when "Romanticism" is seen as a Western movement beginning in the eighteenth century. Sufficient unto the present moment of intellectual unrest are the evils of intellect misapplied. What is always at issue is the recovery of the particular soul's proper relation to complex reality, which is a relation possible only in this present moment. That recovery is by intellectual vision restored, a recovery of intellect to its proper engagement to reality.

And so I value Josef Pieper's cautionary words to the point: in respect to intuitive knowledge as it may be distinguished from rational knowledge, he reminds us, there is no "tension toward the future" in the intuitive intellect, one of whose functions is to call a unified intellect to the exigencies of this very moment in order that it may see reality as beyond the limits of time. Now if the stirring in the poet's intellect caused by his intuitive gift fails in his rational exercise of it through a confused excess, neither his attempt nor the intuition are themselves wrong of necessity. Notably, when our Romantic poet fails in consequence of intuitive stirrings, it is likely to be because he has wrongly associated the intuitive with the temporal circumstances through which he struggles toward vision. That is, the failure is likely to be occasioned by a rational distortion of the nature of the soul's presence in time and place, the nature of this crucial present moment of the soul's being. He inclines to make time the enemy, whereby he only becomes time's pawn, increasingly enthralled either by nostalgia for an imagined moment in the past or an imagined moment in the future: enthralled by an Eden lost or by some Eden yet to be established, the one occasioning passive lament, the other very often an activist assault upon time future.

The struggle to recover intuited reality through our intuitive nature to a respect by rational intellect, so conspicuous in nineteenth-century literature, is revealed most variously in theme and in genre. For instance, the attempt is very much present in those "Romantic" novels of Sir Walter Scott, which our gnostic humorist Mark Twain makes such fun of in his own attempt to recover Adam as his own possession, namely his *Adventures of Huckleberry Finn*. The failures of Twain's own Romanticism, we note in passing, are forced upon him even as he ridicules the nostalgic Romantic. *A Connecticut Yankee at King Arthur's Court*, pitting a modernist "Yankee" against Scott's medieval dream, ends most darkly, followed by Twain's many dark works reflecting despair in him. Intuitive stirrings such as those in Scott one finds also in Keats's nostalgic texture of "The Eve of St. Agnes," through which sensual details a swooning of the senses is encouraged, and even sometimes effected, at least in sophomores who have not yet lost or had distorted entirely the virtues of their sensual nature. We need to be reminded often that it is through our sensual nature, as St. Thomas says, that we are properly drawn toward the Good by fleeting glimpses of the Beautiful such as that flickering in young love. For who in flowering youth, or even that youth only remembered, can resist moonlight through those stained windows that are ripe with "quaint" devices of "carven imag'ries," falling with "warm gules on Madeline's fair breast." Not only Porphyro grows faint.

But these, alas—both Madeline and Porphyro, the old crone and the beadsman—are gone "ages long ago," leaving one to confront this present, fleeting moment. Both Scott and Keats share in this turning back toward the Medieval world in their attempts to regain faint stirrings of the Good, the True and the Beautiful to present experience. If they ignore or down play unbeautiful particulars in that historical period, our century has been delighted to recover those particulars, in a derision of Medievalism and in support of our favorite epithet for it, the "Dark Ages," only to be left with the recognition that derision does not effect vision, as Twain so sadly discovered.

Our century has exercised a proprietary authority over this dilemma to consciousness, its mislocation in contentions of time future with time past, which though mislocated in time speaks an intuitive hunger for a restitution of a fullness of intellect to timeless reality. Such are intellect's stirrings after its long wanderings in Cartesian shadows of being, though we must be reminded often that such wanderings are not limited to either an age or a country or a literary movement. Which is to remind ourselves once more that, in posing Thomistic realism as it contends with Cartesian Idealism, we are posing inherent intellectual difficulties which are not to be sufficiently accounted for by historical designations. One might with world enough and time discover such contentions operative in the intellect of Homer or Aeschylus or Dante. Here, for an economy, we are interested in it as dramatically represented *by*, as it is *in*, the young T. S. Eliot, up to the final section of his celebrated epic of the human soul on its way in his *Waste Land*. The growing recognition we find pointedly in the final section, "What the Thunder Said." Eliot's is that most haunting Keatsean question: What is the relation of memory to desire? That is the question inherent in self-consciousness, whether we find it in Keats or Eliot, or at the same turning point explored by St. Augustine in his *Confessions*.

Neither motivating presence in consciousness, memory or desire, may be denied a presence. Both are fitfully astir and somehow astir in tandem in consciousness as soon as it turns self-conscious. And memory in relation to desire begs a resolution beyond any explanation as merely psychological or even physiological presences in thought: as merely a residual consequence of one's private history accounted for sufficiently by identification of the "personal," in the modernist reduction of that term by biological determinism. That was nevertheless the thrust of the new science of psychology as intellect became rapidly subsumed by that science's pretending to empirical authority in the first half of our century. But anxious intellect increasingly found that a merely psychological solution to its disquiet, demonstrating analogical parallels of imagery between past event and the event as presently remembered, was more distressing than healing. If desire has as its limited cause, not a hunger for some Good that is both desire's cause and its end—if desire is merely a stirring out of memory of some old personal event from which undesirable elements must be purged, leaving only a golden skeleton of event in memory—if such be so, where does that leave intellect in respect to its present moment? Experience selectively remembered and discretely edited is but limited history in an isolated intellect. Nevertheless, with the emerging "depth psychology" between the two world wars the suffering consciousness was insistently encouraged to recover specific memory of past event as full treatment of desire's anxieties. A more detailed recovery of particulars, buried in memory, was the necessary therapy. And so the lay victim of memory became dependent upon the new priests of memory, the analysts, in proportion as he considered himself a sophisticated modernist.

But even with such a scientifically ordained aid, consciousness remains time-locked. The past so dispelled, one must yet come to terms with the future, and in a final extremity even with that ever-present present. If forced to conclude that desire is but an after-glow of an event once experienced in the past, consciousness hardly finds that propitious to its present experience which is already dissolving into a past. There continues a terror of, or a nostalgia for, a private moment now more or less past or passing or to come. The focus in such a psychologically rationalized consciousness leaves it doomed to look over its shoulder repeatedly at its fading present. The restless looking back to the passing moment, even to yesterday as opposed to centuries ago—to the Medieval or the Ancient world—is insufficient to the deepest hunger of consciousness that time be "redeemed," as Eliot was to speak of the concern.

In attempting to break history's lock upon his own consciousness, Eliot must somehow find a "key" to turn in that lock of time upon the soul. For the violent breaking down of the door by modern psychiatry's heavy equipment seemed fundamentally destructive, not only to the locked door but to the imprisoned consciousness itself. That "key" is to be found "once and once only," *The Waste Land* declared in its final section. It is found in the recovery of a deportment of intellect toward being very like that which John Keats describes as "Negative Capability," a gift Keats found conspicuous in Shakespeare. This deportment is not objective nor impersonal, as sometimes described; at least not in Keats's understanding of what, by intuition, he sought as both man and poet. It is rather an openness to being, which to Keats threatens in its existence to become merely indolence, or so he fears it may if it occasions excessive reaction, excessive submission of intellect. He wrote an ode on that fear, in attempting to exorcise it. But he says of the virtue of openness in a letter: "A poet has no Identity . . . he is continually . . . filling some other Body."

This submergence of "Identity" is a turning from the self as center. It is not an obliteration of the poet's *person* such as Eliot argues for early in his career in a famous essay, "Tradition and the Individual Talent," that very Cartesian, even gnostic, essay which Eliot came to regret. After that essay, Eliot begins to move closer to Keats's understanding, discovering that an open giving (*Datta*) leads to that sympathy in mutual being of the self and creation (*Dayadhvan*), as the *Waste Land's* voice is at last able to say.

> I have heard the key
> Turn in the door once and turn once only
> We think of the key, each in his prison
> Thinking of the key, each confirms a prison . . . .

But at nightfall, still entrapped, come "Aethereal rumors" that revive in memory a "broken Coriolanus," that old soul broken by its prideful sense of integrity, which is not true integrity but only the self locked upon itself, and by that act thus locking out all being else. The key has been turned, but the soul has yet to find its way into a new sunlight.

The necessity of this Keatsean openness is crucial to our understanding Eliot's enthusiasm for Keats after Eliot's conversion, as it is important to our understanding Keats's own intuitive perception of being. On occasion Keats rejoices in and celebrates a Wordsworthean "wise passiveness, " an openness to being, as we see in a letter to Reynolds (February 19, 1818.). It is in a spiritual state in relation to being that one is "awake who thinks himself asleep," in which words there is a note of certainty missing in the conclusion to his Odes. Such is that state in which one is reconciled to his own intellectual finitude, as is clear from Keats's first attempt at defining "negative capability": "I mean . . . when a man is capable of being in uncertainties, Mysteries, doubts, without any irritable reaching after fact & reason." He cites Coleridge as one impatient, "incapable of remaining content with half knowledge." One might add here that intellect, by its nature, is incapable of remaining content so long as it is uncertain of its proper end, for that is indeed to succumb to indolence, the danger Keats fears. But it is also true as Keats suggests that intellect's "irritable reaching after fact & reason" is precisely an impatience that tempts intellect to gnostic action with an intent to power over being, a refusal to come to terms with its own finitude.

Intellect may turn active within a wise passiveness, as Keats remarks in saying that on reading the *Iliad* he finds himself shouting in the trenches with Achilles, or that when he observes a sparrow pecking about the gravel, by an imaginative "filling" of that sparrow's being his own soul is enlarged in a receptiveness to particular creatures. Compare Eliot's sardonic echo of Keats's sparrow in Section III of "Preludes," where the sparrows do not peck about the gravel but in the "gutters," a term which by sound and thing signified is hardly inducive of responsive negative capability. Compare as well a passage from Flannery O'Connor's *The Violent Bear It Away*, in which her rationalist intellectual, Rayber, detached from being by careful fear, is yet affected by a terror of his affinity to existences other than himself. It is an affinity out of the commonality of beings in being (certainly in Miss O'Connor's understanding) which her character would avoid at all costs. For it is an experience of a "horrifying love." "Anything he looked at too long could bring it on . . . . It could be a stick or a stone, the line of a shadow, the absurd old man's walk of a starling crossing the sidewalk." The effect of such encounter, Rayber insists on reason's authority independent of intuitive intellect, is a "morbid surge of love" which is "powerful enough to throw him to the ground in an act of idiot praise. It was completely irrational and abnormal." Or so it must appear to Rayber in his reductionist, "scientific" view of existence. One might suggest that what Miss O'Connor dramatizes, good Thomist that she is, is a limited recovery of a prelapsarian relation to being. That encounter stirs soul's memory of such an encounter with being whereby, as Thomas says, one knows the thing itself in its essence by that preconceptual encounter with being. Such is a knowledge proper to the nature of intellect, not to be accounted for by accidents such as a person's literal years, the limits of the psychologist's science in relation to *person*.

Eliot subsequently deprecated the notes he had attached to his poem, speaking of them once as a display of "bogus scholarship." But to these key lines we just quoted he supplies a telling text, from F. H. Bradley. When considered against the verses, and in relation to the quotation from Dante in the same note, we discover Eliot beginning to break through history's shallow claims upon intellect as administered by that new psychology which had been increasingly supported by philosophers such as Bradley in the train of Descartes. Here are Bradley's words, from his *Appearance and Reality*, which Eliot quotes in his note:

> My external sensations are no less private to myself than are my thoughts or my feelings. In either case my experience falls within my own circle, a circle closed on the outside; and, with all its elements alike, every sphere is opaque to the others which surround it. . . . In brief, regarded as an existence which appears in a soul, the whole world for each is peculiar and private to that soul.

The passage enlightens that sardonic distress in Eliot's early poem "Preludes": "The worlds [spheres] revolve like ancient women" who futilely attempt to keep body about the soul by gathering fuel in a strange land seemingly vacant to any soul. The point Eliot suggests by posing Bradley against the *Waste Land* lines is his rejection of Bradley's "finite centers" (or Leibniz's "monads" as antecedent idea to Bradley) as a sufficient account of the reality of consciousness. Why the compulsion in those philosophers themselves to communicate their concern through signs to other closed worlds, which worlds their argument supposes closed as well? If there is no escape from monadic isolation, why all the bother, or how might one recognize in the bother a concern for one's own disquiet? Somehow there seeps through the walls evidence of commonality. The dawning of this hope in Eliot signals a decisive turning in him, which at that moment was but fitfully seen under the moment's pressures upon him that sent him into retreat to a sanitarium in Switzerland.

His fitfulness of recognition is witnessed by his attitude toward myth at the time his poem is beginning to be widely noticed in literary circles. Though he is beginning to break free of the prescriptions upon intellect out of Descartes and Kant and Leibnitz and Bradley and the like modernist inclinations, he is not yet escaped. I suspect it with some desperation that Eliot summoned myth to the support of the poet's intellect as he turns from being the philosopher he had trained himself to become to the poet as a calling seemingly thrust upon him. Myth seems a reassuring instrument which intellect may use in its attempt to make a thing, a poem, out of the energy pent in intellect, an energy engendered by tension between memory and desire. Myth might serve poetry (so intellect may suppose) as idea systematically extended serves philosophy. In praising James Joyce's *Ulysses*, just as his own *Waste Land* has been published and so surely with one eye upon his work of the moment, Eliot declares that myth is "simply a way of controlling, of ordering, of giving a shape and a significance to the immense panorama of futility and anarchy which is contemporary history . . . . It is, I believe, a step toward making a modern world possible for art." (*The Dial*, November 23, 1923)

Perhaps that is all the poet need know, allowing him a merely pragmatic appropriation of myth to his making of the Beautiful. But as Eliot was to discover increasingly, such an appropriation of myth as "simply" a tool is fraught with peril to the poet's intellect insofar as it is yet alive. It has dangers not unlike those to Keats in his attempt to force his imagination to bear intellect on the nightingale's wing into an abiding season of an imagined spring song, made eternal by the imaginative act itself. It is at this period that Eliot has just gone through an experience such as was rather popularly sought after among his compatriots in London. Aldous Huxley captures the time in his novels such as *Chrome Yellow* and *Antic Hay*, in which one meets thinly disguised persons such as Eliot and that "Romantic" rationalist Bertrand Russell, and many of the enlightened London intelligentsia. Within this social and intellectual gathering, one seemed almost required to have had a "nervous breakdown" and to have been analyzed, along with having access to a clairvoyant as often as not.

Now *nervous breakdown* was a more acceptable term than any other, since it seemed scientifically explained, a term justified by the latest view of man as evolved from animal, man himself differing only by degree from animal. *Nerves* spoke of the discomfort in part as a sort of no-fault explanation of human failure, seconded by *breakdown*, which echoed the

mechanistic view of human existence established out of Darwinian speculation. Those suffering nervous breakdowns were still at the pinnacle of
evolutionary development nevertheless, wherein some self esteem might
thereby be justified. To speak of the condition affecting Eliot in an older
language, to consider the possibility of a *soul in spiritual distress*, was long
since passé. Besides which, such antiquated terminology suggested the
victim's participation as a cause of his difficulty by willfulness, a consideration intellectually confusing at best. Terms like *spiritual distress* revealed
the victim's continuing entrapment in nineteenth-century confusions, indeed well nigh Medieval confusions. Of course, Eliot subsequently recognized his difficulty for what it was, to the general surprise of, and sometimes the pained complaint of, irritated contemporaries. That is, Eliot saw
himself at last as having experienced a spiritual crisis, not merely an intellectual or psychological one such as the times required of at least the
intelligentsia.

One does not deny either physiological or psychological truths about
such a condition of the person by naming the fundamental cause a spiritual trauma of the soul, as our latest researches begin at last to concede
and allow. One speaks of the soul with less annoyance to others at the
close of our century than was allowable at its beginning. We may say
more confidently, then, that Eliot's was a spiritual crisis exacerbating his
physical and psychological state. He understood it as occasioned significantly by his extreme intellectual skepticism about existence. And he
came to look back upon that crisis as signaling his emerging from an
extreme Romanticism. Eliot had in the beginning practiced that Romanticism with the deliberateness of a sophisticated detachment from all being
save intellect itself, supposing that by that deportment he was an intellectual "realist." Thus one might make a virtue of a determined necessity. It
was a condition he found in the ancients more than in post-Renaissance
forebears, though he will in the end reject his own antithesis between
Romantic and *Classical* mind. In that distinction he had at first located
himself as Classical, while his contemporaries were declaring him neither,
but a "Modernist."

Concerning myth's use as a poetic device to the poet's convenience—to
control, order, and shape chaotic experience and overcome futility: what
is problematic in Eliot's attempt is his continuing (though fading) presumption that intellect is autonomous, the autonomy seemingly certified
by contemporary sciences. Those sciences were busily exploring intellect
as a spume out of the nerves, a late moment of disturbed blossom upon
evolutionary history. This was the Age of Freud, for instance, though
Jung as a sort of Bergsonian psychologist would presently alleviate some-

what the heavy shadows of mechanistic determinism that fell on consciousness out of Darwinian theory. The chaos and futility lie in Eliot more deeply, in his person as *person*, than in the self as understood mechanistically. Bergson, to Eliot's early fascination, had attempted a rescue of intellect from mechanistic determinism through his theory of an illusive *élan vital* which permeated a universe conceded to be a closed universe, as Bradley had argued the sphere of individual consciousness a closed "world." Bergson's book *Creative Evolution* seemed the poet's rescue, to Robert Frost no less than to Eliot, though Frost never got beyond an entrapment in Bergsonian imminence. And Bergson is the philosophical source of that celebrated literary movement called Imaginism, a movement which effects a moment's recovery to respectability of the uses of attributive metaphor—a justification of intellect in its modernist isolation as certified and treated by the new sciences of the mind. T. E. Hulme's reading of and translation of Bergson underlie Imagism, a movement largely established through Ezra Pound's initial enthusiasm.[11]

For Eliot, Bergson's seeming rescue proved disappointing, leaving him isolated the more. His dissatisfaction is reflected in his own remarks about his most shocking poem. *The Waste Land*, he said, was a "personal grouse" and not an attempt to speak to or for his age, despite all that age's chaos and sense of futility. The immense panorama of confusion was still pretty much the one already reflected in his "Preludes." That is, the "world" was still rather confined to the little closed monad of the self, with the thousand sordid images haunting consciousness now multiplied by the intervening years. For the images stored in memory had only been increased by another decade of experience, not reconciled to desire, leaving the poet still intellectually desolate. However, there had been a moment's recognition that somehow a key must exist to open that little world. On this recognition Eliot reflects a decade later (in "Thoughts after Lambeth"), after he had come to appreciate more fully the spiritual dimension of his own *Waste Land*. Now he sees better that the poem exhibits the nearly total collapse of himself as a person. "I dislike," he says, "the word 'generation.' When I wrote a poem called *The Waste Land* some of my more approving critics said that I had expressed 'the disillusionment of a generation,' which is nonsense." And he adds somewhat testily, "I may have expressed for them their own illusion of being disillusioned, but that did not form part of my intention."

In Eliot's intent to manipulate chaos to artful order by myth as form, we recognize a deliberate engagement of analogy. As Eliot knew well, analogy is a dangerous though exhilarating intellectual game, a discovery made to us at least as long ago as Plato. It is because it is exhilarating no doubt that analogy is also dangerous, for exhilaration is a side effect of intellectual action, never more endangering than when intellect wavers, in its pursuit of order, between affirming order's cause as intellect's own action and affirming it ultimately independent of that action. As a side effect, in this turning to a pleasure of intellect in analogy as primary, a turning to the delight of likeness in unlike things, intellect may turn a means (analogy) into an end. Analogy as a means toward a recovery of reality becomes an end as the seeming delight for, and so justification of, intellect itself, the danger our century's poets have severely risked. But more than our poets. Analogy as either chain saw or laser—that is, as tool in the gnostic remaking of being to suit a variety of intellectual pleasures—can do terrible damage to being. We need only recall this century's general destructiveness of persons from the gas chambers and the Gulag to Cambodia and Iraq.

But analogy abused, whether by poet or gnostic manipulator of the world of being itself, most centrally damages the being of the acting agent—the poet or philosopher or state director—insofar as he submits to this intellectual error of making analogy an end rather than a means of the soul's recovery of reality.[12] That is why, of course, the sign and its use has been the primary battleground over *being* in our century, an age in which propaganda through sophistications of technology has so effectively appropriated power by seducing intellect from reality, whether in support of political program or moving mass-produced products. This recognition leads Eliot to realize the poet's importance to community: the poet has as his particular concern "speech," and so finds himself called in a confused age "to purify the dialect of the tribe" in relating the word to reality, against the essentially diabolic manipulation of speech aimed at enslavement of spirit. The "Romantic" poet, then, must recognize and accept as his proper calling this struggle through speech to recover intuitional volition to the soul's proper end, that common property to the "tribe" in its discrete nature as a gathering of persons. This reality of intellect's proper relation to being, properly common as community, Eliot found radically dislocated through Cartesian Idealism in its various species, the cause of disintegration of the "tribe." And so, above all, the poet is required to recover the sign as viable in the dialect of the tribe.

In our century "Romantic" poets have flourished, largely under the disguise of being anti-Romantic. Joyce, Pound, Stevens, Eliot: each is more Romantic than he would have us know. But it is Eliot who survives spiritually beyond the intellectual entanglement of their common intuitive desire for the Good, the predominant characteristic of Romanticism as I am using the term. As "modernist," as intellectual child of Cartesian

Idealism, each holds that desire suspect, usually fearing it a temptation to sentimentality in art. Joyce and Pound cultivate a sentiment toward rationalism, making them more directly children of Enlightenment rationalism against which certain Romantic poets—Wordsworth for instance—set themselves than like their nineteenth century "Romantic" fathers. The flight from that spectacle of art, namely sentimentality, under the pressure of a rationalism which holds intuition suspect will fail to realize that a sheer knowledge of the True when reduced from the understanding to the province of strict reason may easily become mere knowledge sheared from the Good. That is always a danger in "facts" isolated from complex reality by gnostic error, whether that error be deliberately embraced in the interest of power over being or merely submitted to by confusions of thought about the source of, and the nature of, the Good. Such a control may even be attempted with the best of intent, in the interest of grounding intuitive desire by remaking the world as it "ought" to have been made. It is this aspect of the use of sign that occupies Pound's thought for so long, as we have suggested. If we are to see how these two poets, Eliot and Pound, differ radically we may do so if we understand how each differs fundamentally in understanding what is at stake in the poet's responsibility to "purify the dialect of the tribe." For Pound, the issue is a secular social order. For Eliot, it is a necessity if one is to remove obstacles to grace in the interest of the salvation of the soul.

12

The Poet, Indifferently
Pruning His Nails

The awakening of the intelligence coincides with the apprehension of
things, which, as soon as they are perceived, are classified according
to their most evident similarities [their likeness, though unlike
things]. This fact . . . is something that theory has to take account of.
. . . That is why every form of realism is a philosophy of common
sense.

—Étienne Gilson, *Methodical Realism*

Shared knowledge will allow an admiration of the Beautiful, but it will
be able to account for the Beautiful only as an effect of intellect's own
making. It tempts the poet to dream of a "paradise/ terrestre," in Ezra
Pound's phrase, whether called the Utopian state of Dioce as in the *Cantos* or in a poem named "Notes toward a Supreme Fiction" by Wallace
Stevens, who would elevate intellect's fictions, built by attribution, as the
only acceptable absolute. Joyce's Stephen Dedlaus dreams of making such
a world as Stevens posits for poetry. In *The Portrait of the Artist as a
Young Man*, young Stephen would declare a world into existence by the
power of his own words, on sole authority of intellect. He would then
choose to turn from that made world, himself the god who created it, to
a bored indifference, "pruning his nails" to prove indifference. What is
revealed in Dedlaus's intention is the pathos of indifference that haunts
Joyce himself, the spiritual state our age glorified as ennui, whose shadow
Keats anticipates with fear as *indolence*.

But where may such indifference leave the poet but with the bitter ashes
of Keats's aphorism: "Beauty is truth, truth beauty"? The sad dying of
desire in these always dying poets suggests that such a principle as autonomous intellect is far from being all they wish to know, though it may
well be the sum of all they think they know with any certainty. The pa-

thos of ennui, so pervasive of our century's art, is but a disguise of that old spiritual failure once called *acedia*. Kierkegaard spoke of it as the "despair of weakness," which we find often enough pretending to the strength of a god. Such indifference may be manifest as if true art, when it is rather despair elevated by a severe intellectual sentimentality. Such, for instance, is the state of mind of such an unmaker of the self as J. Alfred Prufrock, whose agitations Eliot brilliantly pins wriggling to the walls of Prufrock's own consciousness.

From Eliot's portrait of the "poet" as indolent among the ladies we might conclude that indolence managed by a stoic resolve of spirit such as Prufrock pretends to adopt is little suited to indifference as *acedia*. But *acedia* is not so simply reduced as *sloth*, meaning laziness, for it is rather a willful revolt against reality in the interest of intellect's autonomy. It is hardly surprising, then, that Lucifer, the Unmaking Maker, becomes the artist's patron again and again, beginning with Marlowe and continuing through Joyce's sentimental vision as embraced by Stephen Dedlaus, who takes Lucifer's motto as his own: *non servium*. The practiced indifference to a spiritual engagement of reality—that practice of a certain sort of art which elevates the artist over all—requires a considerable busy-ness, for the artist must conceal from himself the corrosive despair in his address. We said Keats feared indolence as the consequence of an openness of spirit to reality, which we see in his "Ode on Indolence" as a rejection dooming him to oblivion. In the poem, an openness to existence is agitated by figures beckoning his spirit into reality, but in most dangerous ways. One is reminded of that mystical moment Wordsworth recalls in "Tintern Abbey" when laid "asleep in body" he becomes a living soul, seeing "into the life of things." Keats in such an "idle" moment has himself experienced the "blissful cloud of summer-indolence" that so "Benumb'd [his] eyes" that his "pulse grew less and less," the effect being his own drowning into existence most disturbingly. For in that experience of openness to existence he finds that he must deal with "Love" and "Ambition" and "Poesy." They are fearful temptations to spirit, bearing for Keats something of the ambiance of that Presence which the disciples encounter on the road to Emmaus. Keats's epigraph to the poem, incidentally, is Christ's, "They toil not, neither do they spin," in which is celebrated a perfect openness to reality at the lily's elemental level of being. What is disturbing to Keats is the reality of a visionary moment markedly counter to the indolence of *acedia*, and Keats fears this positive hour of openness. Stirred by "Love," "Ambition," "Poesy," he might succumb to being "dieted with praise," and so become a "pet-lamb in a sentimental farce!" What he desires in this new and desperate fear is an indifference to existence, an indifference raised to the power of intellectual indolence, which would amount to his being raised beyond any response to being. That way even his "sense" would be left "Unhaunted quite of all but—nothingness." He is, in short, more than half in love with easeful death in that moment, desiring only the sod's oblivion.[13]

Indifference, we may remember, is not openness, any more than indolence is a passive yielding to Love or Art or Ambition. Nor may we forget how actively agitated either indifference or indolence may appear in those actions of a spirit threatened by despair. We might note that such active indifference as Dedlaus's may buffet our world. *Acedia* may be stormy beyond what we may think, if we take *indolence* to be merely a spiritual arrest. Josef Pieper makes this point effectively in his "Obscurity of Hope and Despair," pointing out how much is lost to understanding by the term *sloth* as a synonym for *acedia* (*Anthology*, Ignatius Press, 1990) Sloth does not mean laziness in relation to "work." Kierkegaard's "despair of self-assertion," says Pieper, is capable of an amazing range of activity out of a "roaming restlessness of spirit." Such a distraught person may surround himself "with the immense effort of a forced optimism, of a radiating trust in life, of a noisily proclaimed 'progress.' " It is in such a condition of despair that the poet may so easily mistake himself as god, and his made thing (the poem) a world whose First Cause is his own intellect.

What is overlooked by the acediac poet is the reality of his participation in being as himself a "made" creature, that recognition the necessary corrective to such a facile definition of himself as became popular in this century: the *poéte maudit*. The defense against an acknowledgment of the self as a given is the elevation of the poet as exile, accursed as Verlaine has it, for (says Verlaine in *Les poétes maudits*, 1884) "is it not true that *now and forever* the sincere poet sees, feels, knows himself *accursed* by whatever system of self-interest is in power?" Such is that new element in the poet as Cartesian Idealist that proved more congenial to our century's Romantics than to their nineteenth-century English forebears. It is a misreading of the poet in relation to human nature which justifies him as member of a race apart and forever accursed, envied, and hated. But embracing that characterization of himself as maker, such a poet may the more freely turn to the sordid dimension of existence, for thus it allows his self-mythologizing through shocking spectacle while at the same time disguising even from himself that the position is in fact one of sentimentality. Pornography as art has here its origins. By an abusive self-love, then, he would maintain the illusion of his authority as autonomous "maker," losing the mystery in that truth about any man, even the *poéte maudit* in his revolt, that he is created in God's image.

With that loss of vision it is inevitable that he conclude that as creator he is not "like" God the Creator, but *is* the god of the thing he makes. And so there is lost to him the insight St. Thomas gives us upon art, through his understanding of man as maker: art is not an imitation of nature, but an imitation of the action whereby nature (creation) is. In this respect, the proper habit of man as maker, the habit of his own being according to his own nature, is his participation in existence creatively. Insofar as he so participates, there will be evident in his art a dynamic presence such as we recognize in nature itself as we experience creation. It is a recognition which Gerard Manley Hopkins speaks of, in character-izing his own habit of making as an attempt to praise the "instress" of being dynamic in art, the "inscape" of art. In whatever degree of failure of intuitive recognition of this nature of the soul as maker, the failure loses dynamic presence in the made thing, the effect of which is a pathos echoing the loss of vision, however much glorified the *poéte maudit* may attempt to make himself by the sentimentality of his self-exile as accursed, hated, despised, rejected—epithets suitably ironic when we remember they echo our lamentation of man's response to God Incarnate which left Christ in that sad estate.

In moving beyond his "Romantic" beginnings, including appropria-tions of the continental Romanticism he found in Verlaine or Corbière (one of Eliot's early favorites) or Rimbaud or Mallarmé, Eliot comes to this recognition of error in his early stance as *poéte maudit* as Joyce and Pound do not. That recognition is dramatized as a recovery from *acedia* and a new recognition of an ordinate action by intellect in its makings is recovered in "Ash-Wednesday," which recognition we must explore on another occasion. Here we add only that Eliot, unlike Joyce or Pound or Stevens, comes to witness his own having moved beyond dislocated, sheared knowledge. That is, he sees the inadequacy of knowledge sheared by gnostic acts of intellect from being itself. The witness to this significant change in Eliot is movingly made complete in his last considerable poem, *Little Gidding*.

The error of knowledge dislocated from reality by gnostic intellect, in the interest of making a thing of art, brings us back to the Romantic intuition toward the Good as pursued by the poet through likeness in unlike things. We come back to the problem of metaphor as encountered in signs, in words. Here I mean metaphor generically, a term naming those attempts by the poet upon reality in the things he makes, in the words whereby he makes his poem. Those signs have a first effect by revealing to the poet himself at least a shadow of his own intellectual action in response to his encounter with reality. This proves especially so where his intent, as with our prototype Stephen Dedlaus, is self-liberation. For the poem as an imitation of the action of nature is inescapably a reflection of the action of the poet's nature as "maker," an inescapable presence in the made thing. Stephen's attempt upon self-liberation constitutes a rejection of reality. Keats to the contrary would have his to be an openness to reality whereby he would be "continually . . . filling some other Body." Dedlaus's is a feeble praising of the self as creator. Keats, could he but recognize the import of his desire for openness, might realize that his desire is for a festive acceptance of creation. Not that such festive acceptance would mean of necessity a "happy" poem, for "happiness" as popularly dreamed is but a chimera, very like that elusive Beauty that fascinates the poet. When Eliot comes to an acceptance of the mystery of existence by his own openness, he writes *Little Gidding*. It is a joyful poem, but it is not a "happy" one.

What the poet may discover through his poem is his deepest desire, which may be but tacit in his recognition of it and so the more unsettling: a desire for a vision of order beyond the threatening chaos with seems always, in any time or place, subscribing the poet and seeming to call in question any belief he may cling to about his ultimate authority over the word. And he may find intellect never more besieged than when it presumes its own actions and devices to be unaided by any power other than its own. We have said that some "Romantic" poets know this desire intuitively as motive to their art. Wallace Stevens has his imagined poet cry it to an imagined companion as a sudden vision *in* intellect, not *to* intellect, a bubbling to the surface of conscious thought out of the poet.

> Oh! Blessed rage for order, pale Ramon,
> The maker's rage to order words of the sea,
> Words of the fragrant portals, dimly-starred. . . .

It is, we contend, an innate hunger in intellect itself which the maker, if he choose as Wallace Stevens does through Cartesian assumptions, may accept without any confusing questions about that innateness. Thus intellect assumes priority in respect to order, order itself not at issue but rather, as Stevens's title emphasizes, "The *Idea* of Order at Key West" or wherever intellect may chose in building that *idea*, in erecting its "supreme fiction." The *where* is inconsequential: Key West, or "in Tennessee" ("Anecdote of the Jar") or on a garbage dump which "is full/ Of images" to be appropriated ("The Man on the Dump").

However much the poet may become confused or willfully stubborn about the stifling idealist oppressiveness that is subversive of his hunger for order, that hunger continues in some degree present in his actions of making. So long as one is a maker, he has not yet completely lost a certain likeness to the Cause of his given nature as maker. That is, he will not have lost that aspect of his existing which is "in the image of God." Existence itself is of necessity an image of the cause of existence in some degree. And so there remains in his concern and action as maker an awareness that it is the good of the thing made that is the guiding principle of making. The good of the poem as poem is at issue, but within that principle to his nature as maker there is also implicit an intent to his own proper end through his participation in being by the action proper to his nature, the action of his making. We recall St. Thomas's insistence that "Art does not belong to moral knowledge, which concerns things to be done *(agibilia)*, since art is right reason about things to be made *(factibilia).*" (*Summa* 2–2, Prologue) The maker as judged by his making is commendable by virtue of "the quality of his work." The work does not demonstrate a moral good as its primary principle of being but a good in itself in respect to order, proportion, and the like. For the maker himself, however, the maker in his own person, there is an inescapable moral dimension to his actions whereby he is realized through his participating in actions of making. The practical intellect, governed by the virtue of prudence, is necessary to the act of making, so that making, in its effect upon the maker, can never be absolutely removed from the necessity of moral order. Art, like fire, is indifferent in itself to the moral dimension of existence, but that is only to speak of art itself as removed from culpability in respect to the spiritual agent, the artist. The relation of beauty to truth for Keats's urn, as concerned with any moral dimension to the truth or beauty that is proper to art itself, is irrelevant to the urn or the poem *as art*. But the habit of making as perfected by the maker is relevant to the good of his spiritual state as person, a state realized in part through that habit of making which is salient in that creature, the embodied soul of the maker. For in a fullness of his making, according to his gifts, lies a fulfillment of his potential being.

While we may not justly indict either an art or a science which happens to be pervasive of a particular age as the cause of a person's failure in his calling as a "maker," his failure to fulfill his person as a gifted, particular, specific being, nevertheless the complex of intellectual circumstances, the intellectual climate coincident to his particular history as a person, must be recognized. A person's failure as maker is ultimately a spiritual consideration, and rests in his own will, but he must engage, as a soul in progress, those conditions impinging upon that progress. That is because his "calling" as maker is circumscribed by the finitudes of existence, not only those of his own limited gifts which are potential, but also, though less decisive to his soul's prospects, those in the immediacy of history as the context to his nature. Thus in his own deportment as person, which he bears residually as his personal history, there is also his response to the history of his age and to the history of his civilization toward which he has responded by actions of his intellect. At issue, then, is his prudent response to circumstances.

Pervasive of our age's history is the idea, contrary to reality, that one is *determined* in his response by circumstance. Such an idea is quite distinct from saying that a person is circumscribed by circumstances, natural and historical. For the deterministic idea is reductionist in its logical extension, making man an effect of nature and history. One may argue the determinist's *idea* by logic, but the evidence of experience underlines persuasively the innate resistance to that determinate pressure of circumstance. One need only pursue the argument with such an advocate of determinism a little way before discovering that, while he may hold all other men determined, he himself will not consent to external determinations as the first and final principles of his own existence. In this respect only his silence in the face of our argument would be his strongest argument, since the purely determined creature has no necessity to describe his determined state. The very description is already intellect's taking a stand beyond the principles he insists are inclusive. Nevertheless, untenable ideas have effects seductive of imprudent intellect, and the deterministic principle has been generally operative in modernist sociology and psychology in particular. It has seemed to justify the proponents in exceeding the descriptive limits of their science by presuming philosophical authority in the question. As intellectual creature, one is required to understand the position as a circumstance to the pursuit of the truth of things.

One remarks by such reflections the stifling oppressiveness upon the "maker" in our world, affecting his breathing through the virus of Cartesian Idealism advanced as if fully established by empirical science. Since the Enlightenment especially, intellect in its necessarily empirical address to the circumstances of being has tended to a communal authority by declaring a reductionist end of idealism. This is to say that idealism and empiricism have too much cooperated in the divorce of intellect from reality, nowhere more conspicuously than in the academy for this past hundred years and more, and with dire effect upon community. Like Chaucer's Physician and Apothecary, each has made the other for to win in their struggle to wrest being from the realist purview. That struggle requires from their position a domination over other intellects. To understand this circumstance of our recent intellectual history is to safeguard ourselves against our own abuse of knowledge. For empirical science yields truth not to be reasonably denied. And even *cogito ergo sum*, as Gilson says, expresses a philosophical truth, though "it is not the starting point" to any acceptable epistemology. To understand the limit in particular knowledge as learned through science is at once to value that knowledge in its limits and to move toward an understanding of that knowledge, for understanding and not knowledge is the responsibility peculiar to intellect. It is the tensional response to circumstance by intellect, in its freedom of response and within the mystery of limit, that is thematic in what we recognize as that historical movement, Romanticism. And what it has tended to abandon is the relation between knowledge and understanding, too often willing to reject knowledge as if that rejection were the most immediate way to understanding. One might say here that this "Romantic" maneuver is that of an intellect which has abandoned prudence.

13

Reflections, the Trimming of Reality

> When reflection becomes a method, it is no longer just an intelligently directed reflection, which it should be, but a reflection which substitutes itself for reality in that its principles and system become those of reality itself.
>
> —Étienne Gilson, *Methodical Realism*

Art, says St. Thomas, is right reason in making and is an intellectual action under the providence of the practical intellect. As such it is governed by prudence, the "practical wisdom of the highest degree of practicality." We have just remarked a danger to the "Romantic" poet, his abandoning that knowledge which practical intellect provides, in the interest of an understanding, which is only properly earned, we have argued earlier, through the ordinate actions of practical and intuitive intellect. Now, since art is so intimately associated with the idea of Beauty, it might be well to suggest in what sense Beauty itself may be approached through the practical intellect, for such an approach does not mean, as it might be understood to mean, an approach through the rigors of rules, as if by rule Beauty could be commanded. Maritain, in his *Creative Intuition in Art and Poetry*, and specifically in his "Art as a Virtue of the Practical Intellect," says, that art "is the straight intellectual determination of works to be made," which statement might suggest at best a remote relation of prudence to art.

As Maritain might admit, however, the art of making, if divorced from prudence, is likely to lead to violations of being itself. It is our purpose here to require that admission, lest being be at risk for the lack of prudence in the artist. I do not think that Maritain in his important work sufficiently guards against this possibility. He says, for instance, that the artist "totally yields to his cherished demon, to develop, for the sake of his art, a peculiar morality and peculiar moral standards of his own, di-

rected to the good of the work, not of his soul." We have already argued
that the artist, so conducting himself as maker toward the thing he would
make, may indeed make a thing good in itself. But we made a distinction
here: such a thing (a poem such as Stevens's "Sunday Morning") may be
good in itself inasmuch as it bears a true witness to the potential imagined
for it by the artist. It is, however, another question whether the truth of
the poem in itself is significant of the truth of reality in respect to the
possible perfections in realities. And the possible perfection of that reality
called the *poet* includes moral rectitude. So, if we agree that the poem does
not, in and of itself, speak primarily to questions of moral rectitude, we
may nevertheless say that, insofar as it is a reflection of the action of
making on the part of its maker, it bears a true witness to the nature of
its maker in his actuality as a specific nature. This means, to put the point
somewhat at an extreme, that a good poem may be good because it bears
true witness of the actions whereby it comes to be, which actions themselves are not thereby certified as good. To put it even more starkly, a bad
man may make a good poem, but in some aspect of that poem the action
it imitates may be discovered as not good in itself as an actuality. A good
poem, in other words, may reflect in some degree, and necessarily will in
some degree I contend, inadequacy in the maker, a limit in his vision of
truth and so some limit of the beauty in the thing he makes. For in this
arena of our concern, we are dealing with a relative relation of a particular
being to an absolute possibility of being in him, the possible perfection
of the gifts of being in him. (It may even seem probable that such an
intellect, as it approaches its own perfection, relinquishes more and more
its actions of making, a condition one perhaps senses in St. Thomas's
giving over the writing of books.)

The concern here is that the artist, if he gives himself "totally" to his
art for the sake of his art, will reveal in some degree what must be concluded a turning from his proper end as person to a mediate end as artist.
The poem is affected because of (in Maritain's phrase) "the human ambience of the activity of art," and if that ambience of creative action is reduced to art as end, it is understandable that the artist may develop "a
peculiar morality and peculiar moral standards of his own." Which is to
say, in truth, that such an artist must be said to put his soul at risk for
the sake of his art, a Faustian version of the artist. It is a concern to be
pursued.

If art is an effect of the action of a practical intellect, the poet's, then
art is dependent *in* and *on* what is in turn a dependent agent, the poet.
Which is to say that art is rooted, if indirectly, in a fundamental good or
a potential good, namely existence itself, which must be said to be inclu-

sive of art. It is in this sense that we may say that the made thing, the poem, is a thing among things and so shares in degree in the common ground of things, in essence, in respect to the principle of proper proportionality. It is in this respect that Thomas says that art is an imitation of the action of nature. Since this is so, and since existential reality (the complex of existing *things*) is itself necessarily good insofar as they *are*, they are good in consequence of being effected by a Good Creator. The goodness of existence is a necessary aspect of the action of being, and that goodness cannot be absolutely removed for that reason from the poet's action of making, however radical his pretense to "peculiar moral standards" for the good of his art. The good may be diminished, however, in that will is the determiner of "works to be made," and will may be willful in its response to the good of reality. So long as action is possible to intellect, it is not solely determined by will, indeed is fundamentally determined by the good of existence itself, a point which Milton's Satan had considerable difficulty with, since his intent was absolute evil.

As for the poet and his poem, one might wish to separate the role of goodness in art from art, especially moral goodness, which relates to the perfection of the soul. I do not think the separation possible at last, for art is an effect of a moral agent, man, whose nature affects his actions, whether those actions tend to perfection or away from perfection of his nature. Indeed, goodness is an aspect of all things perceived by intellect, whether intellect perceive the goodness or not. And insofar as intellect is in conformity to what things are, that function of intellect involves moral function, which is more immediately the province of speculative intellect, though the speculative and the practical cannot be absolutely divorced. For practical intellect is dependent upon speculative intellect, in that the knowing of things precedes the practical intellect's recognition that it knows. The artist as maker then is inescapably affected by the good of things, without which no making would be possible to him. And it is in this aspect of knowing the good that the question of the beautiful intrudes. If the poet does not recognize the dependence of the beautiful in the good, if in his obsession with the beautiful he "totally yields to his cherished demon," as Maritain says, he will become determined upon beauty as a thing caused by his intellectual obsession. We shall presently examine Shelley on this point, but must first remark something of beauty in relation to the good.

If beauty is that which, when seen, pleases, as St. Thomas says, then the beauty of the thing seen is somehow involved with the good of the thing seen. But here we may realize that one does not, as a matter of actual experience of things, see *beauty*. One sees a beautiful thing. Beauty as an indicator of thingness touches the truth of the particular thing, the essence whereby the beautiful thing is the thing it is. Beauty is not itself an essence, it is *of* an essence. To see the thing as it is, is to respond to its existence. To perceive the beauty of a thing is to perceive its wholeness. And insofar as it is, it is that far beautiful. This is a truth of things, whether the thing be a creature of nature or the poet or his secondary creature dependent in his own nature—that is, the poem. When we attempt to speak of the beauty of a thing, the poem, we find ourselves speaking in terms of order, proportion, clarity, aspects of things in themselves that satisfy a need in the soul. That is why it is not quite precise to conclude, as Maritain does, that "beauty, which is of no use, is radiant with intelligence and is as transcendent and infinite as the universe of intellect." The enthusiasm for beauty, though understandable, makes one somewhat uncomfortable, since it does not acknowledge that beauty as desired by the soul is intimately involved with both the true and the good. In addition, experience which returns one to reality shows that beauty is only infinite in God Himself. It is otherwise intrinsic to things in themselves. If finite intellect fails to recognize the intimate relation of beauty to actual existence, it will presently suppose beauty a gift intellect itself bestows upon being, from which deportment of intellect comes the conclusion that "beauty is in the eye of the beholder." Indeed so, but only in relation to the degree whereby the eye *sees* the truth in things, the being in things. Otherwise the poet will be led, as Wordsworth recalls was his early inclination, to "add the gleam,/ The light that never was, on sea or land,/ The consecration, and the Poet's dream." That, we shall contend, is the use Shelley would make of beauty, commanding beauty as a thing transcendent, then reducing it as servant to his own intellect by an intellectual sleight of mind.

If order and proportion signify a Beauty that is, with the intellect's admiration and courtship through language, that order and proportion must rest at last, and in an ultimate way, in an absolute, lest the concepts themselves be left merely floating in the air, tenuously attached to that intellect which has found for itself no firm ground in being. This is to say that if the "Beautiful" is merely sprung from intellect's primary assertion of the "True," which is an assertion as well that the "Good" is also determined by finite intellect, then intellect alone seems necessarily the primary cause of the good, the true, the beautiful. It creates for itself the desired, the known, the admired. And, lo, the object required: intellect itself as cause. But despair must be the final end of self-love. Narcissus may at first be captivated by the illusion of his own beauty, but the spiritually debilitating effect of *ennui* the most ancient and darkest of dragons waits upon him. Wallace Stevens came at last to concede the point at the end of his life by his conversion to Christianity, having spent a lifetime as poet denying all power over being except that of the poet's imagination, the "necessary angel" as he called it, an agent at finite intellect's command executing those "supreme fictions" as the only absolute. Eliot realizes the danger earlier than Stevens, and from "Ash-Wednesday" to the end treats as the central issue to intellect the contention of hope and despair for his soul, a contention in the soul of the "maker" who cannot escape the reality of his existence as properly resting in the image of the First Maker. If one were to put the recognition in Thomistic terms, one might say that Eliot recognizes as the poet's danger a temptation to a rivalry with the Holy Ghost over the power *to make*.[14]

The necessity of some source of Beauty beyond the poet's own absolute power to make a beautiful thing is fleetingly recognized by Keats, as his great Odes discover to us. The urn seems to echo an abiding Beauty and Truth, though those transcendents as transcendents are prevented from Keats's visionary power. They are prevented largely by the reduction of his flickering vision to rather desperate aphoristic shibboleth—words clasped in a moment of intellectual despair which crowds out the virtue of hope. Despair consequently makes dead ashes of his personal history, which by a forced imaginative act he prematurely scatters onto the static, teasing urn. He is trapped in a reduction of himself as person by the accidents of his immediate circumstances. Similarly, that moment of transport in another Ode in an English garden, that erratic flight by willed imagination as if on the nightingale's wings, stirs intellect to the border of a strange vision-held country which is suddenly lost. And because lost, that country is declared illusional, is declared a shadowy "thing" sprung from helpless daydreaming.

As if rebuking Keats's weak faith in art as saviour to the finite intellect, William Butler Yeats is adamant. Art is the one possible transport of finite intellect beyond the clutches of time. In "Sailing to Byzantium," Yeats insists that intellect by its own power of making, or by its power through a Keatsean negative capability to enter other poet's made things of art as vehicles of transport, may transcend its temporal and corporal entrapments. Keats's aphorism is thus certified as holy vision to the maker of things, though abandoned by Keats. Art, the "golden bird," transforms the natural bird and thereby becomes a timeless medium to transcendent reality. "Set upon a golden bough" beyond nature's decay, it sings a truth beyond "what is past, or passing, or to come" in the decaying world. Through its beauty, time's and space's seeming authority are reduced by a transcendent truth: the beauty of Idea—that old Platonic shadow concept that has haunted Western thought since the Renaissance in one guise or another. For Yeats, truth is the transcendent beauty of form faintly perceived through art, revealed as separate, self-subsistent forms beyond the ravages of temporal finitude.

Art, those artifacts strewn through history which Yeats in a memorable phrase calls "monuments of unaging intellect," thus solves for him history's enigma. Or so Yeats insists. But for Eliot as for Keats, Beauty must have primal cause more real and immediate to the world than an imagined or faintly remembered self-subsistent form among forms, even as it must be more real than an effect certified by the poet's assumed autonomous power of imagination in the making of monuments to itself. The truth of the soul's existence seems not sufficiently spoken to by art so conceived. Yeats's monuments therefore still leave in doubt for Keats and Eliot the makers of those monuments. One might, as maker, as well be sod to art's high estimate of transcendent truth and beauty, if truth and beauty are gnostically separated from the here and now of things through which intellect acts. In time and place, art if understood as by Yeats becomes at best but requiem for that collapsing sod, the poet. In brief, what is sensed as lost, as not rescued, is the *person*, the peculiar discrete maker, this poet whom the world knows yet awhile as John or Thomas Stearns or William Butler, even though by those names they are pinned to the wall of our common memory in time with their own piercing verse.

Of course some Romantic poets hold a quite contrary faith, as does Wallace Stevens. Order and proportion, this faith holds, are decreed effects through signs projected by the discrete intellect. Thereby intellect certifies its self-sufficiency in manipulation of the thing made, the poem, to a specific decreed end. If Wordsworth represents the first sort of Romantic, with Eliot a late companion to the position, Shelley does this self-sufficient intellect, with Wallace Stevens and Ezra Pound being late disciples of that position. One finds evidence to the point in Shelley's "Hymn to Intellectual Beauty," though the argument for appropriating autonomous power to intellect is perhaps better revealed in his "Ode to the West Wind." In that Ode, Shelley acts out what Eric Voegelin has called the modern gnostic intent to power over being. Says Shelley to the West Wind:

> Be thou, Spirit fierce,
> My spirit! Be thou me, impetuous one.

Thus the poet masters the West Wind by seduction, at least to his own satisfaction, for no poet may summon or control a Hurricane Hugo. Still, by intellectual presumption, Shelley assumes the role of director of the world's weathers, or would if only the rest of humanity would grant him that power and follow him in remaking the world.

Thus for Shelley a terrible beauty is born, of which he speaks in his "Hymn" as the "awful shadow of some unseen Power." It is a Power which consecrates "human thought and form," though it is a Power far removed from that orthodox agent of such consecration, the Paraclete. For what Shelley is about is the celebration of intellect itself. His holy power is understood as resident in autonomous intellect, coming to a fruition in his possession of it. It is a Power "which like the truth/ Of nature on my passive youth/ Descended, to be my outward life supply/ Its calm." This intellectual Power, whose effective operation creates "Beauty," is a conjured presence, not conjured *down*, despite Shelley's ambiguous *descended*, but *up* out of himself. One cannot read far in Shelley before discovering that his Platonism is borrowed as a strategy and relocated as if a universal participated in, by that voice which is projecting signs, projecting the poems. To acknowledge the Power as separate from the operative commands of his particular intellect, his particular commanding voice, soothes somewhat the popular mind in which there still resides a suspicion of such presumption to power, and particularly when presumed by the poet. (That is one reason the poet is the "unacknowledged legislator" of mankind, to recall the famous characterization by Shelley.)

As conjured up by Shelley, intellectual Beauty may be understood as derived from an inverted Platonism whereby the transcendent is reduced to immanent, a Poet whose vortex, issuing intellectual beauty into the world, is the poet and his word. To have said this is to be reminded of how close an intellectual kinship lies between Shelley and Ezra Pound in this respect. We remember as well that it is Pound who founds a movement superseding Bergsonian Imagism, a Bergsonian Vorticism. We note as well that this inverted Platonism is also a decayed species of the old Averroist projection of intellect as a substance common to all men while peculiar to none. Intellect thus granted as a universal unity, it will not follow that it is not manifested as peculiar, for the advocate of that principle will presume himself the significant vortical medium of Beauty or Power or whatever designation he may give the principle in whose name he justifies his own authority. The old Averroist modification of Platonic transcendentalism was refuted by St. Thomas long ago, but bad ideas have lingering consequences even when effectively refuted. St. Thomas had insisted *On the Unity of the Intellect Against the Averroists*. Intellect is particular in its unity to the discrete person, a refutation of Neo-Averroists like Siger of Brabant. The distinctions thus made in that old argument disallow our having it both ways: intellect cannot at once be a universal substance participated in and yet peculiar to the particular intellect advocating that position by its assumption of supreme authority over the principle. What Thomas establishes most emphatically is the responsibility of the particular intellect in respect to things intellectual. He was opposing a philosophical determinism decreed upon the discrete intellect.

The Averroist shadow, we might say, lingers in Shelley, though his deportment of argument for universal intellectual Power rather emphasizes not *universal* but *Shelley. Intellect*, like the *West Wind*, is reduced from the wider presence supposed of it as universal substance to its mastery in the vortex of Shelley's mind. We emphasize the point, since Shelley makes an accessible figure as modern gnostic, as a sort of modernist Everyman. He dramatizes the summoning of power by intellect to the purview of autonomous intellect, calling it "Beauty." In that procedure, the particular intellect establishes itself as beholden to no cause beyond its own summoning spirit. In Shelley's assumed authority, then, lies a sufficient justification to himself of the metaphors of attribution, which we witness in operation in "Ode to the West Wind." The West Wind, being *like* the conjuring poet by virtue of his assertion of correspondences, is reduced at last to *being* the poet. The conjurer's trick is accompanied by rising histrionics in the poem's rhetorical progress, in a skillful deployment of signs that once made it a very popular poem for public school recitation. Though this made thing, Shelley's Ode, does not strike one persuasively by the cogency of argument nor as a poetry transcending argument, it does bear a true witness to Shelley's gnostic intent to command power, and it is in this respect that it serves so well as a window upon modern gnostic manipulations of being.

14

Thought and the Suicide of the Self:
From Descartes to Dr. Kevorkian

> It is not all that easy to escape from reality, and the world had to
> wait for centuries before thought contemplated this form [Cartesian
> Idealism] of suicide.
>
> —Étienne Gilson, *Methodical Realism*

The prudent Romantic poet may in the end fear that metaphor is built
only by attribution, thus leaving the poet isolated not only from the transcendent, but also from the immediacy of creation itself, whereby the
potential of *person* moves toward perfections. Its monuments thus built
to celebrate unaging intellect against the despair of isolation may prove
but an effect of fancy, and therefore far removed from the truth which
intellect desires by its very nature. For mere metaphor of attribution
dooms art to fancy's province and so proves insufficient to the intuitive
desire to understand, a perfection of intellect beyond merely knowing.
Intellect, by understanding, might thus be both at home in its own mode
of existence as finitely particularized and additionally more comfortable
with being, with creation, beyond a walled-in autonomy that so much
depends upon metaphor of attribution as the defense of its autonomy.
For by building "supreme fictions" through attributive analogy, intellect
would deflect the intrusiveness of reality as understood Thomistically.

The prudent Romantic, then, may well detect a desperation in a Stevens
or a Joyce or Pound. Or in a Shelley, in whose words histrionics overwhelms poetry. Which is to say, overwhelms signs ordinately related to
the complexity of being itself as encountered in diverse creation when
there is a proper intensity of intellectual attention toward the mystery of
being as known through actual experience of creaturely existences. That
"knowing" is prelude to both conceptual knowledge and to artful articu-

lations of that knowledge. Of course being is not inaccessible to sign: it is only always larger than any concept's or sign's power to contain it through an aggressive presumption of power over it by concept or sign. Shelley exhibits such an excess, as in his "Hymn to Intellectual Beauty." But Keats to the contrary, in a rare moment of vision upon his intellectual limit, speaking of his desire for the faculty of negative capability, recognizes the necessity in that faculty: intellect must consent to exist "in uncertainties, Mysteries, doubts, without any irritable reaching after fact & reason." Intellect is forced by its limits as finite, in spite of its desire, to control that gift of power which Keats calls "negative capability"—the power to a harmony in being.

A species of Shelley's desperation is in the early Eliot, though without Shelley's rhetorical excess against uncertainty. Eliot at first modifies and, to a degree, governs his desperation through ironic detachment, but that irony increasingly turns sardonic, a symptom of a festering intellect. The sardonic reflects an increasing uncertainty in him until he must abandon irony altogether. We witness this change when we read his early poetry against his late poetry, his "Preludes" or "Love Song of J. Alfred Prufrock" against "Ash-Wednesday." Relatively late in his career as poet and critic, we find him recovering himself to a reconciliation with existence larger than the self self-loved which is so fearfully present in the early work. And he recovers through a Thomistic deportment of intellect, the self opened to being.

It is, but not incidentally, consequent to this change that Eliot reports his youthful infatuation with Shelley, whom he now finds intolerable. And along with this late excoriation of Shelley comes his recognition of kinship with Wordsworth and Keats, a kinship that all along has been incipiently present. Eliot's desire has stirred him increasingly toward the Good, the True, and the Beautiful through intuitive intellect, with a diminishing intent to control over them. Thus what he comes to value in Wordsworth and Keats is the presence of their person in the poetry itself, a presence reaching beyond that sheer rationally decreed intellectual autonomy as poetry which so easily burdens art with the merely autobiographical. The principle of intellectual autonomy, which comes to flourish in Western thought with the rejection of metaphysics, Eliot sees as portending spiritual cataclysm such as we ourselves witness pervasive of the intellectual community in our century, the chaos which leaves our intellectual community in disarray at century's end.

It is worth noting as more than an aside to this point that, as we lose the understanding of the *personal* which lies at the heart of Scholastic metaphysics, we become more and more obsessed with the vague ghost of the personal, given a name, the "self." And we observe that the literary genre of the autobiographical becomes dominant, the poet or novelist such as Eliot or Joyce feeling the strain of exorcising his "personal" history in the art, with less success than he desires. Eliot's personal experience of intellectual disarray, consequent upon his embracing modernist ideology, leads him to speak more and more in anticipation of our own pending disarray, after he has overcome an ideological possession by modernism through that exorcism of the "self" from the person through "personal grouses," such as his *Waste Land*. His forewarnings to our intellectual community are in both his *Four Quartets* and his prose. His changing perspective as critic is conspicuous in *The Use of Poetry and the Use of Criticism* (1933), in which lectures he emphatically rejects Shelley as Romantic and embraces Wordsworth and Keats.[15]

We may now recognize as Wordsworth's and Keats's problem the same one experienced by Eliot. Having accepted, if but passively, the reductionist view of intellect whereby intellect is separated from reality, intellect finds itself islanded. It becomes endangered by an overwhelming melancholy, the emotional effect of the soul's growing despair. For melancholy, chemical or physiological causes aside, is symptom of the soul's disorder.[16] In that uneasy circumstance of the soul as experienced by Wordsworth and Keats, we observe, they do not turn back to the "Dark Ages" in their best art. Each is rather concerned to satisfy an immediate hunger of intellect for its present moment in existence—a hunger to be reconciled to that which is not intellect itself but a current to intellect flowing through present circumstances. St. Thomas might say of this disturbing intimation to these poets of some immediate presence that the thing they encounter is a timeless abiding "thing," namely being itself, however much time-designated and determined it might appear to the encountering intellect. It is experienced in *this* time and in *this* place, and so appears to bear an aura of circumstantiality, as if it were ultimately designed by history. But what intellects in their varying particularities discover are rather hints of the ground of existential reality, treasured by memory. Intellect, by its proper operations through concept and sign, must reconcile itself to that knowledge precedent to concept, a knowledge lying in its memory and stirring a desire beyond event. For event itself is always time-trapped.

One understands how the poet, perhaps more than the philosopher, might become time-trapped in such a moment in which intellect finds itself at the border of vision. The absence from memory of the once known appears time-related, since what was present as a knowledge (so memory insists) is now seemingly absent or at best only partially present.

And even this present moment of knowing seems fading, grasped at by intellect through images but held only fitfully in memory as now already "one moment past." Such seem the conditions to memory. St. Augustine speaks tellingly to the relation of intuitive desire as supported by memory in his *Confessions*. The argument in his "A Philosophy of Memory" and "Time and Eternity" (Books 10 and 11) proved a rescue to Eliot in the "Romantic" dilemma of his intuition besieged by time, as they well might have done to Wordsworth and Keats under their own circumstantial labors.

The very finitudes of intellect thus seem to entrap intellect in history, seem to decree that memory in relation to desire dooms intellect to an entrapment by its own past as past event, weighting memory residually and seemingly preventing a present encounter with truth because of the dislocation of desire to its own history as its end, to time past and passing. It is this confused reduction of memory's office that both Keats and Wordsworth struggle to surmount, for they would escape history's entrapment, that graveyard of nature vividly in decay. And so each is in this respect *modern*, if we may wrest that term from its abuse and transform it to a deeper Thomistic dimension. If Thomistic realism is valid, its salient nature is that it is always modern, in that it is concerned most of all with this present moment of this particular, concerned soul. That soul by its concern is always presently vulnerable to the distortions of its realistic position, and most especially so if it fails to orient its inescapable attention to past or future by a return to an abiding present of being. That is the danger Eliot counters when he comes to see at last, with the help of St. Augustine, a dimension to memory larger than the limit of history.

> This is the use of memory:
> For liberation—not less of love but expanding
> Of love beyond desire, and so liberation
> From the future as well as the past.

Such is the "key" that both Wordsworth and Keats almost recover to the rescue of each of their persons person in a present moment bordering upon vision.

Eliot is surely right in praising Wordsworth as a great philosophical poet, since Wordsworth is intent upon the significant question: intellectual existence in its present circumstances. Wordsworth's concern is first for an epistemology that might rescue intellect from its isolation from reality and restore soul to a reality intuited in the present sensual moment. Surely Gilson is right, in *Methodical Realism*, to chide us for a modernist obsession with epistemology. But surely that is a concern to be anticipated once Cartesian Ideology has so generally separated intellect from reality. Happily, the soul is always attempting to come to terms with reality in this moment of its existence—in a presence of itself to being—whatever tangential uses it may make of time past, or passing, or to come. It can do so, it supposes, only if it regains a confidence in its capacity to know reality here and now, beyond the shadowing of knowledge by time. That is, in Eliot's term, the soul first and last (such is the burden of discursive intellect) seeks a *still point* in the turning world. In Wordsworth's less well-known term, it seeks a *spot of time*.

What these prudent Romantics, Wordsworth and Eliot, reach toward intuitively through such metaphor, attempting to put time in its subordinate relation to being, is a recovery to intellect of what we term Thomistic realism. They do so at the risk of melancholy, if not a deep despair, should they fail. Moved intuitively, the poet struggles to recover a knowledge of being beyond mere thoughts about being, however ill-equipped he may be as philosopher to do so, or however much he may think himself ill-equipped by the pervasiveness of Cartesian Idealism which thwarts common sense. We ought to note that actually this idealism in Western thought has been principal antagonist to the poet's recovery in community at least since the advent of Renaissance Humanism, a demarcation point recognized to a degree by the nineteenth-century Romantic himself, as evidenced by his attempt to return to the Middle Ages to recover, suspecting that it was there that we began wandering in the darkening woods of this world; a wandering sometimes led, sometimes followed by the poet. We might recall Pico della Mirandola's words in his *Oration on the Dignity of Man*, in which Pico puts words in God's mouth addressed to Man: "You shall determine your own nature without constraint from any barriers, by the means of the freedom whose power I have intrusted [to] you. . . . I have made you neither heavenly nor earthly, neither mortal nor immortal so that, like a free and sovereign artificer, you might mold and fashion yourself into that form you yourself shall have chosen." A sufficient license to the poet as freed artificer is implicit, and Pico here is prophetic of Joyce's Stephen Dedlaus.

And so it may be an irony suited to the amusement of a Socrates that our age, which so highly values its sophistications of intellect, is so much obsessed with the problem of epistemology. For that is a problem early to philosophical approaches to a metaphysics, whose analogy might perhaps be the child's wonderful awakening amid multitudenous existences, his struggling to keep straight the names of things. Eliot of course shared with his nineteenth-century predecessors—as do we all—a capacity of recovery to reality at first limited by inherited epistemological confusions. That is why he at last sees himself like the Romantics and not superior to them as he had at first supposed. For he comes to know all too well that the poet's and the philosopher's medium, the sign, much decayed from its authority as anchored in reality, proves increasingly uncertain in its manifestations. It is one consequence of idealist dislocations of thought. But uncertainty about knowing does not prove the uncertainty of that reality itself, toward which poet and philosopher reach through signs:

> Words strain,
> Crack and sometimes break, under the burden,
> Under the tension, slip, slide, perish,
> Decay with imprecision, will not stay in place,
> Will not stay still.

But that weakness in the sign, the word, does not now, in the *Four Quartets*, make the signified not to exist. The weakness of man's word does not deny the Word. And so we must, Eliot adds, despite our being caught "in the form of limitation/ Between un-being and being," move on toward our possible being, though handicapped in our "raid on the inarticulate" by the "shabby equipment always deteriorating." To do so is to continue undefeated, but only because "we have gone on trying."

It will never occur to the Thomistic realist, Gilson says, to make "thought the starting point of his reflections, because for him a thought is only possible where there is first of all knowledge." Such is the truth lost to Keats and to Wordsworth, leaving them threatened by thought as somehow an alien intruder into their true nature. Indeed it sometimes seems to them that thought intrudes as if an invading malignancy, reducing intuitive knowledge to an illusion. The truth which is held as knowledge out of an intellectual experience of being is thus obscured, leaving only an ephemeral "Beauty," faintly remembered from past experience, a forlorn means to rescue. As Keats puts the concern, here in this time and place we find that

> but to think is to be full of sorrow
> And leaden-eyed despairs.

The experience of being per se which is anterior to thought appears to thought itself as always "past," just how long past not the issue. Only its *pastness* seems of concern. Thus Wordsworth returns to his childhood in an attempt to solve the mystery of memory. Keats in the instance of his "Ode to a Nightingale" remembers a transport through the nightingale's song freed of thought's curse. But it *was* a moment, a past, though "but one moment past."

It is only by the wavering faith in "Beauty" that this illusive truth may be certified as having existed if one loses the experience of that truth which is the gift of being per se to intellect. It is a gift requiring no desperate certification by thought. What is required first of all is an open acceptance of that gift. But, alas for ephemeral Beauty, the ghost of truth! It is inadequate in that "Romantic" arrest to establish Truth. In an arrested perspective as divorced from reality—the recognition to the soul of its exile—Beauty cannot be itself established intellectually as resting in any Truth. And merely to interchange terms, to declare that "Beauty is Truth, Truth Beauty," is to bite the ashes of being, empty sign. Intellect is thus reduced to that Keatsean condition wherein *person*, either as poet or as man, "grows pale and spectre-thin and dies" toward the oblivion of non-existence, through having declared all existence illusional. That is Keats's personal prospect as a young man struggling to reconcile Beauty's fading attraction to intellect as he has experienced it in the world's conspicuous decay. It is also Gerontion's prospect as Eliot dramatizes this Keatsean dilemma in the "little old man" who speaks his poem, and in "Gerontion" Eliot is himself still endangered by despair.

A reconciliation of mind and heart, of rational and intuitive modes of intellect, is not satisfactorily made by assertion alone, by the will's forcing signs beyond their proper limit in a measure of reality by finite intellect, however strong the desire for reconciliation or how moving the words that would justify the unsatisfied desire in the user of words. Very soon after "Tintern Abbey," Wordsworth we noted experienced the shock of a death close to him, the death of a person who apparently at the moment of her death was approaching the age Wordsworth remembers as his own when "like a roe" he

> bounded o'er the mountains, by the sides
> Of the deep rivers, and the lonely streams,
> Wherever nature led.

Nature, through death, seems at last to have betrayed that child, despite her opening love for creation. The experience left the high sentences of "Tintern Abbey" empty, those that declare that "Nature never did betray the heart that loved her." The famous "Lucy" poems are in this respect a recantation of the argument of "Tintern Abbey," and after those poignant poems Wordsworth turns somewhat desperately toward a vague Platonism reflected in his "Ode on Intimations of Immortality from Recollections of Early Childhood." In that poem he attempts to go back earlier than the roe-like stage that had seemed visionary at the time of "Tintern Abbey." Such a visionary moment, he has now come to believe, was actually an illusion advanced through the trickery of thought. Lulled by thought's "remoter charm," thought's seeming separation of consciousness from reality (or so it now appears) he must now conclude himself to have been seduced into a "slumber" of spirit in which his intellect sojourned by being disjoined from waking reality.

That is the way Wordsworth puts it in those two moving quatrains beginning "A slumber did my spirit seal." In that slumber he had "had no human fears," since he saw "Lucy" then as a "thing that could not feel/ The touch of earthly years." Now she is a "thing" in quite another sense, being dead: a thing with no "motion . . . no force," who "neither hears nor sees" her loved things in nature. A pathos of loss in the words prevents self-excoriation, or even a direct recantation of those high, now seemingly empty, pronouncements recorded in "Tintern Abbey," though even in his lamentations Wordsworth cannot at last entirely reject the old memory of visionary moments. For in that recovery of emotional balance called the "Intimations Ode," itself heavy with illusional high sentences, he cries that loss as once real. This present May day world and a memory of other days in glad nature now speak to him only "of something that is gone."

> Whither is fled the visionary gleam?
> Where is it now, the glory and the dream?

Let us anticipate that the Wordsworthean gleam out of nature, the "glory" hallowing creation, will be spoken to more persuasively by a later "Romantic" poet, Hopkins. Meanwhile, it remained to Eliot to pick up Wordsworth's "Tintern Abbey" slumber in his opening gambit as anti-Romantic poet. Wordsworth had declared the "mind" a "mansion for all lovely form" and "memory . . . a dwelling place/ For all sweet sounds and harmonies." This metaphor Eliot gives a sardonic twist. Not a mansion, but a run-down tenement wherein are housed "a thousand sordid images" holding awareness itself hostage. It will not be until Eliot reaches the point of view upon reality reflected in "Ash-Wednesday" that he will be prepared to rescue from Wordsworth and from Keats their intuitive inclination of intellect which they allowed their "thought" to reduce from truth to illusion. And in that rescue intellect becomes enabled to move the soul beyond nature and history to see them "for the first time," the poet having learned at last both "to care and not to care."

In that movement which Eliot experiences, vision is a possibility to intellect in its pursuit of truth which is relatively independent of nature and history, a possibility through which the soul, through grace, may at any moment or in any place of its journey find light in its dark woods. Such is that "still point of the turning world" in which the world and history and time are "redeemed." Thus intuition restores a present vision, aided by memory but beyond a memory supposed limited by history, personal and general. Memory is thus no longer circumscribed by and reduced to the world, including that little world of the finite particular intellect seemingly confined and "peculiar and private" to itself as F. H. Bradley asserted of it. What is restored is a possibility of a present experience of reality through which the soul may recover its prospect upon timeless being: this *very* present, in which alone intellect ever sees truly the truth of things, sees into "the life of things," to quote again from "Tintern Abbey." In that recovery, intellect beholds all things sustained in being by their cause and proper end, each thing according to its given nature. Intellect, thus having made a journey from its pre-conceptual harmony with being, discovers itself possessed of a knowledge antecedent to its conceptual awakening which initiates its necessary journey toward the soul's proper end. It is enabled thereby to return, as Eliot has it, to the "place" from which it set out and "know the place for the first time." Such is the possible reconciliation of the soul to time and place, once it is freed of the entrapments of time and place. Then the soul may conclude that, in the words of Dame Julian and Eliot, "All manner of thing shall be well." For it will have learned how "to care and not to care."

It is in this circumstance of intellect, alive to being, that one may also conclude with Gilson that "the Good, the True and the Beautiful are in the fullest sense real, since they are simply being itself as desired, known and admired." As for the poet or philosopher, this new life of intellect depends for its proper feeding upon those correspondences discovered in existent things as proper to the thing in its own nature and limit, and not as an attribution *upon* the thing by intellect. For intellect can no longer maintain itself as dictator of the order of conception after such vision. Conception is anchored in reality, it now must admit, and not imposed by the willed desire for order by intellect. What is thus to be discovered are the limits of the truth of particular things within a community of being. It is here that significant metaphor at last must rest—*significant* signing of the thing's truth rather than *form* imposed by intellect upon the thing and declared the thing's truth by virtue of the intellect's imposition. Or so Thomistic realism holds. There must follow, from poet or philosopher, the obligation of his peculiar art whereby he recovers sign. He receives metaphor and analogy beyond the impatient inclinations to mere attribution. In brief, the labor is to recover sign as oriented by being itself, being as seen in the light of the concept of that proper proportionality whereby things *are* as they *specifically* are.[17]

That growth to intellectual liveliness requires no formulaic concept, though intellect may profit from concept prudently formulated, a necessity to intellectual community as distinct from the reflective and meditative harmony possible to the separate, distinct soul. Nevertheless, the end suitably issuing from communal intellect, from minds engaged in a common recovery of the meaning of the mind's journey in reality, a recovery on the soul's behalf, is a rediscovery of the meditative state suited to the solitary, though not lonely, intellect in its reflective journeying. This is to say that the discrete participant in intellectual community tends, intentionally if but tacitly so, toward a postconceptual harmony of soul such as contemplation sometimes allows the solitary soul. That is why St. Thomas sets contemplation as the intellect's highest office. Intellect moves toward contemplation through metaphysical reflection, aided by such rationalized pursuit of a metaphysical vision as St. Thomas's "principle of proper proportionality" designates.

In the end, each of us is "Romantic," whether poet or philosopher, and may be strengthened in our intuitive journey, through which in the end we return to the place from which we set out intellectually. Return to a recognition that intellect possesses knowledge as a gift from an initial and initiating experience anterior to the movement of intellect through concepts. That recognition justifies, in a Thomistic sense, the journey, accommodating the will to knowledge as always to an unself-warranted gift to intellect. One of the immediate ways of strengthening intellect on its journey is to turn to St. Thomas's *On Being and Essence*. The poet will find there a protection against the temptation to constitute his awareness as a little world revolving either arrogantly or helplessly on the uncertain axis of his own self-awareness, as it seemed to do to Wallace Stevens and Eliot at their setting out. Nor will he feel justified by the illusion of autonomy, as if freed by awareness of all worlds other than the signing self, supposing the self thereby empowered to reconstitute being by attribution. That, we suggested, proved an irresistible temptation to Joyce and Stevens and Pound as poets, about which each had second thoughts later.

If we fail to determine this proper point for intellect's embarkation, we shall be endangered by an illusional state of mind whereby thought attributes being to the intellect as being's causal agent. To make that error is to find in our signs only a reflection of our lone self, an intolerable company to keep in the increasingly isolated state. In that isolation, intellect finds itself more and more separated from the inexhaustible wonder of that encompassing being through which one properly makes his way toward the end of a perfection of his gift, an end which the Fathers and Doctors call Beatitude. Failing that drawing of our intuitive inclination to its proper end, one can hardly escape the despair that threatens Keats, "where but to think is to be filled with sorrow and leaden-eyed despair." Joyce at the end feared himself misled by himself. He feared that as maker he had succumbed to *fancy* over the gift of liberating *imagination*. Pound, in the final fragments of his *Cantos*, feels forced to confess, "I am not a demigod,/ I cannot make it cohere" and to call for "A little light, like a rushlight/ to lead back to splendour." *Splendour* here seems to touch, whether intended by Pound or not, on Wordsworth's lament over having lost that "splendour in the grass," that halo of presence in being which is beyond the power of attribution.

Symbol, sign, has for a hundred years and more gradually turned mirror of the self, rather than a window opening the self to reality. For the most part, our poets, however much entrapped by confusions out of Cartesian Idealism (a generic term we have said, and not a historical one), continue disquieted by the entrapment in their own signs. That is why our age in its letters has been the Age of Melancholy, the Age of Alienation from being, the Age of Emotional Pathos. Such is a state of intellect little propitious to the highest prospects of art's celebrations of "Beauty." Our "Romantic" poetry nevertheless, even in its failures, bears witness to a truth to be pondered beyond Beauty's allure. It bears witness to the timeless, continuing hunger in intellect that always stirs it toward recovery of a key to open intellect to reality, both to its own reality and to the diversity of that modernist philosophical mystery, the Other. For intuitively it knows its disturbing isolation from the Other and knows thereby that it is less as a Self.

That opening may at last issue upon the transcendent as intellect's proper *causal* end no less than its *giving* beginning. Such is, I believe, always the proper "future" of Thomism, which is not a future of temporal implication but a present still point in which the soul is reconciled to time past, passing, and to come. In such still points come visionary glimpses of an abiding Presence, which Eliot came to speak of as the "Word in the desert." Those glimpses, which are knowledge understood (however limited that knowledge and that understanding by intellectual finitudes) are a glimpse of the reality of that Cause of intellect and of its journeying. We may well say *glimpse*, rather than *vision*, for such is our impatience that vision seems to promise a continuing rest of the intellectual eye upon truth. St. Thomas might well remind us that it is given only to the Eye holding all creation to rest in vision, in what is metaphorically an unwavering and everlasting "seventh day." Intellect, then, is granted only glimpses of that Presence, from Whom all things have (as Eliot saw of those roses in a garden at Burnt Norton) the look of things that are looked at beyond our limited sight. Granted only such glimpse of being seen as we struggle to see, as struggle we must. Only in this unrest we may be content to rest while journeying. Thus one may, as Eliot found necessary, be at once "still and still moving." Or, in Keats's version, one may find himself "being capable of being in uncertainties, Mysteries, doubts," content in *knowing* if not fully *understanding* that all manner of thing shall be well at last.

15

The Still Point: A Light in Reality

"The apprehended" is the extrinsic already inside the intrinsic, whereas the intellect tends directly, intentionally, towards the object as it is in itself and not as it is in us. . . . Scholastic realism does not rest on metaphysical reasoning. . . . [It cannot because between] one kind of contigent being and another there is always a metaphysical gap due to the analogy of being. . . . [T]he only solution is to admit, as experience suggests, that rather than the subject finding its object through an analysis of knowledge, it discovers its knowledge, and itself, in the analysis of the object.

— Étienne Gilson, *Methodical Realism*

We have explored, in various ways, the poet's problem in maintaining a confidence in the reality of his own intellect in relation to the reality of that which is not his intellect. It is a complication to his thought in consequence of his apprehending the Other through his senses, though given the dark seed of doubt he will question apprehension itself. Common to the "Romantic" poet as we have tried to discover him in his poetry is a desire which, in its initial manifestations in his poetry, he again and again associates with light, or with a glowing, and very often that light he at least supposes to be, not an attribution figuratively made but a recognition of a reality perceived in things. It leads Hopkins to declare, for instance, that "The world is charged with the Grandeur of God" that flames out. Such is the visionary moment to the poet, but it is not a moment easily sustained, so that in his struggle with thoughts about the visionary event, about the sufficiency of signs to thought or thought to event, he wavers. He will then propose possibilities to that light, concerned with whether it ever was on land or sea or in things, as Wordsworth comes to wonder.

Is the light bestowed by intellect upon things? Is it bestowed upon intellect out of things? Is the vision a mutually complementary bestowal in an event, whereby, as Wordsworth has it in "Tintern Abbey," intellect half perceives and half creates? But underlying all of these speculative questions about intellect's awed response to the Other is the darkest question of all: whether the light is but illusion, an afterglow of spent intellect, which is itself destined to oblivion and so caught by desperation in a wishful desire of light, even a "little light, like a rushlight/ to lead back to splendour," as Pound asks for in Canto CXVI. And since Wordsworth proves such a central subject to our Thomistic perspective upon these questions as they trouble the Romantic poet, and "Tintern Abbey" a poem central to his own difficulties, we might look somewhat more closely at that poem. For him, it became evidence of his own slumber of spirit soon after he made it. It may well be that, though we have argued it a poem reflecting his having come to the borders of a Thomistic realism, the poem itself reveals why he could not cross into that country.

Let us begin by recalling some of our earlier exploration. We made a considerable point about our common moments of wonder in response to things, those moments when a light larger than intellectual light seems operative in experience. We cited the particular instance of the small child's encounter with a litter of rabbits as an initiation of her intellectual experience of the Other. It is a moment in which self-awareness is submerged. It is a moment, I would have it, of love perfected, a visionary moment effected by an openness, though as love perfected it may not be sustained. There must follow a falling away, and the falling initiates intellectual action, a consequence I suggest as inevitable to man in his fallen nature. But I would urge that such moments are not given to the child alone in the presence of small creatures, nor to the youth bounding by rivers and up steep mountains. They are moments we each experience so long as we are in life, and even when we do not recognize the moment as visionary. There is wonder often enough. We experience the thing in itself and "Ah! This thing *is*!" There lies a wakened watching, which even affects those who but witness others so waking, as I witnessed my granddaughter's response to those rabbits.

I have also suggested that there is at least an analogous relation of such moments to what we think of as prelapsarian relation of intellect to being, in that in the moment there lies an openness allowing love perfected. That is the sense of his own experience which Wordsworth describes in his poem as that of "seeing into the life of things." But since such a moment cannot be sustained, thought itself attempts to regain the moment, initiating a falling away into self-awareness, an awareness of the self as having been interrupted in a visionary union. We should note, in relation to Wordsworth's "Tintern Abbey," that it is at precisely this point that his Keatsean doubt intrudes. For no sooner has he testified to having experienced the "life of things" than there suddenly intrudes a fragment, never completed: "If this be but a vain belief. . . ." Was it a vision or a waking dream? Such is the undercutting doubt, which Wordsworth then sweeps aside on the authority of thought itself. And it is at this point in the poem that the experience along the banks of the Wye becomes imperiled.

The danger here, as Gilson says of it, is that thought may itself replace the reality. "The fact that everything is given me in thought in no way permits me to assert that everything is reducible to thought." Nor is that thought itself sufficient to establish and certify reality. For if thought supercedes response, becoming the center of the reality for intellect, then by that very centering, intellect can but be increasingly removed from the arena of reality, separated unto itself. That is the direction idealism takes, leading Gilson to observe of it that "the order and connection of ideas replaces the order and connection between things . . . . [I]dealism can justify everything with its method except idealism itself." Idealism allows, as Gilson says in its praise, a perfect system. The difficulty with such a perfect system, he then adds, is that it is a closed system, removed from reality. Thus its completion is out of the temptation to substitute thought for the object of thought. Thereby thought becomes the isolated object. It is in disappointments out of such turning that intellect will turn upon thought itself as having betrayed it. Thought may thus be declared somehow an alien intruder, as it seems to Keats. Thought in intellect thus appears like a virus in sinuses. One knows the experience of such infections, as when we say we are left in a fish bowl, submerged from our usual activities. It is a physical state sometimes like dream-waking. It is, in respect to thought as the center of being, like a "slumber" of spirit, such as Wordsworth will declare his own intellectual isolation. His attempt at a recovery to the world of *being* is only an exacerbation of the condition because of his embracing an unexamined Platonism. Thought in relation to reality, in his "Intimations Ode," reveals the thinker very much in a fish bowl set apart from reality, and that thinker is aware of it himself, trying by Platonic terms to break free.

That Wordsworth cannot break free is evident, for reasons Gilson speaks of in our present epigraph concerning the gap in metaphysical reasoning between intellectual creature and the thing it would apprehend, even should that thing be yet another intellectual creature. The solution, the epigraph suggests, is the admission that intellect discovers itself and its knowledge through an analysis of the object and not by an analysis of its own thought. This attaches to that other observation fundamental to Thomistic realism: knowledge precedes thought, out of the experience of things. These observations serve admirably to enlighten for us Wordsworth's struggle to recover a knowledge he can but vaguely recall as a possession of his intellect, and we may discover him turning *from* that knowledge as possessed to his *thoughts about* that knowledge as the center of his concern.

In "Tintern Abbey" Wordsworth explores memories of past experiences in relation to this present experience, all the experiences having in common his own specific presence as an awareness. It seems, then, that time itself is the variable. A proper issue of his thought's attempt to understand itself is obscured for him by a confused understanding of image in the mind, image now divorced from that reality experienced which was the cause of image in the mind. Through image, a past experience is brought into conjunction with present experience, but that present experience is already internalized by reflection and, after the poem's opening lines, less and less anchored in the actual experience in this place. We might observe that the poem as poem has a certain intended unity, signalled by the deliberate return in the concluding lines to the images initiated at the opening. But the actual place, both at the beginning and the end, lacks concreteness such as must have been sensually registered. We note the important words in the conclusion are those attached to the nouns, words heavy with connotation of thought's priority in elevating event. He speaks of "these *steep* woods and *lofty* cliffs,/ And this *green pastoral* landscape." The arena of the event proves to have been within the intellect. The observation by intellect is dominantly of its own thought. There is, then, an undeniable "slumber" of spirit out of the actualities of the event accomplished by poem's end. By thought, Wordsworth is removed from the actual.

Through image held in mind, a past experience is brought into conjunction with an image held in mind out of a present experience. The images are submitted to thought in an action which seems effectively to put aside the intrusive doubt, "If this be but a vain belief." The images in mind are for Wordsworth virtually a palpable residue of experience, almost as if truth when known literally weights the mind. He is unable to break free from inherited imputations upon intellect which decree it an isolated autonomy which commands image as a possession peculiar to itself. For such is the philosophical bequest to Wordsworth from Descartes through Locke and David Hartley. Thus image is seen to linger as a residue of experience, insufficiently modified as a knowledge of truth as maintained through the offices proper to memory. Consequently, Wordsworth is unable to accommodate thought to knowledge as knowledge is properly refined and ordered by thought, as opposed to being *caused* by thought. We see evidence of his difficulty in the projected signs of the poem, some of them emphasized by the text in his attempt to recover reality to intellect, and the emphasis begins early in the poem.

Wordsworth asserts that "forms" come into the mind out of and through sensual experiences of the external world, through experiences in "nature." And those forms "so inform/ The mind that is within us, so impress/ With quietness and beauty, and so feed/ With lofty thoughts" that one is raised beyond the threat of any evil thereby. In respect to intellectual actions as recorded by words, we might remember that Wordsworth reports his poem composed immediately out of the experience. The lines are ordered in his head as he walks on from the noonday experience toward lodging for the night. The composed words are set down on paper that evening. What is of continuing importance to Wordsworth is the actuality of thought, of which the set words are historical witness—to which he may return as bearing an immediacy which memory unaided by the words might not recover. It seems certain that Wordsworth, considering the skillful rhetorical strategy of his thought as controlled by blank verse, is attempting to recover feeling to the present necessity of thought. He is attempting to heal that "dissociation of the sensibilities" that Eliot subsequently made famous in our criticism, the "separation of thought and feeling" within his own mind. Such words as *inform*, *impress*, and *feed* by their emphatic position at the end of lines strain somewhat under the burden of the attempt to force them to an actuality beyond mere metaphor of attribution.

There is an attempt at an underlying literalness, almost physical imposition of palpable image upon the mind, which one finds as well in his *Prelude*. There he remembers his youth: "Fair seed-time had my soul, and I grew up/Fostered alike by beauty and by fear." It is such a time as that remembered in "Tintern Abbey" when

> more like a man
> Flying from something that he dreads, than one
> Who sought the thing he loved.

Terms like *seed-time* and *inform* and *impress*, then, seem an attempt to catch a lingering *sense* impression seemingly palpably to the mind, a continuing effect upon the mind "Felt in the blood, and felt along the heart." Such is the blow, now faintly perceived, whose perpetrator is not recognized, though requiring a naming beyond such a vague term as *nature*. It is a touching of mind by something personal but not one's own mind itself. It occurs through the body, both within and outside the body. The agent is "something" he now affirms with the aid of thought, a something "deeply interfused" in all creation.

Those "wild ecstacies" of his roe-like youth are now subdued into a "sober pleasure" through the offices of thought, which summons out of memory those past events into a presence as thought. But Wordsworth is caught in a linear time, in a growing up whose progress is designated by lapsing years. He thus argues that one must absorb experience in youth, as if intellect were a sponge but a sponge for once only, in youth. At that stage of mind's growth, mind is unhampered by the necessity of that thought which will settle upon it with age. And so it is then in youth capable of an immediacy to existence whereby mind becomes *in-formed* by images through a mystical immediacy to things. There is a correspondence between mind and that which is not mind which will never be the same again once thought becomes mind's necessity. Visionary moments seem possible only to the "growing boy," who at that point hovers between "thoughtless youth" and thought-full manhood. Past that halcyon point, one must surrender to thought. After that surrender, vision lingers only through the grace of memory.

In "Tintern Abbey," then, Wordsworth re-experiences by thought an event now five years past, an event he remembers to have experienced in this same place on the banks of the River Wye. What now troubles him is that he is not in this present moment aware of an immediacy to things as in that old moment when freed of thought's necessity. He is still willing to believe, however, that perhaps somehow beneath the level of conscious thought a correspondence between his mind and present things may be occurring. And as he turns to his sister Dorothy, he is encouraged to believe from the evidence of her response that a "something" permeating all existence is itself steady in its attempt to enjoin correspondences. Dorothy, incidentally, is a presence to the poem who up to this late, unexpected turning (line 112 of the poem's 159 lines) has not been suspected by a reader, and it is almost as if the speaker has himself forgotten her presence. That the speaker is himself the paramount presence to his thought is further indicated by Wordsworth's later remarking the "elegiac" mood of the poem, its concentration upon himself in whom his own youth seems but a faint memory of a now dead self. Wordsworth turns to Dorothy at an anxious moment and sees in Dorothy's eyes evidence of her present receptive state, suggesting that her experience now is very like his once was, though now only remembered. The two share a present experience of the same world, but not in the same manner nor to the same effect. As he was, so she now seems. The difference he recognizes seems to doom Wordsworth further to a linear perspective upon intellectual growth, and so further entraps him in history. For those remembered "spots of time" wherein time seemed transcended in vision are forever lost, to be treasured in memory by thought. Thought is itself (it now seems) the present experience, nor does it allow any sense of mind as caught up in a "spot" out of time.

We have already spoken of a passage in St. Augustine, in relation to Eliot's concerns, which also bears analogy to Wordsworth's on this point. St. Augustine's "Vision at Ostia," we remarked, precedes his extended consideration of the nature of memory, which is next followed by an extended consideration of the relation of time to eternity. Those extended considerations follow from his account of his having experienced a "still point" or a "spot of time" at a visionary moment. St. Augustine is able to turn from his visionary moment toward eternity, remembering the moment's vision but not memorializing it as if himself trapped in time by the event recalled. The vision as vision is his concern, and not the circumstances. That is, where Wordsworth will define the poem in his title by the historical data, St. Augustine turns to the meaning of the vision, to the soul in respect to the soul's proper end. There is nothing of the elegiac about his recollections, though he clearly remembers it with delight.

Wordsworth had no sooner finished his "Tintern Abbey" than he sees in it the elegiac, tempted to put that term in his title. The elegiac note Wordsworth finds is in the poem, and we discover it at this very juncture, where the moment's vision seems dissolved by the fading of the present moment. It is the same sense of event memorialized, though less pronounced, that we find in Keats's Odes. For both these poets continue time-trapped. The same is a danger which Eliot recognizes, as we may witness in his verbal attempt to escape it in the opening lines of *Burnt Norton*. These convoluted lines, so challenging to explication, may yield their dramatic effect more immediately perhaps as a struggle against time's entrapments, which issues into the present moment of the "rose-garden" in a present, freed of time's webs laid in memory to catch the intellect. Compare the dramatic strategy here to that in Prufrock's fog passage, the speaker there intending an entrapment of the "you," as the speaker in *Burnt Norton* is rather struggling against a similar entrapment, though the web that almost holds him is spun of fine abstractions about time. It is only when intellect effects an escape from the intricate web which it has itself built with concepts of time that it finds itself at last in the actuality of a rose garden, released from such matters as time which with itself intellect too much discusses, too much explains, as Eliot came to see in "Ash-Wednesday."

Wordsworth is at last inclined to accept, and to try to be comforted by, past event as actual, held now in memory. He is unable, as St. Augustine is, to explore beyond memory. For memory is that aspect of the gift of intellect which, when properly understood, becomes the very instrument to intellect whereby it is enabled to move out of time. At least—so Wordsworth would seem content to maintain at last—at least the past event was actual, which means that this present event is actual, and from that knowledge I can reassure Dorothy of the reality of her own present experience. I can assure her that in some sense this present reality will accompany her in time beyond this moment. For surely the sparkling light in her eyes witnesses to him here and now an event not only certifying the validity of his own memory as bearer of past event, but also providing evidence that she will carry this present experience in her mind as a memory. The memory he has summoned to this present event is at least dependable in this respect. Thus desire may not be simply nostalgia for the old self but a desire for a relation to existence which the old self seems to have experienced. That possibility seems very nearly certified empirically by Dorothy's response. This recognition by thought stirs the thinker emotionally and in that degree makes the past experience a present value to thought. Since her eyes speak so much of his own earlier emotional state, now five years past, and since she is five years younger than he at this moment, then surely memory is dependable. The past experience as remembered was real and not merely a present wishful thinking. In turn, that must certify an abiding reality in the conjunction of mind and nature at some point, held together by a "something" deeply interfused in both. There nevertheless remains a disturbing sense that things to the mind are not now as they were of old. But the change must be in his own mind and not in nature itself, as witnessed by Dorothy's roe-like response to their present mutual experience. One notices a seed of doubt already present in "Tintern Abbey" that will grow into uncertainty for Wordsworth: he cannot by thought witness himself, know himself at this moment as participating in a reception of form as be believes Dorothy to be doing on the evidence of the "wildness" of her eyes. Thought separates him from intuitive knowledge, though Dorothy seems not prevented.

That doubt does not at the moment overwhelm Wordsworth, though thought itself, like words, may slip, slide, decay with imprecision. Against thought's uncertainty, he celebrates this present moment. He assures his dear companion that her present experience will sustain her in future years, when she too must resort to the thought as a defense against any growing doubt. But the way in which Wordsworth puts his assurance introduces again the Keatsean fear. He does not say to Dorothy that perhaps five years from now she may not have him beside her but will nevertheless be sustained by her memory of this moment. Rather, "If *I* should be where *I* no more can hear/ Thy voice, nor catch from thy wild eyes these gleams/ Of past experience . . . ." (my italics) The urn of your mind, impressed by nature will remain. But what of the poet or philosopher saying these words now if he be dead then?

16

Things as They Are
Versus the Poet's Blue Guitar

Since knowledge presupposes the presence to the intellect of the
thing itself, there is no reason to assume, behind the thing in thought,
the presence of a mysterious and unknowable duplicate, which would
be the thing of the thing in thought. Knowing is not apprehending a
thing as it is in thought, but, in and through thought, apprehending
the thing as it is.

—Étienne Gilson, *Methodical Realism*

Wordsworth's mind as a mansion for all lovely form will receive ironic
commentary in Eliot's "Preludes," which shows the mind more nearly a
run-down tenement house inhabited by a "thousand sordid images."
Such is the inevitable decay, one might anticipate, if the intuitive heart
that loves nature would but be innocent of a necessary modulation of that
intuitive love by the rational intellect. For the *ratio* orders intellect in
relation to actualities, to the limits of being, in relation to the finitudes
prescribing existing things. That structure of reality requires of intellect a
metaphor grounded in proper proportionality as opposed to attributive
metaphor, if it is not to mislead itself. For Wordsworth, there is not a
sufficient perspective upon the failure of a being from its potentiality, and
so no prospect upon the problem of evil. And yet evil proves inescapable
to Wordsworth. Its consequences as fear, pain, and grief cannot be
avoided, he concedes, but they are assuaged by form supplied by nature
and stored in memory against such fateful moments, to be used as spider
webs upon open wounds as it were. The fund of images out of recollections of adolescent joy in nature are good forms in mind, acquired by a
loving heart, and so sufficient to alleviate future wounds. Sordid experiences may come, but their source is the city of man, which Wordsworth
approaches at the level of its present existence, the squalid London of

1800. What is not addressed is the implication that the sordid city, the proximate cause of sordid images, must somehow have origin in man's mind, since it is the city of man. Failing this pursuit by thought, Wordsworth is quite unprepared for that event, the particulars of which are not quite certain in his history. One knows it as the death of a young person, memorialized in the "Lucy" poems, a someone assumed by Wordsworth to have had a loving heart toward nature but to have been cut down before blossom time, in and by nature, not in the city. It wakes Wordsworth from that "slumber" of "spirit" reflected in "Tintern Abbey," in which state he had "had no human fears." Now that dead person is seen from a state of mind arrested by shock as a "thing," mechanically "Rolled round in earth's diurnal course,/ With rocks, and stones, and trees."

That is a shock from which Wordsworth never sufficiently recovers, though there is that weak attempt at accommodating evil in the "Intimations Ode." That poem borrows a Platonism to take the place of the Aristotelian perspective on nature that introduces "Tintern Abbey." That is, "Tintern Abbey" quite clearly finds that it is through the senses responding to external objects that mind becomes harmonized to corporeal existences through the corporeal body, a point generally overlooked by critics who would declare Wordsworth Platonic too early. It is through, and only through, his "corporeal frame" brought into a harmony with nature's corporeal existences that in moments of vision he has been able to "see into the life of things." Inadequate to the requirement of thought out of such knowledge, to "thinking" as the means of organizing such visionary knowledge of being, as Gilson might put it, he is unprepared to deal with this antithesis to order, the manifestation of which is the death of that young girl at her blossom time. As there had been a turning to the natural world with innocent zeal in "Tintern Abbey," despite the warning stirred in thought that there has occurred a significant change in the relation of intellect to experience, so now there is a turning with some desperation to the transcendent, away from the existential world. Wordsworth is still in pursuit of an epistemology adequate to experience, an experience now intolerable. Gilson reminds us that "the object of epistemology is not *thought*, which is only the consciousness of an act of knowledge, but *knowledge* itself, which is the grasp of an object." All realism, he adds, "implies an analysis of knowledge; all idealism derives from the analysis of a thought." Because of his emphasis on thought as opposed to knowledge in "Tintern Abbey," Wordsworth was unprepared to deal with the certain knowledge of death out of the immediacy of experiencing the death of "Lucy." In "Tintern Abbey" an undeniable change implies impermanence, but by juxtaposing past experience to present experience,

Wordsworth concludes that "Nature" does not change. It is only his own mind that has changed. In the "Intimations Ode" he is still attempting to come to terms with change, but now he must admit that Nature is no longer the steadying medium to mind he had thought it. "Whither is . . . sped" that "visionary gleam" once seen in Nature and celebrated as a "life of things" earlier? The old "Splendour in the grass" seems now lost forever, through no fault in himself that he can name.

And so Wordsworth seizes upon a ready Platonic solution, though it is significant that he is able to do so only after a hiatus of two years, following those famous lines that conclude his fourth stanza lamenting the loss of that "visionary gleam" in Nature, "the glory" in it and "the dream" in him from which he is now disturbingly wakened. The halo in nature, the "glory," is but the light of ordinary day upon a shadow world. The "Nature" so beloved as rescue of intellect in "Tintern Abbey" has now become antagonist. We might compare the dramatic structure of those first four stanzas of Wordsworth's "Ode" to that in Keats's "Ode to a Nightingale." Treating those stanzas as if a poem, remembering that it will be two years before Wordsworth completes the "Ode," we discover an arresting parallel. The question in each is virtually the same, expressed by Keats in relation to a present moment just passing from the immediacy of experience, the moment when transported by the bird's song. Wordsworth's lines address a past moment of experience as well, now held vaguely by the memory of his own past experience through nature. If the dramatic parallels, the rising and falling actions of thought tensionally developed, in the two are similar, however, the significant difference lies in Keats's sense of having been transported beyond nature, while Wordsworth's is a sense of having entered into nature through the senses only to become entrapped by time. It is as if, by the time of his "Ode," he is decided that his understanding of that experience reflected in "Tintern Abbey" was in error, leading to an entrapment of intellect in the world, which has closed more and more about him until this shocked awakening. Was that experience of a "Splendour in the grass" a vision or a waking dream?

What our juxtaposition allows first of all is our underlining of Wordsworth's forced solution by his borrowed Platonic Idealism to the intrusion of a death close at hand. Through that borrowing, Nature now becomes the cause of all evil to the soul. His new beginning, stanza five, sets out with conclusion, with an assertion beyond reflection or meditation: "Our birth is but a sleep and a forgetting." The "slumber" that sealed his spirit in Nature, from which he is waked by Lucy's death, is now seen to have begun at birth. It deepens so long as the "Soul" is entrapped in the body and by the world called Nature. Death is thereby declared birth, as birth was a death into the shadow world of Nature. It is a solution applied out of thought's desperation. And the desperation is suggested not only by bold assertion unexamined but by stylistic devices as well, especially the heavy capitalization of terms. Thus we have Creature, Tree, Child, Bird, and so on, a stylistic device not encountered in "Tintern Abbey," nor, I think, sufficiently accounted for as the formality one might expect of the "Ode" as a form, nor the general practice in nineteenth-century typography. Such difficulties of solution aside, what we still must recognize—what Eliot recognizes in his new discovery of kinship with Wordsworth by the time of "Ash-Wednesday" and the "Ariel Poems"—is the continuing stir of intuitive intellect in Wordsworth in its attempt to escape Cartesian closure. If Wordsworth in some desperation seizes upon Platonism, he is attempting to escape from the despair of the self as closed upon itself.

Here, then, is the perennial problem to intellect, leading to its oscillation to extremes out of the fulcrum point of this present moment. It discovers its seeming isolation and would leap beyond entrapment through a desperate turning from the self. But, alas, reality holds fast, however tenuous the skein anchoring the leaping soul. In recent intellectual history, from Pascal to Kierkegaard to Eliot let us say, we find our philosophers struggling with the problem of this excessive agitation in intellect, to which Wordsworth succumbs on the evidence of his "Ode on Intimations of Immortality from Recollections of Early Childhood." Not recollections as of five years ago ("Tintern Abbey"), but recollections of that point nearest birth so far as memory may approach that point. It is as if by that retreat Wordsworth would gain a running start for his leap out of the present moment, which is always the inescapable starting point—a leap beyond time and place, beyond any "point" which may anchor soul to its immanent being. Thus the illusion: a dream of a leap beyond actuality, borne on the wings of Platonic Idealism in Wordsworth's late attempt. But the "fancy," Keats says, cannot cheat so well as some poets claim it can, a claim made out of either their desperation or their comfort in isolation. In the event, the soul seems always thrown back into the actual moment in which it seems tethered beyond escape. By such recovery to the moment, it is endangered again and again by that excessive burden upon intellect out of its failure, that burden called *melancholy*. Melancholy is the shadowy burden upon intellect cast by the spectre of aloneness. And, lacking the power either to light that shadow or to enlighten it by intellect in the limit of its own power, the shadow may deepen about the past. Is it not valid to say that, as a generalized observation, it is usually the most "intellectual" among us who seem most susceptible to melancholy? For, again and again, we discover that intellect in and of itself lacks a rescue through that superadded light of intellect which St. Thomas speaks of, a light to which one must be open intellectually. Without the gift of that light, ours to refuse, one is repeatedly reduced to one's "sole self."

In the refusal of such light, intellect turns toward extremes. But it is not the desire itself that is the cause of excessive turning, the swinging from the thread of reality holding intellect in arcs out of its immanent, finite being. The problem is intellect's address to its desire through will. And the response may be made, as we illustrate with Wordsworth's "Ode," as if intellect could bypass *being* itself and thereby rescue the soul to Beatitude by its own agency. That was Dante's initiating action in the *Divine Comedy*, in which we distinguish the Agent Dante from his maker, the Poet Dante. We see that pathetic figure, Dante the Agent, in some panic, moving out of the dark wood in which he has begun to awake. He climbs the mountain, running directly toward the sun. As fictive pilgrim, imitating the actions of our intellectual nature, he has the advantage over us actual pilgrims: his creator Dante has already gone through the spiritual quest, seeing the necessity of the soul's turning back. Dante the Pilgrim is intent upon the rescue of sunlight, so that a sequence of rebuffs must turn him back down the mountainside: a playful leopard, succeeded by a fiercer lion, giving way to an insatiable, ravenous "She-Wolf," the combined effects at last turning the pilgrim back. But that desperate Pilgrim Dante, we must note, does not go back into the dark woods. His progress, even that through Hell, is an advance upon the mountain in Dante the Poet's clever turning of *down* into *up*. St. John of the Cross provides a mystical analogue to that journey Dante makes so palpable in *The Divine Comedy*. Eliot, lessoned by St. John's *Dark Night of the Soul* and by Dante, and by St. John's Gospel as well ("In the beginning was the Word . . ."), leaves his own testimony to the necessity of our returning to the point from which we set out, this present moment and this present place of the soul. That return is more complex in its meaning, of course, than when we understand it superficially, as if we should ask why, given the conclusion of Eliot's *Little Gidding*, he did not return to Harvard or even to St. Louis, Missouri.

St. Augustine, too, dramatized that necessity of a return after vision in his account of that vision he and St. Monica experienced at Ostia (*Confessions*, Book 9, Chapter 10). That vision revealed the truth of things in relation to the Cause of things, and after it St. Augustine underlines its meaning. The end toward which fallible, finite intellect would lead the soul is Beatitude. In that state, desired by the soul through its intellectual nature, the state of Beatitude of the soul, St. Augustine says, "to have been and to be in the future do not belong to it, but only to be . . . ." And that recognition held firmly, "we turned back again to the noise of our mouths, where a word both begins and ends," in contrast to that Word without beginning or end. That is, we return to the sensual level of our existence in this present, in which alone the soul may make progress toward Beatitude, toward its Be-ingness which is the perfection of its gift of being. That is a recognition Eliot testifies to in Sections V and VI of "Ash-Wednesday," a recognition of the soul's state of "betweenness" in reality. The soul is now shepherded, in Eliot's view, by the Word, against which and around which the "unstilled world still whirled" and still whirls.

These are the lines in Eliot which best reveal his deepening, personal sense of what is meant to the Christian by the actuality of his "Inbetweenness." It is the state he says in *Burnt Norton*, "Between un-being and being." To that state, circumstances are medial, feeding the desire for a perfection of being. In that condition of reality, he must not violate the limit set by reality through an excessive hope or excessive despair: that is, by the futility of despair the self turns upon itself; by the presumption of hope, there comes the premature attempt to transcend reality and escape the circumstantial necessities to the soul's particular being. This latter is the illusional leap toward Beatitude, such as Dante dramatizes in his pilgrim rushing up the mountain. No wonder that Eric Vogelin, whose own most central concern is the necessity to consciousness of coming to terms with the Platonic *metaxy*, the "Inbetweenness" of the soul, was drawn to Eliot's later poetry. And the importance of Eliot's witness to the Romantic inclination, through intuitive intellect as he experienced it, is of importance to our understanding the complexity of "Romanticism."

For that reason, it is of interest to compare Wordsworth's attempted solutions to the desire and despair embattled in his own soul to Eliot's gradual exploration of his own awakening to the difficulties of *seem* in opposition to *is*, of *illusion* in opposition to *vision*. Both witness the circumstantial inbetweenness of the soul as an existing thing in motion toward perfection. Eliot, too, awakens with some difficulty from his dark wood, from his Wordsworthean slumber. Like Dante, Eliot moves toward a light of which the sun is more shadow than true sun. Wordsworth, unlike either, seems rather to have succumbed to the dark wood, however bathed in neon light making all that world green. Eliot makes his way toward a Thomistic realism, stirred in Wordsworth but abandoned in the panic of loss. In "The Hollow Men," a shadow falls "Between the idea/ And the reality," between "the potency/ And the existence." These are quite deliberately traditional scholastic terms, as we have noted. That continuing shadow is engaged in "Ash-Wednesday" and in the "Ariel Poems," poems in which the light begins, though it is not yet dawn.

It is at these points that a stranger, stronger light glimmers—a light that intellect may have mistaken in the world as a shadow, in the Platonic sense. In that mistake, intellect will turn in panic toward the light of the sun, the light of rational intellect. But to do so is to lose a recognition that patience in intellectual adversity allows aid through the offices of intuitive intellect. For if one sees as through a glass darkly, perhaps confusing trees with men walking, it becomes decisive to the recovery from such wavering perceptions—it becomes decisive to the intellect's seeing the truth of things—to know whether that glass is in oneself, is perhaps even the eye of rational intellect, or the eye of intuitive intellect, the one or the other disjoined from understanding and so allowing only a partial vision. For one may look through the window of the rational, and find the view modified by those moments when the window is opened and we see, or believe we see, as if no window glass intervenes. That is, the intuitive supports the rational. Such are the visionary moments, the still points or spots of time experienced beyond our enhousement and so most difficult to articulate "through the words of our mouth" to those similarly enhoused. The shadow, such is the visionary moment, may be *in* the world, and may be indeed rather a Light, which Eliot calls the Word, after St. John's Gospel. In the recognition of this light, which seen darkly through the glass of finite intellect may well seem rather a shadow: such it was to Wordsworth's disappointment, once he had lost the "visionary gleam," followed by intellect fading "into the light of common day." For as we recognize, through reason's coincidence to intuitive intellect in the act of our "seeing," that nothing—*no thing*—is common in the sense of the term whereby we reduce a thing to the condition of our rational management of it by the practical intellect. Every *thing*, when seen in the truth in which it stands, is *un*common—is itself sustained in its being. Even if so lowly a thing as the sparrow pecking about the gravel of an English garden or in the gutters of a decaying tenement in Boston. Even if but the hazel nut held in the palm of the open hand.

And so Eliot would seem in this light to have Wordsworth's "Ode" in mind also when he opens "Animula" with a quotation from the *Purgatorio*: " 'Issues from the hand of God, the simple soul'/ To a flat world of changing lights and noise" and to the other accidents of beings contingent to that "simple soul."[18] In the "Journey of the Magi," the harsh journey through nature to the city of man, through habitations of man in nature, brings thought's confrontation with a question, the Romantic question put in a new dimension by the Incarnation: "[W]ere we led all that way for/ Birth or Death?"

Such is the beginning of a journey, sensed (intuitively, out of the given nature of consciousness) as an obligation. But not yet *understood* in its obligatory nature. For there is a distance between this immediate knowledge of evil and an understanding of the meaning of exile. Understanding must come in the recognition of a restoration of the self out of exile, expressed in the paradoxical word: *service* as *perfect freedom*: freedom perfected, which is the accommodation of finite existence to the gifts of finitude whereby *one* is (consciousness, soul, person) the thing one *is*. That freedom perfected is quite other than *untrammeled freedom*, though the temptation to autonomy in pursuit of an infinite, untrammeled freedom, is the always-present temptation to consciousness. What the "poet" (i.e., the intellectual creature, man) must deal with, then, is the temptation to a willful subversion of authority through the instrumentality of thought, centered in the words of his mouth and the meditations of his heart. What "untrammeled thought" intends is the violation of its own finitude in a usurpation of that Authority in whose keep lie all finitudes, and it is in this sense that one is "fool." One says in his heart, as heart is encouraged by mind, "there is no God." That is, one substitutes an illusion of understanding (whose seat is traditionally the heart) for true understanding, supported by the limited knowledge of intellect in its rational mode.

Our "poet" recognizes words (signs) as the necessary instrument toward that understanding which would recognize an accommodation of its own particular finitude to the finitudes of creation, in which understanding rightly acquired there is the movement toward that cause of finitudes. In this respect the word is brought into *conformity* (with literal implications, expressed also as *perfect freedom*) with the Word. For it is through this conformity that a perfection of intellect occurs—that is, a coming-to-be out of the potential of finite intellect. And it is in this perfection that the particular intellect discovers what is meant by the mystery of its being created "in the image of God." What is necessary to the good of intellect, then, is the deepening of knowledge to understanding. Understanding encompasses and transforms knowledge. That understanding is a consent to the creaturely nature of intellect—that is, to the limits of its finitude whereby alone *limit* makes the thing to be the thing it is. The omnipresent danger to intellect (recognized as a judgment not merely its own of itself) is that it become "fool" through a willful subversion of proper authority managed through the "false words" (of which the psalmist speaks often). That is, the special gift to intellect is its potential becoming though the instrument of sign, whose mystery lies in the power of sign to reconcile the exiled intellect to being, and through being to remove obstacles to the gifts of grace whereby it becomes reconciled to the Cause of being. The difference between the intellect thus freed and the intellect of the "fool" is the difference between a *living toward* (a becoming) and a *dying away from* (an un-being).

That dying away from is an illusion which, by will gone astray, is made to appear a living toward, under the auspices of a supposed untrammeled freedom. So that what occurs to the intellect is its establishing its exile as its own kingdom. Such is the end of gnostic perversion of those finitudes founded in *being*, in *esse*. It is in this complex of self-discovery that the poet comes to recognize his gift with sign as requiring a *sacrifice* of song: not of bulls and calves (for which all sorts of modern signs in the secular world may be substituted) but of a contrite heart. Here lies the proper relation of the poet as maker to God as Maker, within that proper analogy founded in St. Thomas's principle of proper proportionality.

It is here, precisely, that Jacques Maritain's divorce of art as an action of the practical intellect removed from moral implication requires a more careful tuning as it were—requires the addition of moral dimension supplied practical intellect and its actions by speculative intellect. Maritain's divorce, in *Creative Intuition*, that rich and influential treatment of the creative process, requires a reunifying more emphatic than he seems to give. For in separating the *good* of the *thing* of art from the good of the poet himself, one may lose sight of the embracing dimension of the moral *in the poet* and his act of making, which proves consequential to the good of the thing made. It does not follow that the order of art and the order of nature—the order of the poem and the order of the soul of the poet—are not to be considered discursively as constituting separate orders of being. Only that in perfections of being, such separations are finally inadmissible. We should no doubt have little difficulty with the problem here were human intellect angelic and our intellect thus excused the struggles of discursiveness, and indeed one of the intimations of Beatitude is the soul's arrival at such a state of perfected being which no longer requires the entrapments of a discursiveness whose battleground is the sign.

This is to say that art, in the end, may not be denied as an effect out of moral cause, the poet in his prudence as person, through a desire to execute art as moral effect will again and again result in a made thing which is not properly art, but a tract or program or some such other form of made thing. In respect to the problem of covenant, that abiding theme for any poet—the abiding question of the proper relation of virtuous intellect to sign (which is the same with any made thing through sign, whether vegetable garden or *Divine Comedy*): there is always an incomplete, and so unwilling, initial action of intellect, a hesitant submission to the "law" intuitively known but only partially articulated and uncertainly understood. That "unwilling submission" to the law is in the Psalms accompanied by a constant importuning of God to give *understanding* of the law beyond any *knowledge* of the law. (It is arresting how often "understanding" is said in the Psalms.) That full knowledge, that understanding, alone may effect a full consent to the law, lost to any save the saint. Still, the poet knows intuitively that a full submission is appropriate to the fullness of the gift of his intellectual being.

Practical intellect, whose operation removes obstacles to understanding (which is always beyond the limits of sign, beyond full articulation and so a reality of intellect in the realm of mystery): practical intellect too easily mistakes its actions as cause of understanding, which is the condition of pride. Between this inclination and the recognition of grace as the cause of understanding is the nexus in intellect—the arena within which intellect must struggle toward perfection, always in a tension of falling away. "I believe, help thou my unbelief" is one way of saying the point. Another: I know; pray transform my knowing to understanding.

17

The Poet as Drowning Emperor, His Clarion Signs

"Thinking is obviously our coming to know, and when formed from it our word is true. And so the Word of God (Christ) should be understood without thinking, but not as having something formable in it, which could be unformed."
[Thomas's quote from St. Augustine's *De Trinitate*, to which he adds]
"[I]n this way, thinking is properly said of a motion of the deliberating soul that it is not yet completed by the full vision of the truth [in contrast to Christ who is the full Truth]." *Summa*, I-II, Q 2, Art 2

Keats recognizes the effect of what Gilson calls thought substituting itself for knowledge, though to the extent that he would take thought as alien, even as malevolent, power, he does not discover his own participation in that division in his own intellect. There is in him, as there is in Prufrock, a "you" and an "I"—an inclination deeply attuned to the soul's appetitive relation to creation (the "you") in respect to the soul's sensitive nature, but deeply fearful of that inclination and so resisted by the rational intellect (the "I"). As poet, he is most celebrated for the sensitive use of words, through which he comes very close to the thing itself. It is this aspect of his art that foretells as inevitable that he will be the poet hero to the Imagist Movement when it comes along nearly a hundred years after his death. His desire is for a close union of intellect and thing, a desire which leads him to talk about "negative capability," a capability he possessed to a more considerable extent than perhaps he himself realized. In fearing an incapability, he envied Shakespeare, or perhaps it would be better said, he admired Shakespeare, an admiration which led him to desire as poet that he might write drama rather than the lyric poetry which was peculiar to his tortured gift.

I say tortured gift, for his capacity for negative capability, which drew

him close to the sensual world, inevitably thereby drew him to the prospect of nature's decay. It is perhaps at such a point of response to the
actuality of created existences, which are and then are not, that the recognition of existence as always "between un-being and being" (in Eliot's
phrase) becomes intolerable. One knows that condition as fundamental
to existence, a knowledge spoken of poignantly by Old Testament poets.
The Preacher (Ecclesiastes 3) addresses the knowledge in Keats's and
Wordsworth's and Eliot's own experiences, declaring that "To every thing
there is a season, and a time to every purpose under heaven," illustrating
the inevitables to existence, the good and bad. "A time to be born, and a
time to die; a time to plant, and a time to pluck up that which is planted."
The catalogue of universal conditions to any being in time is extended in
that memorable passage, leading to the enigmatic verse which Eliot will
echo in *Burnt Norton*: "That which hath been is now; and that which is
to be hath already been; and God requireth that which is past." The passage is heavy with the oblivion of dust.

There is this same knowledge of the conjunction of death to life, not
merely with Achilles shouting in the trenches, but in that scene where
Hector bids farewell to his child as he goes out to be slain. The action
of negative capability joins intellect to the universal condition, through
things—sparrows or Achilles or Hector. But it seems that again and again
thought intrudes upon that action, whereby appetitive virtues are arrested
by reflections on death as the end to those virtues. To surrender to
thought, Keats says, to surrender to that intrusion upon the soul's participation in existential event, is "to be filled with sorrow and leaden-eyed
despair," effectively arresting life in the presence of death. Keats is very
much an Old Testament poet in the concern, unable to discover that
prophesied redemption of time which Eliot embraces, the Word that is
both the beginning and the end. His own recourse lies in his gift as poet,
in his imaginative virtue as he sees it, through which he might escape both
nature's decay and thought's subversion. But always, thought cripples
imaginative flight, words themselves so heavy with the matter of reality
as to prevent desire. Words are burdened by the mundane, whether the
joys of birth—of spring and summer—or the sorrows of death—fall and
winter.

Under the threat of thought, then, Keats is uncertain about metaphor's
dependability. For, though there lies deep in his desire a longing for a
reality beyond time's decay, what he experiences again and again is the
rebuff of that desire by the circumstantial realities of creation. Fancy cannot cheat one free of entrapment. However delightful that entrapment—in
wine or in the beauty of the morning rose—it is still an entrapment.

Fancy, the imagination, seems thus burdened inescapably to rely on attribution, so that the moment of seeming vision ends always as bitter illusion. The play with metaphor in its relation to this difficulty is played out impressively in "La Belle Dame Sans Merci." If Wordsworth, in "Tintern Abbey," is arrested by the middleness of his experience so that a "something" in nature speaks out of nature metaphorically, to his delight, Keats finds no such assurance in his "fiction" of the Knight at Arms. Wordsworth, in the middle of a day, month, season, year beholds the sunlit world, he only shadowed in his middleness under the sycamore (for he is at that magic turning of his three score and ten). Keats's Knight, confronted by an innocent, youthful questioner and bearing knowledge perhaps too heavy for that questioner, tells a parable, whose meaning will unfold for the youthful questioner only in his own Knight's journey. The questioner sees the circumstances as literal, not figurative, making him concerned that this old Knight is wandering in a season when he might catch cold. All nature, save the Knight, is prepared for winter, which to the innocent eye is but prelude to spring. But such readings into nature (we remember Shelley's cry, "If winter come, can spring be far behind") are not sufficient to the dark actualities of nature. And so the Knight spins a "supreme fiction": which bears a dark message to be understood by the young questioner long after. It is a tale with all the old metaphorical elements: journey, seasons, days, beautiful maiden, and so on.

Ah that beautiful maiden! Some readers would have her too simply Death. Keats, I believe, saw her as Life, as Life's deceptiveness. She fascinates the Knight with her beauty and with her singing, so that for him the only world is the world she sings and seemingly makes by that singing. He does not notice the road at all, so fascinated is he. For she "leans sideways" to sing her "fairy song." He does not realize the nature of the journey until he wakes "on the cold hill side." He does not notice, because he also leans "sideways" to her, enthralled. The beauty of Life is bitter at last. The message the Knight has for the young questioner is something like this if he would be cruel: "You think you have been living for twenty-one years, when in truth you have been dying for twenty-one years." The beautiful lady without mercy is Life itself, so that to be drawn to life is to be led unsuspecting to the trophy halls of Death.

Such is Keats's version of the Stevens's "supreme fiction," in which the actual or the metaphorical both have the same end, decay into death and oblivion. Keats's own experiences of moments of happiness, such as that conjunction of mind with the nightingale's transporting song, must be in retrospect an illusion. The bird sings with "full-throated ease," but not the poet, so that he might better have been the actual, natural bird, as

Prufrock would be a pair of ragged claws scuttling across the floors of silent seas. For only in that condition of being does it seem possible to defeat thought. No prospect of a Yeatsean return for Keats, but if there were, he would no doubt reject that golden bird singing to the emperor in favor of the fading, actual, unthinking bird whose desertion leaves him now desolate. He is, as poet, deceived by illusion, which as poet he exacerbates through the "fiction" of attribution which is doomed to collapse. It is a deception engineered somehow by that old enemy thought, and not a visionary experience at all. He *had* seemed to escape the agony of thought, but that was the moment before the words of his poem set out to rescue the illusional moment. And the crushing irony, given his calling as poet, is that the very attempt to postpone the fading moment through signs results in the signs themselves becoming only memorial to an illusional moment. Again, those very signs are hopelessly mired in what he would escape, "nature," his own nature and the world's. Little wonder, then, that words leave him more than "half in love with easeful death. Even if sensually pleasing as with so near a presence to the senses through signs as wine "With beaded bubbles winking at the brim,/ And purple-stain'ed mouth," the moment the wine touches the taste buds. Worse, palsy shakes "a few, sad, last gray hairs" or spectre-thin, pale, dying youths. And just how devious thought may be, through the stalking horse of language, is suggested by the ambush effected through words that seem spontaneous, out of himself, and almost achieving the word-user's escape from nature. There is the instance of *forlorn* in the "Ode to a Nightingale" and *desolate* in "Ode on a Grecian Urn."

That moment of escape is always just past. It now *was*, and so is already a memory whose visionary dimension may be merely the effect of nostalgia infesting the new present moment of awareness with longing turned back in time. Nor may that past moment now be fully accepted as ever having actually been what it but seems to have been in a present lamentation for it. Is it, at this present, but a vapour of wishful thinking raised by subversive thought to tease uncertain desire? To raise that question, as thought seems to do most insistently and deviously, leaves Keats in his present moment of awareness most acutely aware of his isolation from all but consciousness itself, in which always lurks in ambush thought. There drift uncertain images in consciousness, arrested by thought to confront awareness, but even those images are ghostly, faintly remembered and fading by the act of remembrance itself from any actuality. Those presences, as they fade, serve only to make more certain the isolation of his "sole self." His imagination cannot cheat consciousness beyond the entrapment effected through song's discursiveness. Discursiveness dooms his poetry to fail, being only such a sad soft music as that supposed upon the musician on the urn. Neither words nor the visual arts may accomplish imaginative rescue. The urn's insistence that beauty and truth are the same is cold comfort to those on earth caught by living, breathing passion—caught by life as opposed to images caught by art. (Emily Dickinson expounds Keats's final line and half of his "Ode on a Grecian Urn" in her "I Died for Beauty," a discourse which ends when moss reaches the lips of the dialectitians hymning beauty and truth ["Themself are One"] and covers up their tombstone names.)

For Keats, the music flees with the moment. A music which is only remembered in this present may easily have been only an illusion out of his desire, like that illusion of music from those "soft pipes" on the urn, piping "ditties of no tone." A perfect music, in that it does not and cannot exist in nature as the flutist and poet must. A dark reading of intellect's experience indeed. What is valuable to us as thinkers, attempting to recover thought from Keats's suspicions of it, is not his skepticism, not his failure to affirm a visionary moment. For all he has to show for his attempt is only that residue of his thought, melancholy despair. But Keats, as does Wordsworth, bears witness almost despite himself to the flickering life of intuitive desire that intellect be opened to the Beautiful, the True, the Good. And we find that life which Keats desires bursting into flame in a later Romantic poet, in whose poetry there is a reconciliation of memory to desire, of thought to feeling. His poetry glows with that reconciliation.

Gerard Manley Hopkins began his own literary interests with the poetry of Keats, as William Carlos Williams was to do. And he was also much aware, in his phrase, "of the pathos of nature and landscape" such as that in Wordsworth's poetry. Thus he was alerted to recognitions of the Virgilean tears of things in Wordsworth and Keats. But Hopkins looked close and more closely at things than they. There is not so much a reconciliation of those tensional poles by the rational intellect in his poems as there is in the scholastic direction we detect in Eliot's poetry. Rather we have an immediate celebration of the thing in response to the poet's experience of the thing. Of course Hopkins was educated in the scholastics, Duns Scotus contending with Thomas Aquinas in his formal, philosophical thought toward a rationalization of the pathos in the human experience of the natural world. But with the exception of his first great poem, "The Wreck of the Deutschland," Hopkins's poetry tends increasingly to the moment's response to a revelation in things, rather than to meditative exposition bearing a philosophical burden.

That is a virtue in Hopkins's poetry which Eliot recognizes as sometimes absent in his own, his own tendency to discuss things too much. Eliot writes John Hayward about an early draft of *Little Gidding*: "The

defect of the whole poem, I feel, is the lack of some acute personal remi-
niscence (never to be explicated, of course, but to give power from well
below the surface.)." It is the power of personal response to things, and
we notice how far Eliot has come from his early rejection of the personal,
his insistence on the "depersonalization" of the poet's mind in "Tradition
and the Individual Talent." That is the essay in which he also remarks,
concerning this "science" of depersonalization, "The ode of Keats contains a number of feelings which have nothing to do with the nightingale,
but which the nightingale, partly, perhaps, because of its attractive name,
and partly because of its reputation, served to bring together." It is almost
as if Eliot prefers a perfection of correspondences which would, in the
event, dissolve the tensional poles which make the poem the great ode
that it is. For the drama in that tension is precisely in the incompatability
of some of those correspondences, which the poet attempts to force to
the end of his transcendence through art of bird and garden and even
poetry itself.

"The Wreck of the Deutschland," a response to the deaths in nature
inviting comparison to Wordsworth's "Elegiac Stanzas, Suggested by a
Picture of Peele Castle in a Storm" and to his "Intimations Ode," is a
reflective engagement of nature's seeming betrayal in the drowning of
exiled Franciscan nuns. There is an exploration of the mystery of death,
whose issue is not, however, solved by Platonic Idealism. (Hopkins had
been earlier touched by Platonism). Nor does he descend into a despair
over nature's relentless decay, as Keats does again and again. Wordsworth
is responding to the death of his brother John in "Elegiac Stanzas," as he
had responded to the death of a child in the "Lucy" poems. Both these
persons are nearer to Wordsworth in nature than the nuns to Hopkins,
but death is not the new experience to Hopkins that it seems to Wordsworth. Hopkins had ministered to the dying in Dublin and elsewhere
often.

What we observe in Hopkins's response to death is his return, after
meditative reflection, to this present moment in the midst of nature's
decay with a joy in that decay, celebrating things as they are. For him the
"shipwreck" is "a harvest" in Christ. For it is in death that life itself is
fulfilled for Hopkins, as it will be for Eliot beyond that uneasy magus'
question, "were we led all that way for/ Birth or Death?" Hopkins turns
in concluding "The Wreck of the Deutschland" to comforting words spoken by the poet as vatic priest:

> Let him [Christ] easter in us, be a dayspring to the
>   dimness of us,
>   be a crimson-cresseted east,
> More brightening her, rare-dear Britain, as his reign rolls . . .

It is the Word that is Wordsworth's "something" in nature, recovered to Hopkins's vision as Christ.

There is in Hopkins's testimony, then, a recovery of hope out of despair, which is the recovery Wordsworth and Keats never quite satisfactorily accomplish through their poetry. There is a very *personal* attempt at recovery by all these poets. Hopkins accomplishes recovery through the intuitive faculty of intellect operative in his poetry, severely testing the rational intellect's support. Perhaps in that accomplishment he makes it possible to value the more the failed attempts of those earlier Romantics. For it is of considerable value to us as particular intellects pilgrimaging, struggling with our own "Romanticism," to have recalled to us the proper question. We have met that question through philosophical explorations by Gilson, Maritain, and Thomas Aquinas, and by the dramatic explorations of Wordsworth, Keats, and Eliot, those poets standing personally in the action of their art. But it is Hopkins who sings it out to us with joy.

The question recognized by the Romantic, lest he surrender all claim to the *ratio*: how do I *stand* in relation to what I stand *upon*, and in relation to the full *context* of my standing as myself a thing in being? That is a question haunting the rational exploration of it. And that rational exploration proves to be an intuitive desire in intellect for community in being. When that desire is not understood as properly under the auspices of both the *ratio* and the *intellectus*, however, intellect will attempt all sorts of perches upon which to sing the Good, the True, and the Beautiful. Eschewing realism, however, though differing in particulars, those intellectually made perches attempt to justify the operation of ideology—the making of false idols out of the intellect's singing. That is an act conjuring being to intellect's own province. Thus one may be moved by nostalgia to build perches in the past, idealized as historical moment, whether one moment past or five years past, or in earlier childhood, or even in the Medieval world or Rome or Greece. Or one may project perches into the future by presumptuous actions of power over the future of being.

If we look at Keats's "Ode to a Nightingale" or lines from Wordsworth's "Tintern Abbey" in relation to Hopkins's "Windhover" or "Pied Beauty," we discover each concerned for a completion of the intellect's intuitive inclination to the Good, the True, the Beautiful—intellect's action toward a worthy thing desired, to be known and admired. The decisive differences among them, affecting even their prosody in the end, is not simply a matter of technique, though technique is always symptomatic of the poet's vision or illusion. In this sense, technique is the accident of art. We have remarked, for instance, in Wordsworth's "Ode" his use of capital letters as symptomatic of his disappointment bordering upon de-

spair and leading him to the edge of that despair. Even the formal manner
of the traditional ode, though irregularly adapted by Wordsworth, supports his detachment. It reflects a deportment which the speaker recognizes, his sense of being removed from the world he observes and longs
to enter. Hopkins in "The Wreck of the Deutschland" writes quite a different sort of "ode," whose verses strain to hold the growing recognitions
in the journeying speaker. The stanzas hold the lines to a form, with even
a certain durational measure of corresponding lines in different stanzas.
But there is throughout the threat of explosion growing within the line
itself, as if the matter at issue were itself the form and the formal line, as
it struggles to come to terms with that matter, doomed to explode with
the brightening vision in the maker's intellect, the poet's intellect, as it
moves to that encounter with the cause of all "eastering." Form as understood fitfully by human intellect is so incommensurate to Form as the
cause of all form that the poem dramatizes a submission to finite inade-
quacies of intellect. And behold! That yielding yields the visionary moment. And it is a submission to form as the name signifying that only
Perfected Form for Hopkins, Christ, who is both man and God.

> Double-natured name,
> The heaven-flung, heart-fleshed, maiden furled
> Miracle-in-Mary-of-flame,
> Mid-numbered He in three of the thunder-throne!

Such, for Hopkins, is his "something deeply interfused in nature," superceding finite intellect and all creation, reducing history—event in time
and place—to a present. In the poem the drowned Nun is "Dame, at our
door/Drowned" but thereby Christ's harvest home. In "Tintern Abbey,"
Wordsworth cannot surmount history. Indeed personal history seems determinant, through his recollections of his own personal events in nature
and in the city of man. He calls up past event, attempting to certify an
unchanging reality as the Prime cause of experience and hence of the history of his own person. But his "something" is never for him that Person
"past change" whom Hopkins finds in nature and by the finding is himself found out. Still, Wordsworth desires something beyond change, since
a change in himself proves inescapable, and since change seems most
likely a falling away. Only through thought as the measure of change, or
so it seems at the present moment of Wordsworth's poem, is it possible to
recover the earlier, and therefore (for Wordsworth) the stronger intuitive
response to an unchanging "something." Rational intellect is forced to
the support of the intuitive, but the intuitive is already surrendered to

history, to his own youthful past in which he remembers it as active but cannot find it active in himself in this present moment.

A similar parabola of past experience in its present effect upon intellect prescribes the dramatic form in Keats's "Ode to a Nightingale," as we have seen. Keats attempts to hold onto the dissolving moment of transport, a moment made possible, it now seems, by a forgetting of the self as *being*, thus transported in the full-throated ease of the bird's song. The bird's ease is that of an art beyond man's, an effect of the bird's natural and continuous unself-awareness at its song. That condition alone seems to promise steadiness beyond change. The moment of transport for Keats is remembered in an action of intellect, which exacts as its effect a decay into self-awareness out of self-forgetfulness, fast fading now like the flowers at his feet. It is a moment prescribed by the finitudes of self-awareness, bounded by that awareness, and thus reduced from its enduring beyond the reductionism of a "moment." We might compare on this point Robert Frost's playful treatment of the Keatsean dilemma in his "Boundless Moment." That is a moment of illusion occasioned, as with Keats, by a natural object: March walk in the woods, a bush burning in blossom, May's "Paradise-in-bloom" it seems. The speaker "stood a moment . . . as one his own pretense deceives," [i.e., submitting to the *as if* we considered in Frost and Stevens earlier]. He is deceived to a consent to *is*. But then "I said the truth (and we moved on)./ A young beech clinging to its last year's leaves."

I introduce Frost here as one of those "Romantic" realists, in the sense that he is governed by the *ratio*, and always most suspicious of the *intellectus*. If Eliot and Pound are direct in their early rejections of Wordsworth and Keats, Frost admits to that rejection, but he declares himself more subtle about it. He sees in them only a Platonism. E. A. Robinson is one of that lot, believing "that what we have here is an imperfect copy of what is in heaven. The woman you have is an imperfect copy of some woman in heaven or in somebody else's bed." And he adds, "Many of the world's greatest—maybe all of them—have been ranged on that romantic side. I am philosophically opposed to having one Iseult for my vocation and another for my avocation." So much, then, for Dante and his Beatrice. Frost, like Stevens, is charry of prose defenses of his anti-Romantic position, though not reluctant to reveal a distinction he sees between himself and those poets ranged on the Romantic side. And he writes a good deal of literary criticism, he says. It is (he says) in his poetry, though he adds "I won't admit it" if pressed. Still, we may press the poetry itself, as when we see his Shelley-like rebuke to Wordsworth's Platonism of the "Intimations Ode," in his "Trial by Existence," or his distancing from Keats's vulnerable response to existence as "one his own pretense deceives." One can find that distancing, for instance, by reading comparatively Frost's "Birches" and Keats's "Ode to a Nightingale" or "Ode on a Grecian Urn," exploring the implications in the vision of each of the poets as makers in relation to art's relation to life.

What is missing in Frost's view of the "Romantic" poet is a fineness of perception that might distinguish among "Platonists," and thereby perhaps discover in Keats's "melancholy" response to life Keats's awareness of intellect's loss of community in being. But to do so would call in question the whole of Frost's position, since his position requires that intellect find all that is not human intellect to be its antagonist, in response to which he makes form against chaotic antagonism. "Nothing not made by hands," he says, "is holy." In brief, despite Frost's seeming reservations against science in its modernist deportment, that science justifies him as maker. It is a justification he found in Bergson, who declared, "The universe . . . is a machine for the making of God." Frost as God stands against the universe as mechanistic God-in-the-making, his weapon being form imposed, though with a deference to aspects of that universe. The limits in nature are to be used, not superceded in an absolutist imposition of form as if one were a radical Platonist. Thus in making an ax-helve, "the lines of a good helve" show "its curves were no false curves/ Put on it from without" ("The Ax-Helve"). This is sound aesthetics and, except for the insistent gnostic position of the maker in relation to the made thing, even sound Thomistic aesthetics, let alone sound utile art. But always with Frost is that insistence upon the self as the ultimate god of the being, whether an ax-helve or a poem, and it is an insistence that prevents not only the possibility of a community in being such as Keats senses himself to have lost, but also the possibility of regaining that community. But above all, it is necessary to deny any intimations of ever having experienced such a moment of community. In this respect, Frost's poetry must battle against such an admission, which is always threatening intellect as it does in "Design." The threat becomes almost triumphant in overcoming the maker's control of his making in the final lines of "After Apple-Picking."

Keats to the contrary is aware of intellect's desire for community beyond the sole self. He cannot name that desired state as the scholastic might, of course, though in turning from the moment past to the moment present, there occurs yet another moment of self-forgetfulness. He cannot see the flowers at his feet, standing as he does in "embalmed darkness." But those flowers' images are raised through the very naming, the names called to the poet's lips by their scent so immediate to the sense, mediated to intellect as image. And from image to sign of image in intellect: the white hawthorne, the pastoral eglantine, fast-fading violets covered up in leaves, the musk-rose. Yet thought, in that flow through the senses into words, has again deceived him out of a transport. For to certify the moment by sign proves fatal to self-forgetfulness. Words are thought's Trojan horse for access to intellect, being anchored as they are in nature as history—being anchored in intellect by thought. The history in words robs the moment of its content by the prophecy of the moment's fading, that old lesson of history. The connotations of the natural history of things is that they are *fast fading* and *covered up*. Even the imitation in words spoken of the old sound of bees at summer, foreseen for the coming musk-rose, that "murmurous haunt of flies on summer eaves," leaves him isolated by present perceptions as thus brought to sign. It is a circumstance very like that in Eliot's "Preludes," in which awareness is turned upon the problem of the self by "a thousand sordid images." Keats's images are not sordid. Indeed they are very much akin to Wordsworth's "lovely forms." But their effect is the same as if they were sordid, for in no way do they heal the moment's melancholy by the remembrance of sensual delights in nature. The faded past only serves to exacerbate the fading present, and that shadow but deepens as the future.

"Darkling," he listens but the transporting song, like the transporting scent of flowers, is fled, leaving only death as a seeming solution to the moment's inexorable death, the death of self-forgetfulness into self-awareness. Intellect is burdened by after-images of that moment, and whether sordid or lovely they serve only to effect isolation. Always the word seems to betray. The word is the death sentence to the moment, whether *fast fading* or *forlorn*. Each attempt at full-throated song collapses through words to the hardest, truest word of all for Keats: *sole self*. That malady of intellect, art, can at best only pretend to a cure through "fancy." Indeed, art is but the child of that deceiving elf Fancy, loosed in intellect through images to mock consciousness itself. For the mind is no mansion for all lovely form for Keats. It is an empty chamber in which images, lovely or not, echo in mocking intellect for its separation from the source of image, a community in being.

Keats and Wordsworth, then, are little able to deal with what Hopkins will subsequently call creation's "pied beauty." To speak some sign of the *pied* dimension of the world seems to them to intrude a subversive thought. To recall *violets* recalls their *fast fading*, their being *covered up* by the ditrius of a collapsing nature, which condition of being thought then takes as the only significant end to that amorphous illusion, life. Even the imagination's escape for a moment through the summoning of history, the story of Ruth or medieval "magic casements," occasions the always present threat of alien corn and perilous seas. In the Keatsean perspective, art's monuments of intellect, raised to a Beauty one wishes might never fade, serve only to emphasize intellect as aging toward oblivious death. Art thus is at best artifact, a tombstone to the dead maker. Yeats will insist the contrary, through his intellect's draft upon the residual Platonism in Western thought which he inherits, as in "Sailing to Byzantium." But that is not a possibility Keats did not see. It is only that the attempt proves always futile. For he cannot, as Yeats would do, disengage the actual bird, fading now and buried in the next valley glades, and make of it a golden bird in a perpetual mechanistic song.

18

The Fitful Moment—Fading, Fading . . .

> It is the human *person* who enters society; as an individual, it enters
> society as a part whose proper good is inferior to the good of the
> whole. . . . [But] the human person, as a spiritual totality referred
> to the transcendent whole, *surpasses* and is superior to all temporal
> societies. . . . With respect to the eternal destiny of the soul, society
> exists for each person and is subordinate to it.
>
> —Jacques Maritain, *The Person and the Common Good*

Melancholy is not simply the effect of accidents in Keats's personal circumstances, nor his tuberculosis that dooms him as a spectre-thin shell of
youth. For sad last grey heads speak the same judgment of the self's descent to oblivion, against which art's monuments are pale compensation,
whether poem or urn. Nor is melancholy out of the enveloping context
of place in a certain time, a London garden where he hears bird song or
Margate sands opening upon perilous waters. The source of intellect is
rather in the action of intellect, at whose center veiled Melancholy has her
"sovran shrine" in an ambient air of "Beauty." Both Beauty and Melancholy are dependent in "joy," though joy is but ever "bidding adieu."
Pleasure is only pleasure because "Turning to poison." All experience
speaks the soul destined to be hung among Melancholy's other "cloudy"
trophies: through inexorable decay.

Such, then, is the Keatsean condition, the intellectual response of
awareness to itself whose centering fear is the inescapable pain of isolation. We must all, at some moments in our experience, have been touched
by such melancholy. It is as ancient as the Psalms. The psalmist, the poet,
enters upon sung words out of the experience of self-awareness. But what
is most immediately revealed to the self in its self-awareness, in consciousness aware of itself by an accord with its nature, is the sense of exile—an
exile from earth as creation, and from the history of that world. The cry

of this most anciently known exile inhabits the anciently bequeathed signs which poets use in attempting to arrest Beauty beyond decay, from Homer and the Psalmist down to us. One finds it in Odysseus's visit to the "nations of the dead," shades lost to distraught Odysseus's embrace. The marvel of "vistas of the dead" where "shades in their thousands" are "blown together," "rustling/ in a pandemonium of whispers," is at last a "horror" sufficient to sped Odysseus up and back in a rapid retreat into the substantial world. And Homer, at the end himself, revisits that dark world, showing the dead suitors bound to Hades, "all squeaking as bats . . . all flitting criss-cross in the dark" where they cling to rock and "if one falls and the rock-hung chain" of bat souls is "broken," once more there is the flitting and squeaking. It is a prospect upon existence which Eliot's pilgrim must engage in "What the Thunder Says" before arriving at surrender. There history, Cleo, "drew her long black hair out tight/ and fiddled whisper music." History unredeemed yields visions of the end of history in a nightmare vision of civilization's "Falling towers/ Jerusalem Athens Alexandria/ Vienna London/ Unreal." *Unreal* because unredeemed, so that in history's whispered music to intellect, one sees the prospect of *person* unredeemed, echoing Homer:

> And bats with baby faces in the violet light
> Whistled, and beat their wings
> And crawled head downward down a blackened wall
> And upside down in air were towers
> Tolling reminiscent bells . . .
> And voices singing out of empty cisterns and exhausted wells . . .

Such the view of Hegelean history, from the perspective of the Hades which alone such a history may foretell. From that shocking encounter, the *Waste Land*'s voice turns to its "awful daring of a moment's surrender" and toward a world regained, not by intellect, but by a true Word in the desert's center, which is also at the heart of the turning person. Eliot's "personal grouse" (as he described his *Waste Land*) begins to yield in its discontent toward that Word. This is the moment of panic, as ancient or as modern as the contingency of the particular soul described as nature and history. For contingency and not the soul is nature's and history's matter. It is the moment of a self-discovery elemental to consciousness, and therefore more ancient than Sartre or Descartes or St. Augustine or St. Thomas. Here the intellect cries "out of the depths" of its exile, as the Psalmist phrases that condition of the soul.

This ancient sense of exile which the Psalmist knew entraps Keats in melancholy, but it is an experience no less immediate to Hopkins. Hopkins's response is not made in relation to memory born in intellect five years ago as with Wordsworth, or five minutes ago as with Keats. For Hopkins, a temporal measure from a present recollection to the remembered event is not the crucial dimension in the significant relationship of intellect to the thing in the engaging event. For Wordsworth and Keats, event is reduced to history at last. This is so, despite the inclination to color lost youth more agreeably than the present opportunity seems to offer to the present mature intellect in its reflective revisitations. Memory is variable, it appears, in respect to our linear removal from it by time as we progress toward our few sad last grey hairs. Thus there develops the complication of worldly desire in relation to our regret, as our age's popular literary genre, the memoir, might suggest. We are as susceptible to memoir collectively as individually.

For Hopkins, something quite other is encountered in memory than the changeableness of intellect itself which so troubled Wordsworth when he supposed that thought succeeds intuitive vision, like a beard grown on rosy-cheeked youth. Here is an old man young:

> I caught this morning morning's minion, king-
> dom of daylight's dauphin, dapple-dawn-drawn Falcon,
>   in his riding
> Of the rollin level underneath the steady air, and
>   striding . . . .

An emotion recollected, but not in a present tranquility of emotion. A spiritual estate out of an experience of the contention of the lord of the rolling air, who by his rein upon a wimpling wing steadies the moment in ecstasy resolved in the hawk's stooping to catch the heart that is in hiding in this amazed, this bird-struck, poet. In that moment this poet, too, is bird-fascinated, but held in a tensional mystery in which the destruction in nature yields a glimpse of a destruction in his own nature. That is a destruction in him which requires a violent rescue beyond the bounds of nature's finitudes. The hawk's sparrow and the poet's heart are prey to one single action. The actual falcon, like the poet, is "dapple," is (to borrow from another Hopkins poem) "pied." Each has been dawn-drawn, though in different senses, the one to the necessities of its nature requiring it to strike sparrow or lark or plover; the other to the necessities of a vision of its own being stricken from its straying exile and carried beyond the world of history. The mystery in the moment is one of conjunction in actuality, requiring of the poet's witness an analogy of proper proportion. There is no sense of attributive analogy, which would violate the vision which is revealed in an actual, even perfectly natural, event. The conjunction, the likeness in the unlikeness of the poet's heart and the falcon's prey, is adumbrated rationally in St. Thomas's principle of the proper proportionality in the whole of creation. But in the poem, as opposed to the exposition *On Being and Essence*, analogy incarnates mystery in the poet's heart, carrying no necessity of his rational exposition of the event and its effect. He must only command language and, through that command of sign, submit mind and heart to the mystery of conjunction of falcon and prey in relation to Christ and his self. The conjunction is an event born in being. It is this command of sign, and so a command beyond history as determinate through sign, which reveals the experience as it is, beyond Wordsworth's or Keats's gift to realize through words their intimations of such conjunction.

We are not here concerned so much with distinguishing between these poets, with saying of each, as Browning's arrogant Duke might, "here you miss,/ Or there exceed the mark." The concern continues to be that each poet is initially moved by a knowledge of his exile as a "self," the sense of exile consequent upon the experience to the self of its own existence. As such, it is a Cartesian moment, whatever the location in time or place. And this Cartesian moment is attended by the danger that, by the recognition of exile, that self may make exile its end in a confused response to the reality of its circumstantial existence. Moved now intuitively toward a desired rest, whose reality is at least ambiguous because of the given finitudes of intellect, however that exiled self may move, it will do so toward a reality seen at best as through a glass darkly. So, if the desired rest is made to center in the self as exile, thus elevating exile as if the true object of desire, the self-exiled soul will be increasingly enclosed in a darker wood of its own determinations. But if the desired rest comes rather to center upon an end beyond the self, as that exiled self begins to respond to a Calling (to borrow once more from Eliot), however indistinct that Calling to the troubled self, there begins the long journey toward its true home, out of the threatening dark woods and with eyes made gradually stronger in their seeing.

We are not concerned, then, with comparative literary criticism, except as such a discipline in reading may recover to our attention the initiating moment of the journey of the soul out of which grows the poet's song and the critic's response to that song. To do so is to realize these but instances of the myriad responses we each make once initiated upon the soul's journey. This is to say that our intent is to rescue our own discrete, present, engagement of the condition common to each soul out of its given nature. The concern is consequent upon our created nature as intellectual creature, in relation to which time past and time future are at last but peripheral, though not indifferent, concerns. What we discover, and this is a true service in art's intellectual monuments beyond any lasting service in them to "Beauty's" name, is that those monuments touch moments we know as real. They do so through imitation of the soul alive, through imitating the *action* of intellect alive. What they turn us to most insistently is *this* moment of our *knowing*. The only qualification is that the monument, if it is good in itself, shall have been built by its initiating intellect, the poet as maker, with a sufficient craft governed by prudential vision in respect to the limits of art, the poem as a thing made with signs. It is in this ground that one might choose to come at last, if literary criticism is the intent, to distinctions between Hopkins's relative success as poet and Wordsworth's or Keats's relative success, judging their moments as both of and out of intellect.

Each of us experiences moments of vision, and each experiences moments of the loss of such vision. But only when we allow ourselves to become entrapped in the intricacies of the *history* of such moments, as Keats does, do we lose that knowledge we already possess by the experience itself, independent of the thought brought to bear upon it. That knowledge is through a vision of the actual. And that is an experience in a country beyond the entrapments of time's circumstances which we may "think" determine us each as arrested Romantic: on the one hand trapped by time past, in a nostalgia out of time past misunderstood; on the other trapped by the illusion of time future, as determined by consciousness itself. It is in our recognition that both are entrapments away from reality, or so I believe, that we come at last to attempt disentangling ourselves through the *ratio* as complement to the *intellectus*, the head attempting to certify the heart, as the poet so often represents it. It leads to such convoluted beginnings as the following:

> Time present and time past
> Are both perhaps present in time future,
> And time future contained in time past.

And

> If all time is eternally present
> All time is unredeemable.

This is to say that if history is the only arena of intellect, then intellect is doomed by history. The escape lies in turning to the rose garden.

Such is the thought with which we too much and no doubt too often discuss, over-explaining our exile to ourselves in self-justification. And by that turning, we lose the present moment of our being dawn-drawn: of our being *en-visioned* by the moment's grace which buckles our self-isolation in an earthquake. That is the earthquake whereby the little world of self, made cunningly (as Donne says) of "elements and an angelic sprite," ceases to be Eliot's little world doomed to revolve on the axis of its self-awareness, as forlorn as a flat, bare earth. Such is the futile action against a coming winter of absolute zero to that little world. In that entrapment, sardonic laughter is the last echo which that little world hears as it collapses into the abyss.

One meets in Eliot, in "Ash-Wednesday," a confession of intellect as too much dominated by the *ratio*, in a passage already alluded to:

> I pray that I may forget
> These matters that with myself I too much discuss
> Too much explain.

The dangers of disproportion that would result in explaining entrapment in terms of time past and time future, time itself becoming the matter of our explanation, in the mood of lament or prophecy—that is always a present danger. We find ourselves, in our self-awareness, always in the present moment of our "dreamcrossed twilight between birth and dying," as Eliot's poem puts it. That is also the shadow world which Keats would, but cannot, escape. And thus Keats becomes fit subject to the false queen of worldliness, veiled Melancholy. He had had sufficient experience of transport beyond the worldly to enable him to do otherwise. Evidence of such possibility for Keats, as for each of us, is suspended in that pathos which is the dominant effect of his best poetry. And pathos as the effect of his art implies, by our own response to it, our own sense of a possibility lost. The possible recovery, we suggested earlier, is a spiritual one. Its reduction to merely intellectual parameters by thought, thus setting the soul aside, proves to be a reduction of the reality of our own given nature as defended but fitfully by Western philosophy since Thomas Aquinas.

The possibility of recovery does not occur once and once only, to echo Eliot's late recognition of the point at the conclusion of his *Waste Land*. It is necessarily a continuous recovery, through a continuous turning and returning. But that turning and returning is not to the past, nor to an imagined future. It is the return to this present moment in which alone we may recover vision of being itself through an immediacy to our particular, discrete intellect. At issue in every moment, beyond all other consideration, is the destiny of the singular soul. For we are never rescued significantly as a plurality of souls, despite modernism's confusions on the point. And so we characterize an encounter of the discrete soul in its present moment, whether localized in nature or the city of man. We do so through the intricacies of time and place—time past, passing and to come at this point of the incarnate soul as it finds itself at this point of an incarnate world. Inevitably, that soul is besieged in its continuous rescue by thoughts of time and place—thoughts which intellect cannot ignore but to which it must not submit as finalities. To do so is to become but another cloudy trophy hung on Melancholy's trophy walls, an image of the self terrified, which the self pins wriggling on the flat earth with needles of time and place. Soon, no longer wriggling. Left unresolved in that arrest is the significance to its existence of the thousands of lovely or sordid images such as intellect might cast up in sealing the self in its own despair.

Eliot at last breaks out of that entrapment, through a moment of vision not unlike that in Hopkins's "Windhover." It is in his discovery of a coincidence in a visionary moment, a stilled moment of the senses freed of time: the discovery of the world rescued, redeemed from the closures of time. The image which focuses that visionary moment for Eliot is the figure of a woman. But she is not the veiled figure of Melancholy. He sees her beyond a green garden, at its edge. She is seen *through* the garden, a figure who walks at that garden's edge "between/ The various ranks of varied green/ Going in white and blue, in Mary's colors." He sees her not *instead of*, but *beyond* the garden's god, Priapus, whose flute in that moment of vision, "is breathless." One is meant, no doubt, to remember that other breathless flute Keats hears on the urn, those "soft pipes" issuing ditties of no tone. But the circumstances to art here are significantly changed for Eliot. It is not in isolation from actuality, this formal garden with its figure of Priapus speaking "generation," to borrow Keats's sad words, "when this generation wastes." And the figure of the woman: she beckons him to her, but he must approach her (the point is crucial) *through* that garden, through the world's realities as accommodated to intellect through the *ratio* and the *intellectus*.

We must not, in reading Eliot's version of a present moment to be recovered again and again, overlook the rich implications we have prepared ourselves to notice. Eliot has very much in mind not only Keats's disjunction of art from the actions of nature as an attempt to escape nature. He has also in mind the sort of false vision one finds in Wallace Stevens's figure of the woman in "Sunday Morning," or better, the figure of that singing woman in "The Idea of Order at Key West." Her singing makes the only self she has, the only world that is, and so as visionary figure she can only speak to the poem's speaker of the necessity of his own action of making himself his own and only world. Eliot's figure, wearing St. Mary's colors, spoke no word, only "bent her head and signed" her consent to his journey through the garden. We see that *signing* figure beyond another signing figure, beyond the "broadbacked figure" of Priapus, who is "drest in blue and green." One does not miss the coincidence of color anchoring the soul in the garden's actions, the actions of nature in the finite world. But that anchor touches as well the figure rescued to perfection, Mary. Both share a "blue." That choice of color is anchored in ceremonial tradition, for blue is indeed Mary's color, as white was, a tradition continued in bridal traditions until recently. But in Priapus's blue, we find a shifting by allusion, out of that Cartesian Idealism as embraced by Stevens upon which he builds his poetry. He builds it not only in "The Blue Guitar," but with the play of blue and green thematically in much of his poetry. Stevens sets the green of the naturalistic world, accepted as an actuality whose causes he will not explore, as subject to that blue which his imagination would impose. To the tensional pole of the "green" world he opposes his imagination's "blue" as a transformation by imaginative intellect of the green world. Thus the green world is made blue to the interest of his intellect and its singing of itself as the only world. Sign as attribution of intellect upon the world, the blue upon the green, is not enough for Eliot. And of course, as we have noted, neither was it for Stevens in the end, in whom a Keatsean Queen Melancholy proved resident all along, despite the outward show of signs denying that presence. There are sufficient memoirs by those who knew Stevens as a person to reveal what his poetry tends to deny, the most important of which is the account by Fr. Hanley of Steven's conversion. "One writes for one," Stevens long insists, making thereby the only world that is: that is what his poetry declares. But in his end, as Eliot would rejoice to say, is his beginning. What Stevens himself is reported by Fr. Hanley as saying is "I'd better get in the fold now," and when baptized, "Now I'm in the fold."

The green world through which Eliot sees he must move, the green world which Stevens accepts as suited to gnostic uses of the imagination, is Keats's own green world, in which one goes in cruel submission to it, not into fall or winter, but to a "green hill in an April shroud." There Queen Melancholy holds her court, enthroned at the bursting point of Beauty in the morning rose. That Eliot is also aware of this Keatsean world as his own prelude to an encounter with the true Queen of the

World, "going in Mary's colors," is clear enough in the passage which sets a garden before us, through which is at last seen that beckoning figure:

> beyond the hawthorne blossom and a pasture scene
> The broadbacked figure drest in blue and green
> Enchanted the maytime with an antique flute.
> Blown hair is sweet, brown hair over the mouth blown,
> Lilac and brown hair,
> Distractions, music of flute, stops and steps of the mind
>   over the third stair,
> Fading, fading: strength beyond hope and despair . . . .

This is the ground necessary to a conjunction of the timeless in a moment of vision, mediated by that figure going in Mary's colors, the implication of which is that one may not, by desire, escape the green world into vision as Keats attempts on the "viewless wings of poesy," or as Stevens would do by the blue brush of imagination upon the green world. Nor as Dante's pilgrim would, rushing up the mountain. Vision lies in the coincidence of transcendent and immanent, whose principal occasion is the Incarnation, which Eliot has accepted. And the effect upon Eliot as person we may see in a new comfort with the sensual world, in contrast to the discomfort with that world registered in "Preludes" and "The Love Song of J. Alfred Prufrock." For "brown hair over the mouth blown" is "sweet"—the sensual dimension of existence made mete and joyful in this recovery, in contrast to Prufrock's panic of arms "downed with light brown hair." Priapus, dressed in blue and green, is so dressed in art's recognition of the timeless as implicit in the object in time. The blue smolders through the green, as we might put it, and is not therefore attributive in the art, as if a gift of being to the thing by the poet's authority as Stevens would have it.

The end, Eliot will say soon after "Ash-Wednesday," is always such a return, for we are given creation as the context within which our journey must be made. Always, a return to the place from which we started. But, once more, not in the limited literal way. The return is to this present moment in this particular place, at which point only may occur that coincidence of a timeless intrusion into this present through things, a still point to the soul in the turning world. It is in this coincidence, by which we do not mean *accident*, that at last we know this place for the first time. It is a moment in which we discover that roses have the look of roses that are looked at, but with a presence quite other than the attributive presence through art of such looking as Shelley or Stevens might have it. Eliot's recognition, though a quieter and more stilled vision and though differing in the particulars of words and the art of their deployment by the two poets, is nevertheless the same vision of reality we saw in Hopkins's "Windhover."

It is a vision, let us say, which is made possible in the return to reality, to a recovery of intellectual realism which, given our temporal conditions in being, we learn must always be pursued methodically by rational intellect toward the visionary recovery in subsequent moments of grace in nature. It is a return to what we know but have forgotten because of the confusions in our intellectual attempts in its pursuit. Still, those attempts are a necessity to the journey out of the soul's given nature, made manifest in the world as intellectual creature. Though doomed to fail, that doom is only through the failure to perceive, through that "supernatural light" supporting the "natural light" of intellect, the glow—the "glory"—radiant in being. Otherwise that glow is lost and intellect succumbs into the light of common day, the light of finite reason. We shall not be freed short of Beatitude of those confusions to thought, intrinsically probable to our finitude when it is not sustained by the grace of that light Thomas speaks of as "supernatural." In the state of Beatitude, that abiding moment of the soul beyond time which we call eternity, we are promised that we shall know "the Good, the True and the Beautiful" with that fullness of understanding which is the perfection of the soul, no longer seeing as through a glass darkly. That is the promise of the Apostles and the Fathers and St. Augustine and St. Thomas Aquinas. We shall know these in their own simplicity, as imperfect intellect in the world is incapable of knowing this simplicity save in moments of vision that prove always superceding our powers of articulation. Meanwhile, we desire and know and admire, though fitfully.

In the fitful moment, always fading, we are spent toward recovering certitude, prevented through our fallen nature an unwavering certitude, for it is fading always and always to be restored. That is the action which is the life of faith. The restoration is a construction underway in us as persons through desire, knowledge, admiration. Here we describe our present moment, caught in the flicker of a finch's wing, of roses stippled on quivering trout, in the nightingale's song or the hawk's cry. In Eliot's being spoken to through a kingfisher in an English garden or remembering the cry of plover or an image of a bent goldenrod. The moment hovers the green world, from the reach of that high, dawn-drawn and dappled falcon to a stoop as low as the shine of ember-bleak soil turned in from the drawing sun by the sheer plod of whatever plowing we make of elemental earth. Such vision is both actual and, because of finite intellect, necessarily figurative through the limits of sign. And because of these limits, intellect is required always in its action to be governed by that proportionality dependent in our common being.

It is also a moment—lest thought bear too much a sense of guilt within the act of thinking itself, out of an excessive Romantic desire for Beatitude—in our own singing about the possible "future" of Thomism. Such moments occur not only in the coincidence of the seeing eye and kingfisher or windhover, but in those flickering shared moments of the signs we are now using, if graced, when we sense a *now* of our being recovered to intellectual seeing. Indeed, that is a dimension peculiar to our given nature, beyond actual falcons and nightingales or a recovery of the "saltsavor" of the earth. It is a moment *to*, not *in*, the eye of the beholder, a "seeing" through that eye and out of mind and soul, making possible our mutual consent to signs. Whether that shining in sign is from podium or in casual exchanges at the office water cooler or at the cocktail party of festive occasion. Or even at Prufrock's feared tea party. It is the moment of quiet consent among companionable presences, lost from self-awareness even on a front porch at Crawford with night settling the bird's last roosting call, solitary perhaps, but not alone. It is, that is to say, wherever in this dream-crossed twilight between birth and death we find ourselves, always here and now,

> Between two waves of the sea.
> Quick now, here, now, always—
> A condition of complete simplicity
> (Costing not less than everything) . . .
> And all manner of thing shall be well. . . .

Afterword

The purpose of the study of philosophy is not to learn what others
have thought, but to learn how the truth of things stands.

—St. Thomas Aquinas

In our preface we mentioned, almost in passing, the difficulty to our concern in the pages that were to follow posed by the problem of "history,"
the problem of understanding the present in its relation to the past. In
those following pages, we became much concerned with history, particularly in its smaller compass of the specific poets' own lives. For what we
discovered about many of these poets was their problem in coming to
terms with their particular "biographical" history as it impinged upon
the poems they would make. We saw it a problem significant to a concern
for "Romanticism," which we at last attempted to extricate from history,
either personal or general, though history seems always an immediate ob-
stacle to the poet in his attempt to understand his limits as his present
moment of history afforded him, the days of his own life. Not to come
to terms with that impingement of "history," we urged, complicates any
attempt the poet might make to speak for the reality of personhood beyond his own accidents of being, those accidents usually meant by such a
term as *personality*, and especially in our current uses of that term.

What we discover as a consequence, then, is the poet's inclination to
elevate time itself as chief antagonist, whether he addresses that antagonist
upon hearing a bird's song five minutes ago or upon revisiting nature's
panoramic presence five years after, or whether he attempt to address the
full course of his own three-score-and-ten in relation to the flow of similarly limited lives through generations since the Psalmist or Homer or
Dante. It may be forgivable, then, to set out from this problem of history
as we have found it intruding again and again upon the poet's conspicuous

207

concern for the truth of things and perhaps set this problem called "history" in an acceptable perspective.

It is a concern not limited to the poet, of course, since he is not unique among intellectual creatures. His problem with history is the historian's and philosopher's and scientist's as well. Now, any intellectual creature, whatever his special (not *specialized*) calling, seems to deal best with history according to his capacity for a "negative capability" in relation to the things of existence which we locate as displaying their *thingness* in what we call *time past*. If one can, in some acceptable degree, occupy imaginatively a past "thing," here meaning rather specifically "see intellectually with the eyes of a past intellect" such as Thomas's or Shakespeare's or Keats's, one may the better appreciate the past contingencies that rest upon past intellects. That is the attempt we make to repossess a past context to thought. We are constantly encountering superficial exercises in such reconstruction, as in "historical" fiction when it purports to present imaginatively the way things really were on a fateful day, say at Concord or at Appomattox. What one is concerned with as historian is to reconstruct a moment out of the cumulative knowledge of that moment possessed in this present moment. The difficulty of negative capability as exercised through that cumulative knowledge is that one knows not only that collected past but a larger past collected cumulatively up to this present moment, including one's knowledge of one's own intellect. How difficult it is to recapture the way it really was at that courthouse in Virginia in 1865 when we must attempt to do so looking through and beyond the present war in the Mid-East, past Vietnam and Korea and World War II and World War I. It seems impossible that we should be able to discover with certainty, from within our imagined experience of a point or a person in time past, its contingencies to our own present and so do justice to any judgment of person or event in history in relation to the consequences to us. We know present actualities which we believe directly consequent to actions taken in those past contingencies, and our knowing works against our intended "negative capability," making us in our saner moments better content to leave the realities of history to the providence of God. Present effects born in past intellectual acts are not easily put in perspective, though insofar as we may suppose ourselves to possess such perspective, we tend to become gamblers with the future, at least half believing the dice loaded in our favor by our supposed knowledge of cause and effect as certified by history.

And yet there is advantage to such attempt, loaded as it may be with the hazards born of our own gambling natures, our self-assurancy of true prophecy certified by our present knowledge. We must say that, despite such hazard, we do experience a fuller understanding of our present out of our partial understanding of the past. It is only when *fuller* is taken as *full* that the trouble begins. For if from such understanding of partial knowledge of the past and present we conclude ourselves possessed of a surer purchase upon present circumstances, seeing contingency clearly—which it is our concern to accomplish—the danger becomes that we confuse our partial understanding of a partial knowledge as full understanding. We become subject to pride of intellect. By such a disorientation from the reality of our own understanding, we may easily conclude that something called "History" has empowered us. History is then seen as the operative agent in event, more powerful in a determination of event (here our intellectual action in the present) than we should properly allow. That is, we may not so allow, unless we choose to elevate History as determinate of this present more absolutely than is justified by the limits of the knowledge upon which our understanding depends.

But such is our intellectual hunger for certainty that it becomes easy to submit to History as cause of whatever is. Add to that entity History that other procounsel to intellect safely secularized as Nature—seen by that intellect in the same manner it sees History—and one arrives confidently at a determinism such as that which has emerged in various guises in Western intellect over the past few hundred years. With that confident submission to History and Nature, one becomes confident of predicating the future. Meanwhile one may admit, as the eighteenth-century Enlightenment intellectual could do, that indeed some things are not yet *known*, though they will prove already *understood* when we at last certify them as known. Such is the necessary condition of predicating, prophesying, the future when this sort of prophet is questioned by common sense. That common sense, fortunately, is often astir in the generality of mankind upon whom predications of the future are to be executed into a present by that prophet. Such a position intellectually held allows a completion of an Idol suitable to common worship by common sense, if common sense can be relocated. The Idol of History plus Nature, manifest in a variety of intellectual shrines since the enabling eighteenth century, has often enough gained that consent. It is but a breath into the imagined future, however, before that intellect becomes (through its vaunted knowledge) Priest to its Idol. After which intellect itself becomes the Holy Spirit in relation to History and Nature as the other "persons" of the secular trinity, whose banner is Progress. Such is a brief "history" of intellect in its turning gnostic. If that seems an end to gnostic inclination of intellect, however, we must hasten to add that such a paradigm does not circumscribe the *particular* gnostic who advances it. Though a determinist by faith, he is not therefore absolutely determined—to his initial shock and dismay perhaps. We have made some argument, for instance, that Eliot was himself just such a gnostic, but that epithet is appropriate only up to the event in his personal life which biographers talk about as his "nervous breakdown." That he and we may see it as more properly called a spiritual crisis has been a part of our exploration in these pages.

As for the gnostic as prophet: I am quite wary of any readings of the future, recognizing that some necessity exists for such prophecy. There is suggestive evidence that tonight a storm front will move through, leaving an accumulation of six or eight inches of snow by morning. Prudence in response to such prophecy well advises me to lay in a supply of wood and fetch milk and bread from the local grocer. But there is in prophecies of the future, when less guided by the realities of nature, too often not a foreseeing but a forewilling. In that confusion lie old contentions between prophet and king, as Oedipus might say not only against Tieresias, but in the light of his own excessive pretense to understanding based on his inadequate knowledge as suited to either king or prophet. He would himself be more prophet than king, and in the end is neither. I remember Dante's vivid imaginative punishment of Tieresias in lower Hell for his presumption in declaring the future's realities. That prophet is punished by having his head turned backward on his body in Hell, so that his endless circling allows him to see where he has been but not where he is going. One might even suppose that an added fillip of that punishment is his seeing, and re-seeing of what he has seen but only as from the beginning, a retrospection that dooms him to the eternal present with no prospect of any future.

And yet, there is a certain kind of prophecy, which we each practice in some degree, the prophecy which memory encourages us to. It is a legitimate, even necessary prophetic condition to intellect out of intellect's very nature: the recovery in this present moment of known but forgotten things. This is a prophecy I would, indeed, champion as crucial to intellect's survival in its present. It nevertheless has a disadvantage exacerbated by our world's long neglect of it. For it lacks the appeal of imaginative spectacle. It is imaginative spectacle which excites careless interest in the future, as if spectacle were itself substantive, even as "history" or "nature" or "time" are imagined to be substantive through long intellectual neglect of that which is truly substantive. It is most exciting but also most misleading when projected upon time future as if a substantive nature. And thereby it seems the more immune to rejection, as it should be rejected, since more difficult to measure by the realities of time present. Demagogues, whether politician, poet, priest or philosopher, have this advantage in commanding a present popularity.

We see Virgil in the office of such a prophet, as is desirable, guiding Dante down through Hell and up Purgatory Mountain in Dante's *Divine Comedy*. He is prophet teacher, recalling to the pilgrim Dante things he has known but forgotten, in conjunction with what he is observing at the moment. Such "prophecy" requires a conscious attention to what men have said—Aristotle and Plato, the Church Fathers, Old and New Testament persons, St. Augustine and St. Thomas. These teachers are introduced gradually, and in relation to the present circumstances in which they signify, from the Elysian conditions of the great ancient poets to the doctors of the Church in the Heaven of the Sun near the end of Dante's journey.[20] To such "prophecy" as encountered directly, one must bring "history" to the account in order to understand the presentness of the past, the pertinence of what "they" have thought in relation to my present attempt to understand whatever of truth is borne in what they thought.

What Dante learns is to avoid the trap of elevating history to an entity determining the present. For in each instance he is speaking to discrete souls in their eternal present, in which the consequences of what they have thought and done of their free will are made specific. They, and not history, are the proximate cause to their eternal present state. To observe this of Dante's reading of man in nature is to see just how great a chasm opens with modernism, in which growing heresy the soul is progressively exonerated as mediate cause of its being. Determinate causes are sought elsewhere, in history and nature. But such is that nature at risk, the soul, that it cannot at last allow determinism as its own cause, whatever the ultimate or mediate cause. And so the shift occurs whereby intellect, abandoning the soul, becomes itself ultimate. All else is determined by history or nature, but *not* the particular intellect making that determination about existence.

Present effects of past intellectual actions, whether those of Plato or Aristotle or Descartes or Locke, are with us. But what must be signified as the *cause* of those effects is not History as a deterministic force, but rather the particular intellect's actions in response to such causes in its own present, in relation to its present measure of those things by the truth of how things stand. That truth of things is not determined by History, though the way in which we see that truth is affected by our own response to the way others have seen that truth, whether in 399 B.C. or 1300 or 1990. What men have said and done is "history." But the truth in that history is independent of time as it is also independent of what they or we say and dare. It is in recognition of this distinction, then, that we at once find ourselves contemporary to great minds by an orientation of intellect to the truth of things. But we are also able as well to see that some minds are more closely attuned to truth than others, even as a singular mind is at times more closely attuned to truth than it is at others.

It is this burden of history that we cannot ignore, for it is intrusively present in our intellectual life, requiring actions of our own intellect to refine and purify. And only the truth of things is sufficient to that necessary action, out of which we recover our ordinate relation to our *person's* contingency to reality. Without such clarifications, it is little wonder that we make history an entity, as if it were at least coequal to *being* itself. We thereby concede to History a determinate power in relation to *being*. Indeed, this elevation of history to an entity is precisely the gnostic strategy which Eric Voegelin anatomizes as emanating from Joachim of Flora at the end of the twelfth century, a strategy gradually pervading Western intellectual thought with such modern symptomatic issues as our great wars and the general dissolution of society toward chaos. History is couched by Joachim of Flora deceptively in an analogy to the Holy Trinity. First came the Age of the Father, ancient history, followed by the Age of the Son, in which Joachim lives. To be followed by the Age of the Paraclete.

From where we stand to look back from the 1990s, we may have the uneasy sense that Joachim's metaphor, which makes History God's executive angel in time, is rather like the appropriations of the Sacraments to Satanic rites. Certainly, since the elevation of History to the pretenses of that science called Historicism in the eighteenth century, History has become increasingly a dark presence served up in a variety of deterministic dress for popular adoration. Joachim's is a paradigm of History as Creator at last, determining a beginning, middle, and end to being—the end recently celebrated in the name of Hegel. Creation thus is History's determined province, that which nothing else is. But in that paradigm, it is significant that the explicator is always—as in the classical epic—located in *medias res*, though in nothing of that sense meant by Voegelin in relation to the *metaxy* of consciousness, nor of Thomas's sense whereby the soul is immediate to created existence as it responds to contingencies. For in the Joachim paradigm, there is always a necessity of process as lineal, as measured by time in a progression from one stage of History's determination of being to the next. The age of the Holy Ghost is always just ahead, just around the corner. The Age of the Holy Ghost is a future. But that implies that the Age of the Father is a past.

Such is the paradigm which intellect builds to its own ends after Joachim. The one we are currently most familiar with is Marxism. Marx derives his version of history most immediately from Hegel, we say, projecting it by a mystical language dressed as rational exposition out of the fundamental tenant to that faith: History as determinate of being, sweeping all before it in process. Thus begins Marx's (and Hegel's) reduction of all "nature," and especially human nature, to an increasingly egalitarian response to things. In an earlier stage, those particularities such as spoken of by St. Paul as the peculiar gifts to the specific soul which make that soul potentially member in the body of community—those particularities are dissolved into an amorphous condition of "communal" existence. Not in fact actual, but dreamed to become actual in the coming Age of the Holy Ghost of History. The impetus is of the inevitability of an irreversible History, absolute because irreversible. From such a "communal" dissolution of particularities in social structures, we are not surprised at the excessive dissolutions of particularities whose current effect is a divisiveness in what is left of social community: any creature of nature is no less nor any more than any other. The extreme egalitarianism confronts us with a shock of recognition in the extreme environmentalism that emerges as the new religion, wherein—not this thing, *this* spotted owl or *this* whale—is defended, but *species* as an abstraction is defended. There are rare moments to the contrary, in which some hope of recovery emerges. The lost whale swimming inland from the Pacific, into a California bay; three whales isolated in a frozen spot in the far north. A revived hope lies in the necessity to those struggling to rescue the particular creatures of giving them a *name*, a gesture of endearment which Wordsworth would no doubt understand, and Hopkins certainly would. For they are not Whale 1, Whale 2, Whale 3, with the subnames peculiar to their species. When "Humphrey" the whale imperiled himself a second time by returning to the San Francisco Bay and moving inland, the general alarm included the thrill of recognition that this was *Humphrey*, the excitement over that marvel of particularity recognized and caught up by television cameras and in newspaper accounts across the country.

The problem of Marxist communalism, derived from Hegel, is that the principle has removed from it not only the attention to the essence of the thing (the *wholeness* of this *particular* whale or the *personhood* of this *particular* citizen), but its accidents as well, except where the accidents may be used to emotional persuasion of a body of humanity reduced to a "mass" of humanity. Those aspects of the particularity of the explicit creature removed, the possibility of a transformation in intellect through a communion of intellect and thing is redirected to abstractions and thus away from essences. But not simply to species. More destructively, the transformation is made to an abstraction that is never specific except as an empty center constellating accidents of being intellectually removed from actual being. The accidents of personhood are transferred to constellate about an empty center called the State of modernist thought. The rituals associated with the elevation of the State replace the Sacraments that once ordered community in the body of a whole, whose head (St. Paul says) is Christ. (See the machinations in this transformation such as those of Robespierre or Comte.)

The "Head" of the State as body civic in the history of our century is such that out of common sense (failed in its fulfillment as knowledge under the guidance of the rational intellect) there is effected the accelerating decay of those communal remnants still holding the body of community together. How could we expect otherwise? And should we still attempt other expectations of History's issue? The inescapable, present bombardment of intellect by the disintegrations of persons, the collapse of the family of persons, the centripetal explosion of the body social—these are inescapably present to us, eroding our confidence in familial, civic, and religious institutions. The growing cynicism directed to executive, legislative, and judicial sectors of the civic soul speaks of the growing collapse within the particular person who feels more and more at risk, for whom cynicism seems the only defense and alienation, though undesired, apparently the only available refuge.

We know all too well our popular response to the assumption of history as inexorable determinator of our temporal existence, for we encountered it often. Whenever we are uncertain of the future and made fearfully uncertain in the present on the evidence of our past, we say the aphorism: if we do not know our past, we are doomed to repeat past mistakes in the future. That signal warning, from Harvard's recalcitrant Humanist, Santayana, still manages to carry too much the implication of history as an entity. For we still respond to history as if it were an extrinsic determinant upon nature and human nature, against which even our advanced knowledge seems insufficient guardian. The latest "artificial intelligence" seems rather geared to serve intellect as itself the determiner of being rather than to serve intellect as a special gift to the being we call man. Know the past, and that knowledge will free you of the present into a desirable future. Such would seem the conclusion to be drawn. By knowledge, by gnosis, our power over an entity, whether *being* or *history*, is supposedly assured. Until, that is, we must act in the context of our present contingencies. It is at the point of this necessity, as we fear more and more, that we recognize the fulfillment of C. S. Lewis's warning to us, made long ago. For we seem very near the realization of the abolition of man.

What we may discover in that moment is that, when desire has become separated in intellect from its proper end, from its proper movement toward the Good, desperation in the moment becomes the effect. For that disjunction recognized and accepted as inevitable, as determined, the only possible Good must be conjured out of Nothingness by a present action whose cause is a temporal future elevated as desire's only possible end, despite the temporal obstacles, despite the inevitability of death to the particular intellect so desiring. It is not the past as determining cause of our present that is the arena of intellectual action, we may say, attempting to escape History's power. The arena is rather projected as a future. But that proves, in the event of such present projection, merely our whistling in the graveyard of our present to still our panic. Still, that is exactly the counsel of our contemporary Moses to Modernism, Jean-Paul Sartre. Sartre, fascinated by "Time" in William Faulkner's fiction, says what we may learn from *The Sound and the Fury*. The source of Faulkner's title is pertinent, a definition of "life" as "signifying nothing" as MacBeth puts it. The lesson to be learned, says Sartre, is that "Man's misfortune lies in his being time-bound." For this "unspeakable present, leaking at every seam," and confused by "sudden invasions of the past," puts one to confusion. It does so until one assumes a command of the future. "Man is not the sum of what he has, but the totality of what he does not yet have, of what he might have." Thus one can only be said *to exist* in one's own future, which one makes against this present and its interrupting past. In short, one conjures oneself into existence, successfully so if the conjuring is out of Nothingness, which is a new entity proposed, representing intellectual being as freed of time past and passing.

Most intellects are restive with such a metaphysics of Nothingness, wherein action precedes being. For we find it impossible to ignore the continuing sense of the continuing decay of this very moment into a past, certified by our memory of experience of past moments now decayed, which turn us uneasily toward that most uncertain prospect, the future. What refutes Sartre is our ineradicable memory, a presence to each consciousness. Indeed, the enemy Sartre must deal with is not time as an entity but his own memory of himself as an existence anterior to this moment of his remembering. His own memoir, *The Word*, is an account of his attempt to exorcise, not time, but himself, to an emptiness, a Nothingness, within which he would construct his Self. The absurdity of such intent as philosophy, as thought, is so evident that it requires a new philosophy declared *ex nihilo*, the Philosophy of the Absurd, which has been so much a darling term to deracinated intellectuals since World War II.

One's awareness of oneself as held by memory stops at some point. To remember that one saw or did certain things when one was two years old only underlines the point that one even then already *was*. And so one is denied absolute authority as the Cause of one's being. Consider on the point Sartre's own "Wordsworthean" moment, from which he moves in a direction the opposite of Wordsworth's Platonism. In his memoir, he recalls himself as a child in the family library, closing curtains against the world, retreating into books to escape the present, though thereby confronted by the past which always clings as accident to the words of man. Only the Saint, we believe, can rest content in such an assurance of the good of the present that it allows him to believe as already fulfilled that old prophecy about the present as transcending past and future: sufficient unto the moment is the good thereof, which is the issue to any understanding of Christ's words, "Sufficient unto the day are the evils thereof."

Not being saint, one may seek some rescue in the moment out of the experience of it. One may, in other words, seek to come to terms with the evil in it, whatever its particular manifestation. For there is a certain truth in Sartre's description of the "unspeakable present" as subject to "sudden invasions of the past." It is not so much what Sartre sees that is in error, but what he would make of what he sees. Even so, by the very attempt to come to terms with the moment's evil in order to rescue its good, one realizes it already slipping into a past. I stand in this present moment, looking ahead to a future moment, and am both amazed and baffled by the maze of contingency to that action of looking. By my intellectual act, I look back, to my past moment, considering by the offices of reflective intellect my progress into this moment, wondering what contingency must have seemed as complex from that past moment's looking as I stared vaguely toward this actual present. And behold, contingency's maze by retrospection appears a precise path through contingencies, though never a straight path like a highway in Nevada desert, leading to an inevitability of my present moment. If we do not credit the will's guidance in making that way, which is never straight though always narrow, we are misled to the conclusion that this present moment is determined by our own "History," a special accompanying presence somewhat like Socrates' guardian voice, though with consequences unhopeful of issue into the country of the Good.

It is the role that *will* plays in this journey through time that one is encouraged by. I am arrived in this present largely by, though perhaps not inclusively because of, my own determinations in the face of contingency. In that recognition, I may consent to my own "history" in this limited sense as determined, for it is not determined by history but by me. Our aphorisms out of common sense acknowledge participation through will in our present condition of being: as we have made our bed, we say, so we must sleep in it. Thus we conclude, our *personal* participation in our own history—through will, intellect, and ultimately soul—requires our responsible acceptance of active participation as affecting our present. What we have ignored in the self-assurance that I myself am the Captain of my Soul (the Thomistic realist would say) is that not only our will is expeditor of our sailing toward whatever Byzantium we come to desire, but grace as well, and from the initial grant of grace, our inception as person, our creation as discrete soul. But what we have been concerned about is the Modernist will's assurance to intellect that it is sufficient to navigate contingency. That is an act of intellect separating itself from the contingencies of being by the will's denial of grace as supportive of the necessary journey. And in that separatist action there appears the sense of power as primarily the intellect's.

There follows intellect's assumption of its autonomy, by the authority of its own history. Its motto is "I will not serve." And under that banner it attempts to exercise its independence, independent of creation, of the world, whose "maze" becomes thereby but a sort of prime matter to its constructions of dreams. Intellect thus self-justified turns to future contingencies as if the conquering explorer of a Nothingness which it alone may make into a Something, and the "something" deeply interfused in those illusional structures turns out, again and again, to be the isolated intellect, staring in horror at itself. It is against that prospect of discovery of illusional action that the gnostic activist is required to force all to a conformity in the illusion. Otherwise, being cannot be dictated into its dream existence. The gnostic tyrant, whom we recognize more and more as issuing from the Modernist faith, may be as spectacular as a Hitler or a Stalin. But he may also be as near as the champion of any ideology, however much he may camouflage that ideology with the shibboleths of concern for the future of humanity. Gnosticism knows no East or West, no North or South. It cannot, lest it become uncomfortable in its gnostic transcendence of and over being. The points of the compass do not apply to God. The gnostic intellect cannot allow it either, though in his end he must.

Endnotes

1. On the nature of community as vital, see my "Quest for Community Ground: A Scholastic Foray," in *Liberal Arts and Community: The Feeding of the Larger Body*, 1990.

2. The term "modernist," characterizing the intellectual shift from reality as the measure of truth to intellect as presumptuous measure of truth through its power to determine being by presumption, will be a constant in these pages. There is a considerable literature on this "modernism," so that my own meaning in the term may be clearer from my "Modern: Modernism, Modernist—A Preliminary Exploration of Our Intellectual Manner," in press.

3. Concerning Eliot's remark that heresy's problem to intellect is that it is partly right: in our intellectual deportment, in some respect that may be discoverable to clear analysis, we are likely heretics all. And so in that condition of mind we find ourselves in circumstances not unlike that of the "crowd." I have suggested in another context that civilization is the effect of the *crowd* struggling to become a *body*, the necessary struggling preventing perfect correspondence of its reality to its desire. Similarly of our intellectual community: we are a crowd more or less struggling against heresy toward becoming an orthodox body in service to truth. The struggling lies in our intellectual deportment individually, in each person's attempting to draw a line defining an acceptable body. For as discrete intellectual, one recognizes the necessity of a crucial distinction even when the precise demarcation is not always clear. That is, there is necessarily a distinction to be made between *heretic* and *infidel* in respect to the intellectual piety required toward reality. That is why we treasure both St. Augustine and St. Thomas, though there are difficulties in reconciling each to the other on all points. Or Scotus and Thomas. Closer home, that is why we value both Gilson and Maritain, while not always comfortable with the one or the other, as they were not always comfortable with each other. Both, however, were agreed that Descartes was infidel, though they might not agree in the sorting out of degrees of heresy between themselves. We must, as best we are able, find guarded comfort, each with the

219

other, in the amorphous body intent upon orthodoxy, that is intent upon recovering to ourselves a vision of the truth of things.

In the light of this gratuitous homily, perhaps it may be acceptable, if not necessarily appropriate, to say in what respect I value each—Gilson and Maritain—in my attempts to overcome whatever of the heretical lies in my own intellectual deportment. For to struggle at all, I must assume that I am not of the party of the infidel. Gilson is superb in his gift for clarifying what men have said of being; Maritain ravenous for the truth of things. To oversimplify, the one has the dominant inclination of philosopher, the other of poet. *Inclination*: meaning disposition of mind as reflected tonally in their verbal pursuits of truth and the beauty of truth in their mutual desire for the good. It follows from this difference in inclination, I think, that Maritain must prove the more controversial, for he is more audaciously ambiguous, moving with intuition touched by a mystical ambience in his intellectual deportment, so that he must recall himself often to the governance of the *ratio*. It seems inevitable that there should be a lively following of Maritain, an association of diverse intellectuals drawn to conclave. One feels almost cautiously reserved toward Gilson, which deportment I take to be a considerable tribute to him.

Put another way, for mine is an impressionistic distinction, which I nevertheless believe points to a reality of distinction between these two "things," the intellect of Gilson and the intellect of Maritain: Gilson's deportment of thought seems to correspond analogously to St. Thomas's; Maritain's has a touch of the Kierkegaardean daring in it, which raises an enthusiasm that itself requires a caution. Maritain stirs me up. Gilson calms me down. I find I need both, if my own intellectual life is to continue alive, but not excessive of the limits of my gifts in that department. It cannot be either/or for me, but both/and. Happily so, it seems to me.

4. I have explored this recent history in several works, which may in some degree justify this abbreviated summary, especially in *The Reflective Journey Toward Order* (1974); *The Prophetic Poet and the Popular Spirit* (3 volumes, 1981, 1983, 1984); *Possum, and Other Receipts for the Recovery of "Southern" Being* (1987); *The Trouble with You Innerleckchuls* (1988); and *The Men I Have Chosen for Fathers: Literary and Philosophical Passages* (1990).

5. My occasion lies in the work to follow the present one, in which the question of the dangers in attributive analogy as opposed to the Thomistic analogy of proper proportionality are explored.

6. Concerning Eliot and the technical concern for point of view in its relation to poetic tradition and to his own philosophical concerns, see my *T. S. Eliot: The American Magus* (1970) and *Eliot's Reflective Journey to the Garden* (1979).

7. I cannot leave this passage and its preparation without recalling philosophy as feminine, as Sophia, and to recommend in this relation a neglected work by Karl Stern, in which he examines the confusions in modern philosophy in chapters dealing with, among others, Descartes, Schopenhauer, Sartre, and Kierkegaard. The book is called *The Flight from Woman*, and in it there is a possible beginning of our recovery from the present confusions whereby, consequent

upon that flight, "Man" is pursued by "Woman" in an effort to become "Man" under the confusing insistence of the latest spirit loose in our age, "Feminism."

8. The evidence of Stevens's rejection of all save the saving imagination which is his own runs through the poetry and his few essays and letters. Thus from the *Letters*: ". . . instead of crying for help to God or one of the gods, we should look to ourselves for help. The exaltation of human nature should take the place of its abasement," such abasement as in finding *sinfulness* in man in the theological sense. (195) "I ought to say that it is a habit of mind with me to be thinking of some substitute for religion . . . . My trouble, and the trouble of a great many people, is the loss of belief in the sort of God in Whom we were brought up to believe. Humanism would be the natural substitute, but the more I see of humanism—the less I like it." (348) God is "simply a projection of itself by a race of egoists, which it is natural for them to treat as sacred." (349) In the light of such pronouncements, Stevens says nevertheless, "I am not an atheist although I do not believe to-day in the same god in whom I believed when I was a boy." (86–87) (The page citations are to *Letters of Wallace Stevens*, edited by Holly Stevens. New York: Alfred A. Knopf, 1966.)

9. On the importance of Hawthorne as Romantic poet distinct from Poe as Romantic poet, see my *Why Poe Drank Liquor* (1983) and *Why Hawthorne Was Melancholy* (1984).

10. I consider Eliot more directly in his progress toward conversion to Christianity as revealed in his words in a work in progress, "T. S. Eliot and the Still Point of Consciousness: An Excursion into the Four Quartets."

11. The Bergsonian Idea, so important to a recovery out of the mechanistic determinism that entrapped nineteenth-century thought, becomes a sentimental crutch by the end of the twentieth century. One sees it nowhere more clearly than in the environmentalism grown out of an increasingly vague attachment to mechanistic principle, which nevertheless continues an intellectual burden. It is in that movement called "green," within which there has grown a special species of Manicheanism. For in the old manifestation of Manichean doctrine, nature itself was the evil principle and the existence of the created world to be attributed in one way or another to a dark force as opponent to the good and the light. Material existence was the medium of spiritual destruction by the dark force. In the new environmental Manicheanism, the dark force, after first having reconstituted God out of eighteenth-century rationalism, is now reduced beneath nature: I mean man himself. After the supplanting of God as Cause by man's own mind as cause, with nature the instrument through which was established the primacy of man's mind, what now develops is an antagonistic reaction to mind by a new "pagan," the environmentalist, who but reluctantly consents to an identity as "man." Mind requires religious fervor as spark to a combustion of active energy on nature's behalf, but rational mind is rejected in favor of a mysticism only vaguely remembered as an inheritance from empirical science. That is, "scientific" evidence accepted on faith is imbued with mystical authority, seldom rationally tested as truth alive. It is, rather, knowledge abstracted from being and taken as absolute.

In the upshot, what is considered most evil, most to be deplored, is the existence of man himself. One need only listen carefully to the mystical position underlying the typical "Nature" program on public television to realize that the dominant evil spawned almost inexplicably is man himself. For how could nature do this to herself?

In these nature programs, one notes the repeated explanation of color on insect wings, of sexual habits of creatures: adaptation is out of an *intent* precedent to the effect. Marty Stauffer, the personable commentator on PBS's "Wild America" speaks (October 26, 1990) of "Nature's innate will to survive." But that intent is never located in an agent. Intent floats free in the argument of the intentionality of species. At best it is anchored in genetic "memory." One has to conclude that such argument as expressed or implied declares intentional purpose in evolution. Intentionality signifies, however, only as some aspect of mind, and the agency of that intent must at last be addressed. Chesterton, in his works in general but helpfully in his little book on St. Thomas, addresses the vagueness of this unanchored thought about "creative evolution" which is now pervasive of popular, emotional responses to "nature." He says, "It is typical of [such thinkers] that they will sometimes rather timidly use the word Purpose; but blush at the very mention of the word Person . . . .[W]e do not need anything but our own common sense to tell us that if there has been from the beginning anything that can possibly be called a Purpose, it must reside in something that has the essential elements of a Person. There cannot be an intention hovering in the air all by itself, anymore than a memory that nobody remembers or a joke that nobody has made." That in large part explains why nature *personified* is so much a necessity to such thinkers.

In recognizing the impossibility of a floating intention, sentimentalists have therefore made nature a substitute "Person." It is this Person who seems infected by a sort of acne, a disorder to be extirpated, which must be removed if the elected priests of nature, the environmentalist, can do so. That rash on nature's face is man. In those PBS nature programs, widely used in the public schools to educate our young, the metaphysical position implied is the one found in Walt Disney's *Bambi*. Of that subversive film one should note incidentally that the villain is not man transgressing the order of nature as indifferent, brutal poacher. He is a hunter. The implication to be drawn is that man must at worst be vegetarian, though one wonders whether lettuce may not cry out under vicious chompings. It is quite another matter for the lioness feeding her cubs, for the boa catching the monkey. The concern for balance in nature admirably recorded by the devoted environmentalist when islanded from mankind as itself included in "nature," fails generally to indict man for excess. *That* he is a hunter is sufficient. For all the hard empirical information about nature, the revelations of particular creatures in their habitats gathered through evermore sophisticated technology, the virtues in such discoveries are so much distorted as to disallow man a position in the ranks of creation according to his nature.

The origins of this species of sentimentality, paraded in art as scientific truth, we find in Darwin. One passage is worth an extensive quotation, from the 1872, sixth edition, of *Origin of Species*. One notes the inversion in Darwin's account of the eye:

> We know that [the telescope] has been perfected by the long-continued efforts of the highest human intellects; and we naturally infer that the eye has been formed by a somewhat analogous process. [One observes the suppression of purposive agent in the passive "has been formed," the agent avoided.] [W]e must suppose that there is a power, represented by natural selection or the survival of the fittest, always intently watching each slight alteration in the transparent layers; and carefully preserving each which, under varied circumstances, in any way or in any degree, tends to procure a more distinct image. We must suppose each new state of the instrument to be multiplied by the million; each to be preserved until a better one is produced, and then the old ones to be destroyed. In living bodies, variation will cause the slight alterations, generation will multiply them almost infinitely, and natural selection will pick out with unerring skill each improvement. Let the process go on for millions of years; and during each year on millions of individuals of many kinds; and may we not believe that a living optical instrument might thus be formed as superior to one of glass, as the works of the Creator are to those of man?

The presence in this passage of the "Creator" is a concession typical of the mechanistic thought of the late nineteenth century. For the God recognized here is "natural selection or the survival of the fittest." Not the Creator, but "natural selection" is the causal agent, picking "out with unerring skill each improvement." One suspects the process in which Darwin rests faith is that descried in the recent evolution of industrial machinery. With the advantage of our hundred years since Darwin's words, we may observe that the analogy Darwin uses is that of attribution, imposed upon nature from art, specifically from mechanical art. By the time of Darwin's words railroads conveyed 307 million passengers annually in a wonder of mechanistic order. But what escapes the wonder gives pause, as it did John Ruskin: "[N]ow every fool in Buxton can be at Bakewell in half-an-hour, and every fool in Bakewell at Buxton." Unless Ruskin's "fool" can be translated as the unfittest, one well questions a principle buried in Darwin's words: the principle of self-correcting, self-perpetuating perfection of life as machine, whose latest manifestation to us is the current fascination with artificial intelligence.

What the environmentalist of whom I speak does, whether intentionally or thoughtlessly, is assume the authority of Person himself, justified by knowledge as opposed to understanding, a knowledge received uncritically, whereby nature is presented as the supreme Person whose agent is the environmentalist. The confusion is that of an *ad post facto* bootlegging of his own intentionality into nature from his provincial point of view, while suggesting an intentionality of Person out of which alone Purpose may be said to issue. By suggesting such Purpose to be inherent in nature "from the beginning," but attributable to naught else but "Nature," a sentimental ambience is effused whose pretense is of an Absolute

Immanence. That is why I have spoken of this as a modern version of Paganism. We must nevertheless recognize that, despite the shallowness of the thought on the purpose of existence as derived from an emotional embrace of "creative evolution," there has grown a considerable political power by the end of the twentieth century. Though that power is not justified by the soundness of vision, it is highly operative upon the intellectual—and consequently—social fabric. One well notes also that it is an intuitive response through a common sense resident in this creature man. That common sense recalls us to stewardship, but when common sense is not supported by thought in a full exploration of the experience of both humanness and the inclusive creation, it loses the proper orientation of intellect as steward of being—of creation—and becomes highly manipulative and highly susceptible to manipulation by modern gnostic thought. The ideal implicit in thoughtless environmentalism is nature taken to be an unexplained throb in the void, before which intellect is required to kneel. Intellect may do so for a time, but then appears that director, the gnostic intellect, who appropriates collected power from such reduced intellects to the restructuring of being, a far remove from intellect as steward of being.

12. It is an irony of pathetic dimension, though predictable, to hear Joyce near the end of his life worrying over whether he has been victim to this side effect, whether he has become a poet of Coleridge's "fancy" rather than of the "imagination." And we discover in Pound's *Cantos,* particularly in those last fragments, something of the same lament. Has he, by an assumption of autonomous authority of his own intellect, established order?

> That I lost my center
>   fighting the world.
> The dreams clash
>   and are shattered—
> and that I tried to make a paradiso
>   terrestre.

13. Eliot, in *Little Gidding,* is quite aware of this condition of the "Romantic" poet as encountered in Keats or in Joyce, speaking of three spiritual conditions that "flourish in the same hedgerow":

> Attachment to self and to things and to persons, detachment
> From self and from things and from persons; and,
>   growing between them, indifference
> Which resembles the others as death resembles life,
> Being between two lives—unflowering, between
> The live and the dead nettle.

What follows immediately is a recovery of memory understood in its service to the soul. It is for "liberation," for an "expanding/ Of love beyond desire" whereby one is liberated "From the future as well as the past."

14. Consider on this point, the rivalry of intellect and its imaginative making

in relation to the Son as Maker and the Holy Ghost as continuing Lord and Giver of Life, St. Thomas's analysis of blasphemy against the Holy Ghost, *Summa Theologica*, II-II, Q14. This may be a point at which to remark my contention that Eliot's move toward Thomistic realism as more than merely intuitive in him, remembering his long engagement of the difference between *seem* and *is*, between *vision* and *illusion*. Note, for instance, his deliberate use of scholastic terms in "The Hollow Men's" final section. A "shadow" falls between *idea* and *reality*, between *potency* and *existence*, deliberate scholastic terminology in the poem. That "shadow" is engaged in "Ash-Wednesday" and in the "Ariel Poems." It seems probable that Eliot also had Wordsworth in mind, a contrast to Wordsworth's Platonic solution to the mystery of the "shadow," when he opens "Animula" with a quotation from Dante's *Purgatorio*: " 'Issues from the hand of God, the simple soul'/ To a flat world of changing lights and noise." There follows a catalogue of other worldly contingencies to that "simple soul." (The "flat world" is discovered a quite different flatness from that announced by Stevens's "flat and bare" earth.) In the "Journey of the Magi," both the harsh and the sensually attractive aspect of the speaker's journey through that world, through nature to the city of man, comes to focus in the "Romantic" question, now put in a new dimension by the Incarnation: "were we led all that way for/ Birth or Death."

15. Note, for instance, Eliot's remark that Wordsworth's "critical insight, in this one *Preface* and *Supplement*, is enough to give him the highest place." A decade earlier, Eliot had dismissed Wordsworth's argument in this "Preface," without ever naming the work or Wordsworth directly. By 1932, however, he finds in Wordsworth's "poetry and in his Preface, a profound spiritual revival, an inspiration communicated rather to Pusey and Newman, to Ruskin, and to the great humanitarians, than to accredited poets of the next generation." One surely adds to the list Eliot gives Gerard Manley Hopkins.

16. In a concern for melancholy as symptom to the soul's disorder, one does not deny chemical or neurological disorders as affecting one's spirit through the body. What is at issue is the reduction of spirit, of soul, to the mechanisms of physiology. There is emerging at the moment a sort of last battle in the West waged defensively by remnants of Freudian therapists and the ascendent biologically oriented therapists—those who would treat depression with words and those who would treat it with drugs and words in a limited capacity of the "word." The biologically oriented force objects that there is no scientific evidence of the effectiveness of "psychodynamic psychotherapy" based in Freudian psychoanalysis, only opinion. There seems to be some evidence that the use of imipramine or fluoxetine helps patients recover from depression. My own concern is that, in this war between Freudian opinion and clinical statistics, there may be lost that dimension of *person* that is fundamental to the nature of our human *being*. Both positions are a presumption of our being as mechanistic, the one intent on blowing out time's dust with the word, the other with flushing out that mechanism with chemical cleaner. Having so addressed "mind," the question to either becomes, what is the "time" the restored watch of mind is to be set to? For an account of the emerging conflict, see *Science News*, January 26, 1991.

17. The phrase "things *are* as they *specifically* are" intends to catch the relation between *being* and *specific* being, between the thing as it shares being and the thing which is concomitantly—even as it is consequentially—the thing that it is by essence.

18. For a response to Wordsworth's "Ode" approximately contemporary to Eliot's conversion, see Robert Frost's "Trial by Existence." In it, Frost takes Virgilean metaphor to his purpose, which is to justify intellect as autonomous. His use of "myth" is a convenience to his gnostic understanding of intellect in contention with chaos, as opposed to being a denominator of creation.

19. We suggested that Maritain's removal of moral implication in art as an activity of the practical intellect might need qualification. In making the suggestion I am aware that St. Thomas says quite emphatically that "Art does not belong to moral knowledge, which concerns things to be done, since art is right reason about things to be made." (*Summa*, II-II, Prologue to Questions 1–16). Similarly (*Summa* I-II, Q 57, Art 3): "Art is nothing else but the right reason about certain works to be made. . . . [T]he good of these things depends, not on man's appetitive faculty being affected in this or that way, but on the goodness of the work done. . . . Art . . . is an operative habit." It is in this sense a making through the practical intellect. But Thomas adds: "And yet it has something in common with the speculative habits: since the quality of the object considered by the latter [speculative habits] is a matter of concern to them also, but not how the human appetite may be affected towards the object." In this passage, following Article 3, Thomas distinguishes art and prudence as virtues: "art is the right reason of things to be made; whereas prudence is the right reason of things to be done." Citing Aristotle's distinction between *making* and *doing*, in *Metaphysics*: "making is an action passing into outward matter, e.g., *to build*, *to saw*, and so forth; whereas doing is an action abiding in the agent, e.g., *to see*, *to will*, and the like."

We have, I believe, made an adequate separation of the poem itself from the maker of the poem in saying that for the maker, the good of the thing made is the operative principle. But we have also suggested that, considering the maker himself, his action of making involves his action of doing, in that he gives himself to the action of making. It is in this sense, as we have argued, that any made thing will bear in some respect evidence of its maker, evidence of his doing, whereby his being as person impinges upon the thing made. Indeed, given his finitude, given his limits as maker or as doer, he lacks that absolute power whereby God may be said to have created the world without being thereby dependent, in his own being, in that made world. It is this very dream of such an independence that leads the poet so often to exaggerate his own being as maker in the analogy to God as Maker, clouding the limits necessarily involved in the principle of proper proportionality.

Now, we are, as "critic," to take the work of art as good or bad in itself, that is, in a proper address to that thing in itself, for we are judging the poem as poem. But that is always an address that moves beyond mere aesthetics, since the poem is neither created *ex nihilo* by the poet nor does it exist in itself spontaneously *ex nihilo.* What is of concern, in respect to the virtue of prudence as focused upon the work of art in itself, is that it not be declared in and of itself as the cause of any action in intellect. Art's concern, this is to say, is not "the good of man's appetite," St. Thomas says. As for prudence as virtue, "there is need of a moral virtue, which rectifies appetite." "Rectitude of the will is essential to prudence, but not to art." For "Prudence is of good counsel about matters regarding man's entire life, and the end of human life. . . . [O]nly those are simply prudent who give good counsel about all the concerns of life."

It becomes evident, I think, that the concern for virtue in the made thing, the poem or the chair, is a concern for the maker's understanding of his making whereby the thing is made the thing it is by virtue of the constituents of its being, the material and formal causes in relation to the efficient and final causes. The concert of these causes makes the thing the thing it is, this poem or this chair. There is not possible to the thing itself the intentionality whereby it may fail in its being, though such an intentionality cannot be denied to its efficient cause, the poet.

Our concern all along has been less an isolated aesthetic one than a prudential one, in relation to the efficient cause, the poet, and we have argued that, aside from the aesthetic issue as divorced from all other issues, the degree of intentionality in the maker shadows the thing made inescapably. In respect to the thing made, the action is a making; in respect to the being of the efficient cause of that making, the poet, the making is a doing. In respect to the soul of the poet, then, we would argue that prudence is a dimension to his making, in that his making is a doing, as words ordered are a doing of intellect in relation to its knowledge and understanding. St. Thomas recognizes perhaps that one is as a being a *simple* being, however diverse he may appear through our philosophical analysis of his being. For he adds, having separated art as a virtue to intellect from the speculative intellect: "And yet it has something in common with the speculative habits: since the quality of the object considered . . . is a matter of concern to them also, but not how the human appetite may be affected towards the object." The effect of inordinate appetite is occasioned by the will and is not in the object of the will, so that a failure of the will may be occasioned by the poem, but is not therefore to be said caused by the poem. (That excuse proved an insufficient one to Paola and Francesca in Dante's *Hell.*) If prudence requires the will's rectitude, and if prudence is concerned with man's entire life and even more with "the end of human life," and if the poet is a man, then prudence in relation to his act of making can not be excluded as consequential to his being as maker. The distinction, again, is that the poem may not be said the cause of his failure as man, anymore than the poem can be said the cause of the failure of the reader of the poem. If we do not make such distinctions carefully, we shall too easily come to exclude the poet from our Republic because of the poem, instead of because the particular poet is the person he is.

I do not suppose that so brief an address to the problem has resolved it. We should have to consider the relation of the theological virtues of faith, hope, and charity as affecting the being of the poet or of the reader to give the poem its limited independence no doubt. Thomas says, for instance, that "faith completes the understanding" while "hope and charity complete the appetitive part." In this distinction, these virtues cannot be "reasoned about in the same way" (*Summa*, II-II, Q1 Art 3). It is through appetitive nature that the soul experiences being as ordered teleologically, the ordering of the appetitive made through faith, whose good is truth itself. If the "virtues that complete the appetitive part [hope and charity] do not completely exclude the false," then understanding as deepened by faith must rectify even hope and charity. The intention of hope and charity may be founded on false understanding of reality, affecting the appetitive actions. Here, in the complex of theological virtues in relation to both doing and making, lies the decisive unraveling of the nature of the poet himself, insofar as the poem in itself may speak in a limited way toward that nature.

20. Dante the Poet sets the great poets outside Hell, removed from Hell or Purgatory, on the Hell side of the Acheron where they are suspended, knowing no torment except the exclusion from the bliss of God's presence. Among the great poets are Homer, Virgil (who is on leave shepherding Dante), and Horace. And Dante is overwhelmed when he is made "a sixth amid such intelligences." He will meet St. Thomas (not canonized until two years after Dante's actual death) in the Heaven of the Sun, Dante now accompanied by Beatrice, Virgil having returned to his circle below. St. Thomas is first among those intellectual lights, and conducts Dante through that sphere, giving him an abbreviated *Summa*. But Dante is not made a thirteenth amid such intelligences as he encounters there, though Thomas's antagonist Sigier of Brabant is among them. That Dante would so elevate Sigier is sufficient evidence not to elevate Dante (in our estimate) to that high eminence.

Index

About the Author

Marion Montgomery is professor emeritus of English at the University of Georgia. He is the author of numerous books, including *T.S. Eliot: An Essay on the American Magus* and *Ezra Pound: A Critical Essay*, as well as many poems, novels, and critical essays.